500
Little-known Facts
in
Mormon History

500

Little-known Facts

in

Mormon History

by

George W. Givens

BONNEVILLE BOOKS™
Springville, Utah

Copyright © 2002

All Rights Reserved.

No part of this book may be reproduced in any form whatsoever, whether by graphic, visual, electronic, film, microfilm, tape recording, or any other means, without prior written permission of the author, except in the case of brief passages embodied in critical reviews and articles.

ISBN: 1-55517-651-8
v.1

Published by Bonneville Books
Imprint of Cedar Fort Inc.
www.cedarfort.com

Distributed by:

Typeset by Kristin Nelson
Cover design by Adam Ford
Cover design © 2002 by Lyle Mortimer

Printed in the United States of America
10 9 8 7 6 5 4 3 2 1

Printed on acid-free paper

Library of Congress Cataloging-in-Publication Data

Givens, George W., 1932-
  500 little known facts in Mormon history / by George W. Givens.
     p. cm.
Includes bibliographical references and index.
  ISBN 1-55517-651-8 (pbk. : alk. paper)
  1. Church of Jesus Christ of Latter-day Saints--History--Miscellanea.
  I. Title: Five hundred little known facts in Mormon history. II. Title.
  BX8611 .G58 2002
  289.3'09--dc21
                          2002007989

For David and Irene Foote

Great-grandparents of the author,
and now lying in unmarked graves
in the Nauvoo Pioneer Cemetery

Table of Contents

Preface

"Little-known" is, of course, a relative term, depending on the knowledge readers have of a certain subject. My own experience, however, as a long-time member of The Church of Jesus Christ of Latter-day Saints and a former professional teacher of history, suggests that the average Latter-day Saint, although perhaps knowledgeable in Church doctrine, has a less than ample knowledge of the history of his church. This may be the result of a number of reasons, including poorly taught history courses in our public schools and colleges which turn students "off" the learning of history. It is also, of course, the large number of converts who have never studied "Mormon" history, and the little they have encountered outside the church is anything but objective or complete. Outside the cloistered world of LDS scholars therefore, the title seems safe enough and it is to those outside that circle that this book is intended.

One might ask, "How do such little-known facts do much to solve the lack of Mormon history knowledge mentioned?" I believe I discovered the answer in my years of teaching American history to students who grew up on modern media entertainment and had developed little patience for boring instructors. Nothing can be more satisfying to a history teacher than to hear students say at the end of a course, "I didn't realize how interesting history can be!" My philosophy became, "If you can make history interesting, fun or intriguing, a student is far more likely to develop an interest and continue to study or at least read history as an adult. And of course, in an age of shortened attention spans produced by fast-moving entertainment, keeping stories short is an added incentive.

So that is the intention of these brief, unusual facts—to make Mormon history readable and interesting. There are obviously far more details to the stories than are presented here and the footnotes and bibliography can lead the reader to them if desired. On the other hand, to include more details, like any long story can turn the hearers or readers off. These offer, in the author's opinion, enough details to satisfy the average reader— and hopefully in the process turn time-conscious and busy readers into more avid students of Mormon history.

A final cautionary note about the word "facts." As I warned readers in the *Nauvoo Fact Book*, "what is fact or truth to some of us today often turns out to be disputable if not downright false to others." It was not only amazing, but frustrating, to encounter so many discrepancies in the "facts" I compiled for this book. Many of the stories, as short as they are, often required diligent research and valuable time to verify or correct. I am sure there will still be questions about some of the "facts," but that is what makes history, and especially Latter-day Saint history so exciting. It is not an exact science and the discovery of new "facts" and changing interpretations require a humble acknowledgement that this is a field where we are all students.

Introduction

Despite many observations in the preface that most members of the Church of Jesus Christ of Latter-day Saints have a less than ample knowledge of their history, the brevity of the "facts" forced me to make some basic assumptions. I am assuming that most readers will have a general knowledge of the movements of the early Church from its beginnings in New York to first Ohio and while still headquartered there, to Independence, Missouri. When the Saints were forced from Jackson County, they fled north to such places as Far West and Adam-ondi-Ahman before their final expulsion from the state in 1838. They then turned eastward across the Mississippi to settle in Nauvoo and outlying Illinois settlements where they resided for only seven years before being forced westward to Utah. Such basic knowledge is essential to understanding the context of some of the "facts" in this book.

I am also assuming some reader familiarity with the more prominent early pioneers as well as some of the most notorious apostates. Critical readers might perceive what appears to be an extreme emphasis on persecutions and polygamy. It takes little time however, in reading both LDS and non-Mormon sources from the nineteenth century to realize that early Mormon history is a history of persecution—it is difficult to separate the two. It takes little reading in Church histories also, to realize that almost every aspect of Mormon life in the last decades of the nineteenth century inevitably revolved around the doctrine and practice of plural marriage even though only a small percentage of the members were actually involved in it.

Speaking of the nineteenth century, there is a reason to primarily limit the scope of this work to that time period. Like any history, the more remote it is, the less is known about it and there are more "little-known" facts to be uncovered. It might also be observed that as the Church moved into the twentieth century, extreme persecution so typical of the nineteenth century, declined and as the Church developed along more mainstream and familiar lines there are fewer and fewer unusual or unfamiliar facts associated with it.

An assumption is also made in the chapter headings. "The Nauvoo Era" and "Asylum at Last" are easy to understand. "The End of Discretion" and "The End of Autonomy" are not quite as obvious but the time periods listed are certainly a clue when considering the major events in that period. It will also be noted that many of the facts mentioned have little to do with the implied meaning of a chapter heading but they do fit into that era and lend a more balanced picture to everyday Mormon life.

And finally an assumption about that word "Mormons." Latter-day Saints are, of course, urged to limit the use of this nickname. However, when curtailing verbiage was so essential in fitting two facts to a page, I opted for that common but less approved word. Please forgive me for this as well as any other liberties taken which may make your pleasure in reading this book less than my intention.

1

The Beginning
(1813–1831)

A Century Early (1813)

The story of the operation on young Joseph for osteomyelitis usually revolves around Joseph's stoicism. Less mentioned is the amazing surgical procedure by one of the foremost surgeons in the country. Doctor Nathan Smith of Dartmouth Medical School was probably the only surgeon capable of such a pioneering procedure at a time when surgery was not a medical specialty. Much could be deduced about a seven-year-old future prophet from an impoverished family ending up in the hands of such a skilled medical pioneer at that time, but it is a fact that such work as he performed on young Joseph would not be successfully repeated until the early twentieth century.[1]

The Year Without a Summer (1816)

The Smith family's move to Palmyra was prompted by a series of crop failures in Vermont—the last one in 1816. Known in New England as "the year without a summer," there was snow or freezing temperatures every month of that year. Now thought to have been caused by the volcanic eruption of Mount Tambora in Indonesia in 1815, this freakish weather was

---

1   Wirthlin, LeRoy S., "Joseph Smith's Boyhood Operation: An 1813 Surgical Success." *BYU Studies* ,Spring 1981, pp. 131-154.

responsible for the Smith's move from Norwich, Vermont to Palmyra, New York. In fact there was such an exodus from Vermont in that year that it would be nearly a century before the state would recover from the loss. Thus, it was the eruption of a mountain thousands of miles away that led young Joseph to reside only three miles from another mount where Moroni hid up the plates.[2]

Assassination Attempt (1819)

Attempts to take Joseph Smith's life were common, but the most unusual one occurred when he was only fourteen, several months before the First Vision. Lucy Mack Smith mentions the incident briefly in her biography of Joseph but quickly drops the subject without further reference. An assassin fired at young Joseph as he was about to enter his home in Palmyra one evening at twilight. The lead balls missed the target but struck a cow nearby. Neither the suspect nor the reason for the attack was ever discovered and no references in his pre-vision life suggest the kind of enmity that would prompt such a deed.[3]

A Skeptical Minister (1820)

According to the Prophet Joseph's brother, William, the minister who prompted Joseph to ask the Lord which church to join was the Reverend George Lane. Both William and Oliver Cowdery stated that Reverend Lane had preached a sermon based on James 1:5 and that this sermon prompted young Joseph to enter the grove seeking answers. Allegedly this same Methodist minister later rebuked Joseph for claiming he received the answer he did. Ironically, Reverend Lane's older sister, Irene Lane Foote, later joined the Church of Jesus Christ

---

2   Proctor & Proctor, p. 91.

3   Proctor & Proctor, p. 93.

of Latter-day Saints and her LDS descendants are numerous today.[4]

First Prophecy (1823)

After the First Vision, Joseph's mother still felt compelled to unite her family with a local church. Joseph, who had been expressly commanded by the Lord "to go not after them," refused to attend and told his mother, "You will not stay with them long, for you are mistaken in them." As illustration, he said he would give an example, "and you may set it down as a prophecy." Deacon Jessup, a supposedly good and pious local religious leader, he told his mother, would soon take financial advantage of a widow with eight small children. In less than a year this prophecy by the young prophet was literally fulfilled.[5] Lucy did not yet understand that her son, who was to restore the original Church of Jesus Christ, was a prophet in the footsteps of all the Biblical prophets.

Not the First for Heber(1823)

In 1823 Heber C. Kimball received the first three degrees of Masonry and it was as a Mason, not a Latter-day Saint, that his persecutions began. As a member of the Masons in upstate New York during the height of anti-Masonic activities, Heber recalled that because of the persecutions "heaped upon them by the anti-Masons; not as many as three of us could meet together, unless in secret, without being mobbed." But such persecutions apparently made some of the Masons no more tolerant of others. Years later, as a Latter-day Saint, Heber would state, "I have been driven from my houses and posses-

---

4   Proctor & Proctor, p. 106.
5   Proctor & Proctor, p. 122.

sions, with many of my brethren belonging to that fraternity, five times, by mobs led by some of their [Masons] leading men."[6]

Josiah Stowell's Daughters (1826)

Joseph Smith's trial in South Bainbridge on a charge of being a disorderly person in 1826 is well known. Equally known is his acquittal as a result of the testimony of Josiah Stowell for whom he was working at the time. Less known is the appearance in court of certain other witnesses for Joseph – two of Stowell's daughters with whom Joseph had "been keeping company."[7] They apparently gave satisfactory answers when asked about Joseph's behavior toward them, both in public and private. What lends an air of intrigue to this affair is that less than a year later the young prophet was married to Emma Hale, a marriage that had been encouraged and aided by Mr. Stowell himself.[8]

The Right Person (1827)

When the Prophet Joseph made his final visit to Hill Cumorah in the early morning hours of September 22, 1827 to retrieve the plates, he was accompanied by his young wife Emma. Why did Joseph take her? The answer is found in his visit to Cumorah the year previously, before he was married. Moroni told him at that time, he later revealed, that he could have the plates the following year if "he Brot [sic] the right person." Upon being asked who that was, Moroni said he would know. Using a seer stone Joseph discovered it was Emma Hale, daughter of the Hales whom he knew in

---

6   Holzapfel & Holzapfel, p. 80.
7   CHC, 1:207.
8   Bushman, Richard L., p. 77.

Pennsylvania. He married her shortly thereafter. Did Moroni's charge to bring the "right person" encourage Joseph's proposal of marriage?[9]

The Stone Box (1827)

Often ignored in LDS history is the fate of the stone box in which the golden plates were deposited on Hill Cumorah and to which Joseph was led in 1827. Once the plates were removed, neither the prophet nor anyone else appeared interested in the fate of the stone box itself. Almost fifty years later David Whitmer was interviewed by a Chicago Times reporter who wrote that "three times has he [Whitmer] been at the hill Cumorah and seen the casket (box) that contained the tablets and the seer-stone. Eventually the casket had been washed down to the foot of the hill, but it was to be seen when he last visited the historic place."[10]

The Interpreters Taken—Why? (1828)

It is commonly believed that the heavenly messenger took the Urim and Thummim and the plates from Joseph following the loss of the 116 pages by Martin Harris. Actually the plates and interpreters, as they were called, were taken earlier and not as a result of the loss of the translated pages but as Joseph later said, "in consequence of my having wearied the Lord in asking for the privilege of letting Martin Harris take the writings." Shortly after the loss of the pages, the angel returned the interpreters long enough for Joseph to receive a revelation (D&C 3) on the reason for the loss of the privileges, before taking them again. Shortly after sincere repentance both the

---

9   Baught, Alexander L., "Parting the Veil: The Visions of Joseph Smith." *BYU Studies*, Vol. 38, No. 1, p. 31.
10   Cook, *David Whitmer Interviews*, p. 7.

plates and interpreters were returned for the work to continue.[11]

Joseph Attends Methodist Meetings (1828)

Shortly after the loss by Martin Harris of the 116 translated pages, the Prophet returned to Harmony where he was forced to do some farming for his livelihood. During this period he attended some Methodist meetings with Emma, possibly to improve relations with the Hales. It was reported that he even asked to be enrolled as a class member, but a cousin of Emma's, Joseph Lewis, vehemently objected to the inclusion of a "practicing necromancer." Although the prophet remained on the rolls for several months, we find little evidence that Joseph placed much stock in his attendance or even attended very often.[12] He certainly remembered what the Lord had told him about all other churches but he had not yet been told to organize the Restored Church.

The Sealed Portion of the Plates (1829)

Although we do not know what the sealed portion of the golden plates contain, we do know the subject matter. According to Oliver Cowdery, the first Church Historian, Joseph gave a detailed version of his visit by Moroni: "The sealed part, said he, contains the same revelation which was given to John upon the isle of Patmos, and when the people of the Lord are prepared, and found worthy, then it will be unfolded unto them." Being the "same" revelation, it will doubtless be an elaboration and clarification of much that is still unrevealed and obscure in the Book of Revelation.[13]

---

11 HC 1:21-23.

12 Bushman, Richard L., pp. 94-94.

13 Backman & Perkins, p. 80.

Another Witness (1829)

Usually overlooked when Book of Mormon witnesses are mentioned is the name Mary Whitmer, mother of the witness David. Bowed down by the toil of caring for not only her own large family but also the Prophet Joseph, his wife Emma, and Oliver Cowdery as they were completing the translation of the Book of Mormon, the Lord felt her faith needed strengthening. David related that his mother was shown the plates by a heavenly being in the family barn, thus becoming the only woman to have the privilege of seeing the actual plates. One can only wonder why the Lord granted Sister Whitmer such a privilege while withholding it from such apparently worthy sisters as Lucy and Emma.[14]

First Convert Baptism (1829)

The story of the baptisms of Joseph and Oliver at the time of the restoration of the Aaronic Priesthood on May 15, 1829 is well known in LDS history. But that was only the beginning. Now the task of converting others who had not experienced the heavenly manifestations shared by the prophet and his companion began. Shortly after the visit of John the Baptist, Joseph's brother, Samuel, arrived in Harmony for a visit. Joseph wrote, "We informed him of what the Lord was about to do ...and began to reason with him ...He was not, however, very easily persuaded." After much prayer he received a testimony, however, and was baptized by Oliver on May 25th, becoming the "first convert baptism" in this dispensation.[15]

---

14 Ludlow, *Encyclopedia of Mormonism*, 2:955.
15 Proctor & Proctor, p. 187.

Witnesses in Utah (1829)

In 1870 Martin Harris, a witness to the 1829 printing of the Book of Mormon in Grandin's Print Shop in Palmyra, arrived in Utah. But he was not the only surviving witness to that historic event to finally reach Utah. By a strange turn of events, another witness, Stephen S. Harding, preceded him by eight years but with a far less welcome reception. Harding, who had lived in Palmyra as a youth was visiting his old home and spent some time with his cousin, editor Pomeroy Tucker, at the print shop while the Book of Mormon was being printed and was actually given one of the original title pages. In 1862, Harding was appointed Territorial Governor of Utah, and became one of the most hostile and disliked federal officials to hold that office. After a mass meeting by the Saints to protest Harding's policies, Lincoln appointed a replacement.[16]

It Wasn't Joseph (1830)

It would be logical to assume that the Prophet Joseph would have given the first public discourse in this dispensation, but he didn't. Just as Aaron was chosen to be the spokesman for Moses, Oliver Cowdery was given the same privilege for Joseph. Thus it was Oliver whom Joseph chose to deliver the talk to the public, which had been invited to meet in the Peter Whitmer, Sr. home at Fayette, New York, on April 11, 1830. Several neighbors attended that first public meeting of the Church and several were baptized in Seneca Lake following the discourse. Unfortunately, there was no scribe to record exactly what Oliver said or whether Joseph had anything to say on that historic occasion.[17]

---

16   Roberts, CHC, 5:14.
17   HC, 1:81.

Most Honored Woman (1830)

Latter-day Saints are well acquainted with the Prophet Joseph's wife and mother as devout and loyal believers of Joseph's prophetic calling. Fewer are familiar with his grandmother whom he blessed and called the "most honored woman on earth." Mary Duty, the mother of Joseph Sr. accepted the gospel along with her husband Asael in 1830, but neither was baptized. Asael died shortly after reading and believing the Book of Mormon. Mary traveled to Kirtland six years later with the intention of being baptized by her son, Joseph Sr., but died within ten days, unbaptized but nevertheless blessed at the age of ninety-three by her prophet grandson.[18]

Another Emma Mystery (1830)

There are many unanswered questions on the life and events surrounding the wife of the Prophet Joseph. One seldom mentioned is the occasion of her baptism. Baptisms occurred on the day of the organization of the Church and some had taken place even before April 6, 1830. Why was Emma not baptized until June 28th of that year and then under the hands of Oliver Cowdery rather than her husband? Her confirmation scheduled for the following day was put off because of the arrest of Joseph on spurious charges but why was she not confirmed until August? Confirmations did not always immediately follow baptisms in the early days of the Church but certainly in the case of Emma, such a long delayed confirmation into the Church her husband was responsible for restoring is a little strange.[19]

---

18   Proctor & Proctor, p. 436.
19   Ludlow, *Encyclopedia of Mormonism*, 3:1323.

Oliver's Objection (1830)

In 1830 the Prophet Joseph received a very disconcerting letter from Oliver Cowdery commanding him to alter one of the commandments in the Doctrine and Covenants—specifically the portion of Section 20 reading "and truly manifest by their works that they have received of the Spirit of Christ unto a remission of their sins." Although we can only assume the reason for the objection, probably the use of "works" rather than "faith," we don't have to merely assume that Oliver was completely out-of-line in dictating to a prophet. Such an error in thinking was soon made evident to Oliver and the Church. This inexplicable misunderstanding by such an important servant of the Restored Church was necessary in establishing a principle of ecclesiastical government and the role of a prophet.[20]

An Honest Friend (1830)

There are numerous little-noted gentile friends of the early Saints, and one of those was John Reid who, although not a lawyer, acted successfully as defense counsel for the Prophet in his first trials in Colesville and South Bainbridge, New York, in 1830. Although never a convert he journeyed to Nauvoo in May 1844 and publicly described his defense of the prophet and the spiritual experience that prompted him to take the case. Thirty-five years after Esquire Reid defended Joseph, his son Amos Reid (Reed) became acting governor of the Utah

---

20 Ludlow, *A Companion to Your Study of the Doctrine and Covenants,* 1:158.

Territory where he often referred with pride to the part his father had taken on behalf of the Prophet Joseph on those early occasions.[21]

The First Message (1830)

The first message of the Restored Gospel to be taken to the descendants of the Book of Mormon people was to the Cattaraugus Indians near Buffalo, New York. This Lamanite mission by Parley P. Pratt, Oliver Cowdery, Peter Whitmer, Jr., and Ziba Peterson also visited the Wyandots in Ohio and the Delawares west of Missouri. Ironically, the mission's greatest success was not among the Lamanites but among a group of Campbellites in Ohio. There they converted Sidney Rigdon who brought many of his followers into the Restored Church along with Edward Partridge and F.G. Williams. By early spring there were over 1,000 converts in Ohio but they were not Native Americans, which was the purpose of the mission.[22]

"And More Too" (1831)

Much has been said about Martin Harris' loss of his farm to pay for the printing of the Book of Mormon. What is less known is that although the farm was sold at auction in April 1831, supposedly to pay off the printer's debt, the editor Pomeroy Tucker judged that Martin could have paid the bill from other resources. It should also be remembered that Martin had to dispose of his property anyway in making his move to Kirtland. And finally, in an interview given to a Utah missionary in 1853 about the loss of $3,000 dollars for publishing the Book of Mormon, Brother Harris replied, "I

---

21 Cannon, *Life of Joseph Smith the Prophet*, p. 90.
22 Pratt, Parley P., p. 44.

never lost one cent. Mr. Smith paid me all that I advanced, and more too."[23]

The First Splinter (1831)

According to George A. Smith, speaking in the tabernacle in Salt Lake City in January 1858, the first schismatic group in the Restored Church was established in Kirtland, Ohio, in 1831. Wycam Clark and Northrop Sweet, both having been converted by the Lamanite Missionaries in November 1830, joined with four other apostates and established what they termed the "Pure Church of Christ" with Clark as prophet. They believed Joseph to be a fallen prophet and promised to preach "Mormon" principles. After two or three meetings, the group faded away to become only one of approximately 130 splinter groups from the Church of Jesus Christ of Latter-day Saints—merely having the distinction of being the first.[24]

---

23 Reynolds, 1:436.
24 JD, 7:114.

2

Seeking Sanctuary
(1832–1838)

He Walked Out of History (1832)

His name was Jesse Gause and on March 8th, 1832, according to the Kirtland Revelation Book, he was called as a counselor to the Prophet Joseph in the presidency. A week later Joseph received a revelation confirming Jesse in this work. For an unknown reason, Jesse's name in the Revelation Book has been crossed out and that of Frederick G. Williams substituted. Published copies of the revelation (Section 81) also name Williams as the individual to whom the revelation was directed. What happened to Brother Gause? On August 1 of that same year he started east with Zebedee Coltrin, but Zebedee became ill and turned back. Gause continued his journey and simply walked out of history.[25]

The Very First Mention (1832)

The name Paulina E. Phelps Lyman is a name unfamiliar to most Latter-day Saints, but she should be remembered as the source of the very first mention of the Rocky Mountains as a home for the Saints. She signed an affidavit many years later in Salt Lake City that as a young girl she had received a blessing

---

25 Woodford, Robert J., "Jesse Gause, Counselor to the Prophet." *BYU Studies*, Spring 1975, pp. 362-363.

in the home of Lyman Wight in Jackson County in 1832 in which the Prophet Joseph told her that she would live to go to the Rocky Mountains. Only two years later, according to Wilford Woodruff, Joseph told a group assembled in Kirtland, Ohio that "This people will go into the Rocky Mountains; they will there build temples to the Most High."[26]

Teacher and Student (1832)

December 1832 was the culmination of a romance that had started for Elizabeth Ann Whitmer when she was thirteen years old in a small log schoolhouse near Manchester, New York. Her teacher was a young man only twenty-one and now, four years after that student-teacher relationship, they were being married in Jackson County, Missouri. In fact, this was the first Mormon marriage in Missouri and was to be, in spite of the loss of five children, a happy marriage until the husband died in 1850. Thirty-seven years later, she would write a letter to her brother David Whitmer, describing the testimony her husband, Oliver Cowdery, had always had of the Book of Mormon.[27]

Body Snatchers in New York (1832)

On January 7, 1831, Joseph Brackenbury, a Mormon missionary, died at Pomfret, New York, from "the effects of poison secretly administered to him by opposers." On the night after his burial during a heavy snowstorm, Joel H. Johnson, a neighboring Saint, dreamed that body snatchers were digging up Brother Brackenbury's body. He was so convinced that he awoke his brother David and they went to the cemetery, about a mile distant. There they found some doctors digging up the

---

26 Christian, Lewis Clark, "Mormon Foreknowledge of the West," *BYU Studies*, Fall 1981, p. 404.

27 Gunn, p. 211.

body to use for dissection. Upon discovery the body snatchers immediately fled the scene. The brothers were able to capture one of the doctors who was bound over with a thousand dollar bond for his court appearance. Like many anti-Mormons accused of crimes against the Saints, he was never brought to trial.[28]

Code Names (1832)

Some of the earliest revelations received by Joseph were directed at specific individuals in the Church. During the winter of 1831-32, secular newspapers in Ohio, after acquiring some of these revelations, began ridiculing Church leaders whose names were mentioned. To lessen embarrassment to his officers, Joseph began in March 1832 to identify certain individuals in revelations by code names. Joseph himself became "Enoch." He gave such names as "Ahashdah" to Newel Whitney and "Pelegoram" to Sidney Rigdon. Years later the real names were added in parentheses and the 1981 edition of the Doctrine and Covenants no longer listed the code names at all.[29]

A Cautious Future Prophet (1832)

Evidence seems to suggest that Brigham Young had access to the Book of Mormon when it first appeared in the spring of 1830. He read it and obviously prayed but received no immediate witness of its truth. On the thirtieth anniversary of the organization of the Church he described his conversion in a talk in the Salt Lake Tabernacle. He said he "watched to see whether good common sense was manifest." Several members of his family were baptized while he still investigated the

---

28 HC, 7:524.
29 Backman, *The Heavens Resound*, p. 58.

doctrines and the members. He said he waited two years before he embraced the gospel by baptism. Brigham's example should be encouraging to investigators and missionaries who are frustrated when the Holy Ghost appears to ignore requests for immediate answers to the truths of the Restored Gospel.[30]

First Martyr (1832)

The first Church martyr in this dispensation is considered to be Joseph Murdock Smith, the adopted son of the Prophet Joseph and Emma. He and his twin sister had been given to Joseph and Emma to adopt by their father, John Murdock, when their mother died and when Emma's twins died soon after birth. The baby Joseph died on March 30, 1832, at the age of eleven months from exposure caused by the mob at Hiram, Ohio, when they invaded the Johnson home. The baby, sick with the measles and with whom Joseph was sleeping that night, caught cold as a result of the invasion and died four days later. The baby's twin sister, Julia, grew up in the Smith household, but became a Catholic in her adult years.[31]

Slavery in Missouri (1833)

Latter-day Saint history usually mentions Missourians' fear of the abolitionist feelings of the Saints as one reason for their expulsion from Jackson County in 1833 and later the state itself. The actual number of Missouri slaves puts the issue into a more vivid context. Slave enumerations in 1830 lists 25,081 slaves in Missouri, a state that had been legally made a slave state in 1820 as a result of the Missouri Compromise. Most of the Saints were from New England and New York, seven states

---

30   JD, 8:38.
31   HC, 1:265.

that together held a total of 117 slaves in 1830 and were obviously anti-slavery. By 1833 there were enough Mormons in Jackson County to begin wielding political influence throughout a state that had a total population in 1830 of only 140,000. The slave-holding Missourians perhaps had reason to fear.[32]

A Matter of Faith (1833)

After the Saints were driven out of Jackson County, Missouri, in 1833, Bishop Partridge called for volunteers to take the news to the Prophet in Kirtland, Ohio. Several elders were asked if any of them could make the nine-hundred-mile journey, but they all made family excuses and seemingly with justification. When Lyman Wight stepped forward, the Bishop asked him what situation his family was in. He replied that his wife lay by the side of a log in the woods with a baby three days old and with three days' provisions on hand. He saw no reason he couldn't go. Parley Pratt also volunteered and they went together.[33]

Don't Threaten Us! (1833)

Militia General Alexander Doniphan, a lawyer by trade, is fondly remembered by the Latter-day Saints for his refusal to cooperate in the execution of the Mormon leaders after their surrender at Far West, Missouri in 1838. Less known is the reason for his earlier willingness to take on the Saints as clients at the risk of losing the business of the Missourians. In 1833, the Saints asked Doniphan's law firm to help them bring suit against the Missourians who had driven them out of Jackson

---

32 *American Almanac for the Year 1838*, p. 163.
33 Jenson, *L.D.S. Biographical Encyclopedia*, 1:94.

County. The firm agreed, requesting $1,000 to offset an expected loss of business. Doniphan and his partners explained that they could easily be hired by the other side, but they preferred the Saints cause "as we have been threatened by the mob, we wish to show them we disregard their empty bravadoes."[34]

American Violence (1833)

The large scale organized mob violence that began against the Saints in Jackson County, Missouri in 1833 and would continue until the Mormons were driven from the state five years later, was not unprecedented in that era. Scholars on American violence generally agree that the period of the 1830s, 1840s, and 1850s may have been the period of the greatest urban violence in our history. Directed also against Catholics, abolitionists, immigrants, prostitutes, and a variety of other unpopular minorities, it is estimated that "at least seventy per cent of American cities with a population of twenty thousand or more by 1850 experienced some degree of major disorder in the 1830-1865 period."[35]

Three Sacred Buildings? (1833)

On May 1st, 1833, a conference of high priests in Kirtland voted to appoint a committee to raise money for the purpose of erecting a schoolhouse for the use of the First Presidency and all matters pertaining to the Church. It was to be fifty-five by sixty-five feet with a lower and a higher court and considered a sacred building in which no unclean thing was permitted to enter. At the same time a second building, also sacred and with

---

34 HC, 1:425.
35 Ellsworth, Paul D., "Mobocracy and the Rule of Law: American Press Reaction to the Murder of Joseph Smith," *BYU Studies*. Fall 1979, pp. 72-73.

the same dimensions was to be erected as a printing house. A third sacred building, again with the same dimensions and with the same lower and upper courts was to be constructed as a temple. Only the temple was constructed, part of which was used as a school. A smaller, non-sacred printing office was constructed next door.[36]

School of Prophetesses? (1833)

The School of the Prophets, established in Kirtland in 1833, was intended by the Prophet Joseph as a training ground for missionaries, and it did serve that purpose well. It also served however, as a school for young, intellectually inclined sisters. One of these was Sarah Granger, aged fifteen, invited to attend the school with her father, Oliver. In fact, some sources indicate that as many as twenty-three young women attended classes.[37] We are not told of the prophet's reaction to this "invasion" of sister Saints, but we do know they were not expelled. Their presence was a portent of the prominent role Latter-day Saint women would play in their communities and church, a role denied to so many of their gentile sisters at this time.

A Patriarchal Correction (1833)

Asked for the name of the first patriarch of this dispensation, the average Latter-day Saint will say Joseph Smith Sr.—which is what most church histories will say. Actually, he was the second. On December 18, 1833, at an assembly of elders in the printing office in Kirtland to dedicate the printing press, the Prophet Joseph gave the first patriarchal blessing in this dispensation. Since he held the keys of all the authority in

---

36 Smith, Joseph Fielding, *Church History and Modern Revelation*, 2:164.
37 Ludlow, *Encyclopedia of Mormonism*, 2:784.

the Church he was spoken of as the first patriarch in the Church in the minutes that were kept at that time. He then proceeded to give a patriarchal blessing to several, including his father whom he then ordained to the office of presiding patriarch. It should be noted there were other early patriarchs, including Brigham Young's father who was ordained the following year.[38]

The "Voice of God" (1834)

After being driven from Jackson County in Missouri, the Saints appealed to Governor Dunklin for redress. On July 25, 1834, he replied in a letter, explaining his refusal to involve himself or the executive branch of the state government. His reasoning appears totally alien to American constitutional law as we believe it to be today. He explained that the Saints must, by "conduct and arguments, convince them (the mobs) of your innocence. If you cannot do this, all I can say to you is, that in this republic the vox populi is the vox Dei." That is, the voice of the people is the voice of God. This belief that public opinion takes precedence over the laws was a common belief, even by the educated, in Jacksonian America.[39]

An Early Friend (1834)

Missouri militia General Doniphan, who proved his sense of justice and integrity later when he was credited with saving the lives of Joseph and other LDS leaders, proved his fairness long before that. After the expulsion of the Saints from Jackson County, he attended a meeting in June 1834, where he agreed with another speaker that the Saints were better citizens than many of the old inhabitants. Noting that the Saints had armed

---

38 Smith, Joseph Fielding, *Essentials in Church History*, pp. 141-141.
39 Roberts, *The Missouri Persecutions*, p. 171.

themselves, he stated "if they don't fight they are cowards." And then referring to knowledge of the approaching Zion's Camp, he said, "I love to hear that they have brethren coming to their assistance. Greater love can no man show, than he who lays down his life for his brethren."[40]

Zion's Camp—Training Ground (1834)

Although Zion's Camp was initially intended to help restore the Jackson County Saints to their homes and was considered by some a failure, the Prophet Joseph claimed the experience was a training ground for future Church leaders. As evidence of how well this worked, we can refer to the members of the Priesthood quorums in Kirtland in 1836. Nine of the first twelve Apostles were veterans of the march to Missouri as were all seven presidents of the Seventies and seventy-three of the two Quorums of Seventies. Even more significant, it was a perfect training ground for the pioneers who would be making the trek west twelve years later, including Brigham Young, Heber C. Kimball, Orson Hyde, the Pratts, George A. Smith, and Wilford Woodruff.[41]

Remembering Zion's Camp (1834)

Although several members kept journals, there is no extant day-by-day journal of Zion's Camp (Camp Historian F. G. Williams' journal was lost). Most of its day-by-day history, therefore, has come from the memoirs of George A. Smith, a boy of only sixteen when he joined the trek. His memoirs could not be based on his own journals because at the time of the journey, he had not yet learned to write. Ten years later he was

---

40 HC, 2:98.
41 Backman, *The Heavens Resound*, p. 381.

able to furnish a detailed account of the camp's activities and with some help, a list of the more than two hundred members of the camp. George never revealed when he learned to write, but two years after the march, he was teaching grammar classes in Kirtland.[42]

A Warning Out (1835)

Frustrated by the growing numbers of Latter-day Saints in Kirtland, the non-Mormons devised a boycott, agreeing to not hire the Saints, buy from them, or sell to them. Believing this would totally impoverish the already struggling Saints, the authorities issued a "warning out of town" to the Mormons. This was not what it sounded like. It merely meant that, under Ohio law, when a family became impoverished they could not become a township charge but could be forcibly moved to another township. This was the same type of law that had been applied to Joseph Smith, Sr. in Vermont before he left for New York. However, the Kirtland boycott failed and the anti-Mormons were finally forced to resort to more violent and illegal means to force the Saints out of Kirtland.[43]

Life Was Shorter Then (1836)

In January 1836, Don Carlos, younger brother of the Prophet and only nineteen, was called to preside over the High Priests' Quorum in Kirtland. He was ordained and labored as a missionary when fifteen. His cousin George A Smith was active in the ministry when only fifteen, a member of the First Quorum of Seventy at seventeen, and was called into the Quorum of the Twelve at twenty-one.[44] Joseph F. Smith was

---

42 Pusey, p. 17.

43 JD, 13:106.

44 Pusey, p. 19.

ordained an elder and sent on a mission when he was fifteen.[45] Temple worker George W. Bean was made a Seventy at age fourteen. Such charges were not that uncommon in the early days of the Church. Perhaps there was less concern about finishing one's education or maybe it was because life was shorter.

Even the Dead Were Not Safe (1836)

The graves of Latter-day Saints who died during the Kirtland period had to be closely guarded or the corpses would be stolen by medical students from the nearby Willoughby Medical School. Helen Mar Whitney described those students thinking it "no sacrilege to dissect a 'Mormon' dead or alive." One method of guarding the interred loved ones was to tie a "rope to a strong bier, which was turned over the grave and the other end to the arm of someone" sleeping nearby. Such arrangements would be continued for a number of weeks. It is of interest to note that John C. Bennett, the notorious Nauvoo apostate, taught at the Willoughby Medical School in 1834 but was dismissed for being a "promoter." Did he once encourage "body snatching"?[46]

Sustain by Rising (1836)

It is a custom among the Saints to sustain leaders by a show of hands, but this was not always the custom. At the dedication of the Kirtland Temple in 1836, the Prophet Joseph called upon the congregation "to acknowledge the Presidency as prophets and seers, and uphold them by their prayers. (i.e. sustain) They all covenanted to do so, by rising." Joseph then proceeded to

---

45   Smith, Joseph Fielding, *Answers to Gospel Questions*, 2:8.
46   Holzapfel & Holzapfel, p. 94.

call upon the congregation for the same sustaining vote for the Twelve Apostles, the High Council of Kirtland, the bishops, and other officers as is done today. Each time the members were asked to rise as an indication of their support. Records indicate "the vote was unanimous in every instance."[47]

An Infant Wife-to-Be!(1837)

Heber C. Kimball, the first missionary to be called to the British Isles, converted a young couple named James and Nancy Knowles Smithies who shortly thereafter had an infant daughter, the first child born into the Church in Great Britain. Still imbued with a Protestant tradition, the parents insisted their baby Mary be immediately christened so she would not die unsaved. Heber pointed out that this was contrary to the scriptures, but convinced them only when he pronounced the first of his famous prophecies. He promised that the child would not die in England but would become a mother in Israel. The prophecy was fulfilled—she grew to womanhood, went to Utah, and became the last plural wife of Heber himself, giving him five children.[48]

A Temple In Debt (1837)

By April 1837 problems for the Latter-day Saints were piling up in Kirtland, especially the one of debt. At the general church conference that month, Sidney Rigdon was called upon to address that subject, which he did, outlining the principal items that remained unliquidated. When the temple was dedicated, the Church was indebted for between thirteen and fourteen thousand dollars. When Sidney spoke at the confer-

---

47 HC, 2:417-18.
48 Kimball, p. 52.

ence, the unliquidated temple debt alone was nearly thirteen thousand dollars. Such a debt by today's exchange rate would be close to a million dollars, but of course no money is borrowed to build temples today.[49]

Six Times in One Day (1837)

On July 27, 1837, the prophet set out from Kirtland to visit the Saints in Canada, accompanied by Sidney Rigdon and Thomas Marsh. He had gone less than ten miles when the sheriff in Painesville arrested him on some spurious charges. Released for lack of evidence, he was arrested again and before the day was over, had been arrested six times and each time released. He had to postpone his trip until the following day. Brigham Young, who was supposed to accompany Joseph part way on that occasion, later described the legal persecutions experienced by Joseph while trying to build the restored Church: "He never broke a law, yet to my certain knowledge he was defendant in forty-six lawsuits."[50]

Saints and Seminoles (1837)

The federal request for troops, resulting in the recruitment of the Mormon Battalion in 1846, was not the first time the federal government asked the Saints for troops. According to Edward Partridge, writing from Far West to a brother in October 1837, orders had come to "this upper country, (Caldwell County & northern Missouri) to raise 1,000 Indians, and also 150 or 200 volunteers among the white, all to go to Florida to fight the Seminoles." Although evidence suggests that few if any Saints responded, one regiment of "old volun-

---

49   HC, 2:479.
50   Backman, *The Heavens Resound*, p. 322 & JD, 14:199.

teers" responded and suffered severe losses at the Battle of Okeechobee on Christmas Day, 1837. History is also silent as to how many, if any Indians from the area volunteered. Twenty years later, Brigham Young was making reference to the inability of the United States to conquer those same Seminoles.[51]

The Kirtland Apostasy (1837-38)

The so-called "Great Apostasy" in Kirtland was not as great, perhaps, as many histories report. Milton Backman, Jr. in *The Heavens Resound*, estimated that the total number who left the Church was no more than two or three hundred, representing 10 to 15 percent of the membership in Ohio. He based this on excommunication records and reports of those who joined apostate groups. Backman noted that 87 percent of the Kirtland Saints were later identified on records from Missouri, Nauvoo, Iowa, or Utah. The apostasy seems dramatic and perhaps exaggerated because so much of the leadership left the Church at this time—leaders who had the most invested in the Kirtland Anti-Bank and blamed Joseph for its failure.[52]

Joseph's Honesty (1838)

Although impoverished throughout most of his life, numerous stories exist about the prophet's diligence in paying or attempting to pay real or even spurious debts. When Joseph was forced to flee Kirtland in January 1838, he left behind many unhappy creditors, many with fraudulent claims. Although many had been his most active persecutors, he recognized his legal obligation to pay those with legitimate

---

51 Jennings, Warren A., "What Crime Have I Been Guilty of?" *BYU Studies,* Summer, 1978, pp. 521-522.

52 Backman, *The Heavens Resound*, p. 437.

claims. After settling in Far West, he sent Oliver Granger to Ohio to seek out such creditors and pay them. As late as 1843 while living in Nauvoo, he was still attempting, with the help of Church members, to pay off his Kirtland debts.[53]

"Nasty, Dirty, Pettifoggers" (1838)

Sidney Rigdon played a major role in the expulsion of Oliver Cowdery and David Whitmer from Far West and the Church in 1838. Although their church trials listed a number of reasons, Sidney's feelings about their professional activities apparently played a major role. In June he had protested that the two witnesses had come to Far West to "set up a nasty, dirty, pettifoggers office" and in a letter he accused them of stirring up men "of weak minds to prosecute one another, for the vile purpose of getting a fee for pettifogging for one of them." It is of interest that Sidney himself will later shoulder much of the blame for the Missouri expulsions after his July 4th speech, which many said were the result of a "weakened" mind following his abuse at the hands of mobbers in Hiram, Ohio in 1832.[54]

A Turn-about! (1838)

In addition to their 1838 Missouri excommunication, Oliver along with David and John Whitmer, W. W. Phelps, and Lyman Johnson also were the recipients of a letter signed by eighty-four Church members ordering them to leave the community. Although Oliver eventually returned, such a petition seemed to rankle him more than the charges in his Church trial. It is uncertain if Oliver saw any irony in the situation in

---

53 Backman, *The Heavens Resound*, p. 436.
54 Hill, Marvin S., p. 74.

view of the petition he signed two years earlier by nearly as many Kirtland Church members, ordering a hostile justice of the peace to resign and leave town. Unlike the excommunicated Saints, the justice did not leave but served out his term. In 1837 Oliver himself was elected to replace the hostile officer as Kirtland justice of the peace.[55]

Attorneys Joseph and Sidney? (1838)

In early September 1838, as tensions increased in northern Missouri, the prophet sent for General Atchison to counsel with the Saints and help put a stop to the hostilities. On September 4th, the Saints hired David Atchison and his partner, Alexander Doniphan as their attorneys. On that same day, Joseph recorded that he and Sidney Rigdon commenced "the study of law, under the instruction of Atchison and Doniphan. "They think," he said, "by diligent application, we can be admitted to the bar in twelve months." Four weeks later, the Saints were surrendering to the Missouri militia, partly commanded by their friend and attorney, General Doniphan, at Far West. Thus ended Joseph and Sidney's formal legal studies.[56]

Prelude to Haun's Mill (1838)

The massacre at Haun's Mill has often been blamed on Governor Boggs' extermination order signed on October 27th, 1838. There is evidence, however, that the massacre had little to do with the infamous order. On October 25, a number of Livingston County mobbers rode into Haun's Mill and demanded a surrender of all arms. Many were confiscated and

---

55 VanWagoner & Walker, p. 76.
56 HC, 3:69.

a "peace" agreement was made. Confiscation of weapons and disarming peace agreements were apparently a part of the mob-militia plans to eradicate the Latter-day Saints in Missouri. Such tactics would insure that a later attack on such communities would not only be a surprise, but also lessen resistance. Whatever the case, their tactics worked.[57]

A Fiendish Desecration (1838)

After the massacre of Mormon men and boys at Haun's Mill in 1838 ,the bodies were dumped into an unfinished well. Survivor Amanda Smith however, relates a fact that may not be as widely known. As she described in her own words: "Over that rude grave—that well—where the nineteen martyrs slept, where my murdered husband and boy were entombed, the mobbers of Missouri, with an exquisite fiendishness, which no savages could have conceived, had constructed a rude privy. This they constantly used, with a delight which demons might have envied."[58]

An Offer Rejected (1838)

On a mission to gather funds for the Missouri Saints in 1838, George A. Smith and his cousin Don Carlos Smith stopped at a hotel in Columbus, Kentucky. The hotel keeper, Captain Robinson, was so impressed with the young George that he offered him a job, an opportunity to "read" [study] law and the hand of his nineteen-year-old daughter who had just inherited an estate valued at $200,000 from a husband who had been killed in a duel. Although the daughter was described as "not without personal charm" and with an estate valued at

---

57   Baugh, Alexander L., "Joseph Young's Affidavit of the Massacre at Haun's Mill." *BYU Studies*, Vol. 38, No. 1, p. 197.

58   Tullidge, p. 132.

several million current-value dollars, the impoverished young man could only remember a waiting young Bathsheba Bigler to whom he had given his pledge and also his people in distress.[59]

Friends Again (1838)

When the Mormon leaders were delivered into the hands of the mob army at Far West in 1838 by the treasonable George Hinkle, Sidney Rigdon was among them,. Because of his age and poor health, he seemed to suffer the most as a captive. And yet, seven years later, the now excommunicated Rigdon was making overtures to Hinkle to bring his followers and join the church which Sidney had started in Pennsylvania. Hinkle who had started his own church by this time (it seems most leading apostates recognized the truths found in the Restored Church) did join with the Rigdonites, bringing many of his followers, and became a member of Sidney's grand council. When Sidney's group moved to Antrim Township in Ohio, Hinkle went with him but left when the Antrim group lost their property in 1847.[60]

Avard Couldn't Answer (1838)

Sampson Avard, the moving force behind the illegal depredations by the Mormon Danites in Missouri, turned against his fellow Saints upon his capture by Missourians in 1838 and testified against the Saints. Blaming the Prophet Joseph for ordering the illegal activities of the Danites, Joseph was allowed to question the apostate in court. Reminding Avard that he once proclaimed an unshaken confidence in Joseph as a prophet of God, Joseph asked, "What gave you this confi-

---

59 Pusey, p. 31.
60 Gregory, Thomas J., "Sidney Rigdon: Post Nauvoo," *BYU Studies*. Winter 1981, p. 62.

dence? Was it because I taught you how to lie, steal and murder as you have testified, or because you actually believed me a prophet?" Forced to admit that either Joseph was a prophet or that he, Avard, was a scoundrel from the beginning, Avard remained silent.[61]

Make The Bible Treason (1838)

After the surrender of the Saints at Far West in 1838, Joseph and other leading Saints were cross-examined at a hearing to determine the charges for an upcoming trial. Witnesses, including apostates, testified to Joseph's teachings regarding the Biblical prophecy of Daniel that the kingdom of God would roll forth like the growing stone that would destroy all earthly kingdoms. When the anti-Mormon Judge King told the clerk to "Write that down; it is a strong point for treason," one of Joseph's attorneys objected. "Judge, you had better make the Bible treason." He was overruled and a Missouri judge went on record of making belief in a Biblical prophecy treasonable.[62]

Avenging Her Husband (1838)

As the surrounding mobs prepared for their attack on Far West, the defending Saints included more than just the brethren. In the heart of the city was the home of Phoebe Ann Patten, the widow of the martyr, David Patten, killed at the battle of Crooked River. Vilate Kimball and her daughter Helen had sought safety with the widow and reported that Phoebe Ann "was perfectly calm and she shed no tears." At her waist she wore her dead husband's large bowie knife and on the fire

---

61 BYU Studies, Vol. 26, No. 2, p. 9.
62 BYU Studies, Vol. 26, No. 2, p. 9.

was a kettle of boiling water she was preparing to throw on any invaders. Not unlike the spirit of many Mormon widows, Helen Mar Kimball remembered that Sister Patten "only thought of avenging the blood of her husband."[63]

Future Governor and Joseph (1838)

When the Prophet Joseph was moved from Liberty Jail to a hearing at Gallatin shortly before his "escape," he was accompanied by two defense attorneys, Amos Rees and Peter H. Burnett. Burnett, who would become the first governor of California, once offered this assessment of Joseph. "He possessed the most indomitable perseverance, was a good judge of men, and deemed himself born to command...his manner was so earnest, and apparently so candid, that you could not but be interested...He had the capacity for discussing a subject in different aspects, and for proposing many original views, even on ordinary matters...In the short space of five days (at Gallatin) he had managed so to mollify his enemies that he could go unprotected among them without the slightest danger."[64]

Was Expulsion Inevitable? (1838)

As the Saints gathered in 1838 in Caldwell County Missouri, that had been set aside for them, and further north in Daviess County, the future looked promising. The prophet himself said there was no persecution through the month of May and the same seemed to be true for the following month, up until the 4th of July. Rigdon's infamous speech on that day in Far West turned the tide however—against the Latter-day

---

63 Kimball, Stanley, p. 58.
64 Allen and Leonard, pp. 132-133.

Saints. A citizen of Liberty later said "Until July 4th, we heard no threats being made against them in any quarters." On that unfortunate day however, Rigdon, perhaps still suffering mental effects from a mob beating six years earlier in Hiram, Ohio, challenged the Missourians who had persecuted them— "It shall be between us and them a war of extermination." The mobs couldn't resist.[65]

Hinkle's Guilt? (1838)

Was George Hinkle, who surrendered the Mormon leaders to General Lucas at Far West, as guilty of treasonable conduct as he has been portrayed? In 1844, he wrote a letter to W. W. Phelps explaining his conduct in 1838. He said that the Prophet told him to obtain a treaty "on any terms short of a battle." There is also evidence that Lucas wanted the prisoners only as hostages, giving the Saints until the following morning to decide whether to accept the terms of surrender offered Hinkle, after which he would return them. Perhaps Lucas was more guilty of deceit than Hinkle was of treachery.[66]

---

65 Hill, Marvin S., pp. 78-79.
66 LeSueur, Stephen C., *The 1838 Mormon War in Missouri*, pp. 168-169.

3

The Nauvoo Era
(1839–1846)

An Apostle Who Never Knew (1839)

The Prophet Joseph, although imprisoned in Missouri in the winter of 1838-39, still conducted the affairs of the Church. On January 16 he wrote a letter to the Quorum of the Twelve advising them to replace Orson Hyde and Thomas Marsh, who had become disaffected, with two men they had nominated. One was George A. Smith, the youngest apostle ever to fill that position and the other a close friend of the prophet and a veteran of Zion's Camp, Lyman Sherman. Both Heber C. Kimball and Brigham Young knew of Lyman's calling, but for some reason, possibly because Brother Sherman was so ill, they chose not to tell him. Lyman died at Far West in February before he could be ordained or even informed of his high calling.[67]

A Prophet By Thirteen Days (1839)

After the prophet's death many had questions about who now held the keys and must assume leadership. If it was a case of Joseph delegating his leadership duties, it appears that was settled five years earlier when the prophet was in Liberty Jail.

---

67 Otten & Caldwell, 2:236.

On January 16, 1839, he had written to Brigham Young and Heber C. Kimball, the two most prominent members of the Twelve still active in Missouri, saying, "the management of the affairs of the church devolves on you, that is the Twelve." He also told them to "appoint the oldest of those of the Twelve who were first appointed to be the President of your Quorum." Since the senior apostle, Lyman Johnson had apostatized and Brigham was thirteen days older than Heber, he thus became president and used this precedent later in Nauvoo.[68]

Just Quote Blackstone (1839)

While Erastus Snow and some friends were visiting the Saints in the Liberty Jail in 1839, there was an attempted jail-break and the visitors were jailed also, charged with abetting the attempt. When Joseph suggested Erastus plead his own case at the upcoming trial, he pleaded ignorance of the law. The Prophet merely said, "plead for justice as hard as you can, and quote Blackstone (noted English barrister) and other authors now and then, and they will take it all for law." He did, and when he concluded the regular lawyers gathered around him and said they had never heard a better plea. Brother Snow was discharged, and all the rest were held to bail, which Erastus paid.[69]

Optimistic Heber (1839)

In March of 1839 the Church appeared to be on its knees. The prophet and several leaders were in prison in Missouri. The leader of the Twelve, David Patten, was dead. Other members including Marsh, Luke and Lyman Johnson,

---

68 Kimball, *Heber C. Kimball*, p.59.
69 Jenson, *L.D.S. Biographical Encyclopedia*, 1:106.

McLellin, and Boynton had apostatized. Hyde and William Smith were suspended from their offices. Two of the three witnesses had left the Church. Most of the now homeless Saints had already been driven from the state or were attempting to leave, but on the twelfth of that month, Heber C. Kimball wrote to Joseph Fielding back in England: "I can truly say that I have never seen the Church in a better state since I have been a member of it. [Those left] are firm and steadfast full of love and good works . . . and now are ready to go out to preach the gospel to a dying world."[70]

An Ironic End (1839)

In April 1839, while the prophet was still in the Liberty Jail, an ex-sheriff, William Bowman was the captain of a Davies County anti-Mormon mob. Angry that the Mormon prophet still lived, Bowman swore in the presence of Theodore Turley, who was visiting the prophet, that he would not eat or drink, after he had seen Joseph, until he had killed him. Later Bowman was placed in charge of escorting the Prophet and his friends to Boone County for trial. En route they were allowed to escape, probably on the orders of higher authorities who were now embarrassed over the presence of the illegally detained prisoners. In revenge for the escape however, a mob rode Bowman on an iron rail causing his death.[71]

The Blank Sermon (1839)

Jedediah, the father of Heber J. Grant, served a mission in Tazewell County, Virginia, in 1839. Because of the great talks he gave without preparation, he was challenged by unbelieving

---

70 Kimball, *Heber C. Kimball*, p. 60.
71 Proctor & Proctor, p. 402.

detractors to give a public talk on a subject presented him at the time of the discourse. At a packed courthouse in Jeffersonville, he was handed a blank piece of paper. Announcing that this was his favorite subject, he proceeded to tear apart sectarian beliefs about a God creating the world out of nothing; a "blank" God without body, parts, or passions; a "blank" church without prophets, apostles, etc., and a "blank" heaven beyond the bounds of space and time. The inspired audience contributed enough money to purchase a suit of clothes, a horse, saddle and bridle.[72]

Room Enough? (1839)

The Mormon pioneers gave little thought to having "room enough." Martha Thomas, driven from Missouri in the winter of 1838-39, lay on the west bank of the Mississippi with her children, waiting for her husband to return from seeking a passage over the river. There, nearly nine months pregnant, she was found by Brother Wiswager, a fellow Saint from across the river. He told her that they could share his home. "It is twelve foot square, we have five children, you have five, four grown persons, plenty of standing room." Such quarters were not that uncommon. Heber C. Kimball and his wife and three children had just been driven from their home in Far West, an eight-by-eleven-foot cabin with side walls only four-feet high.[73]

Without A Boat (1839)

The Mississippi has received the title of "Father of Waters" for a good reason—it is a mighty river whose floods have received national attention throughout our history. Crossing

---

72   Burton & Burton, pp. 228-230.
73   Backman & Perkins, p. 27.

such a river without a bridge or boat sounds like a bit of fiction and yet that has happened. There is a well-known story of Wandle Mace leaving Nauvoo in the summer of 1846, guiding his family in a boat as he walked most of the way across. (Givens, p. 141) In 1839, Truman Angell and Joseph Holbrook who had escaped to Illinois during the winter heard their wives had reached the river and were waiting for help to cross. Joseph and Truman walked to Quincy, and Angell recorded in his diary that they crossed the river to the Missouri side without a boat, wading "about half-knee deep in mud."[74]

An Unsung Father (1839)

Much has been written about the father of our first prophet but little about the father of Brigham Young. A few quick facts. He was raised as an indentured servant, his father having died when John Young was very small. He ran away and joined the Continental Army when he was only thirteen and fought throughout the Revolution. He investigated and joined the Restored Church before his famous son Brigham. Falling ill in Kirtland in 1834, he asked for a blessing but instead the Prophet Joseph ordained him one of the first church patriarchs so he could bless others. He survived and went through the next five years of Ohio and Missouri persecutions, finally dying in Quincy in 1938, aged seventy-seven, as a result of the hardships of Missouri.[75]

Just Like Joseph Said (1839)

When the Saints settled the town of Commerce in 1839, Joseph made the decision to rename the place Nauvoo,

---

74 Cannon and Whittaker, p. 141.
75 Sessions, pp. 25-30.

meaning "beautiful" in Hebrew. Critics have charged that this isn't even a Hebrew word. However, a teacher of Hebrew named J. Seixas, who taught the Saints in the School of the Prophets in Kirtland, was the author of *A Manual [of] Hebrew Grammar for the Use of Beginners*, dated 1834. Under a "List of Peculiar and Anomalous Forms Found in the Hebrew Bible" on page 111 of that manual, under the letter Nun is the word Nauvoo. In Isaiah 52:7 that Hebrew word is translated as "are beautiful" a word that may apply to a person, thing, or place. The prophet was right, of course.[76]

A Temple In Iowa (1840)

On August 23rd 1840, Joseph and Hyrum preached to a gathering of Saints at Nashville, Iowa, a small town being built up by the Mormons three miles south of Montrose. At that time Joseph suggested a temple be built on the west side of the Mississippi (Iowa) and the members all voted to carry out the suggestion. A little over six months later, a Mormon bishop "with compass and chain," redesigned Montrose, apparently aligning its Main Street with the new temple started in Nauvoo. A perfect alignment can be seen today from the middle of the Montrose Main Street. Some Iowa historians believe a park on Main Street in Montrose was planned as the site of a Montrose Temple, which was never begun.[77]

They Called It Steerage (1840)

In March of 1840 several Saints, including Brigham Young, bought passage on the ship Patrick Henry, bound for England. Like other missionaries they purchased the least expensive

---

76   Seixas, p. xiv.
77   Black and Hartley, p. 197.

tickets, which was called steerage and "you find yourself," which meant they provided their own food. Steerage also meant cargo-hold quarters with no ventilation, light, or privacy. In addition, they had to provide their own bedding, which the local New York Saints made for them. There is no mention of the kind of food, but it had to suffice for at least a month in the crossing and probably consisted of such typical foods as hardtack, salt pork, dried beans, flour, and so forth. The cost was typical—eighteen dollars plus a dollar from each person for the ship's cook. Such costs would be comparable to $800 to $1,000 at today's dollar value.[78]

Getting a License (1840)

When the Twelve began their missions in England in 1840, their first duty, as with all missionaries, was to acquire a license to preach. This was an official certificate that they had sworn to several declarations before the local Court of Sessions. These declarations included the abjuration oath (not to preach heretical doctrines), obedience to the laws of England, and several declarations against "popery."[79] Obedience to England's laws would have been no problem, nor at that time even the declaration against "popery," but there seems to be little question that the abjuration oath should have presented problems. It is no small wonder that any of the Mormon missionaries were allowed licenses once their doctrines were known.

"Next to Catholicism" (1840)

Jedediah M.Grant was on a mission in Tazewell County, Virginia in 1840. A well-to-do and prestigious young woman,

---

78   Young, S. Dilworth, p. 245.
79   *Contributor*, vol. 4, 1882-83, pp. 122-123.

Miss Floyd, was prompted to attend one of his public meetings. Impressed by what she heard, she invited the young Elder home for dinner. She is reported to have said, "Mr. Grant, I am a Catholic; and if Catholicism is not true, Mormonism is. I am fully persuaded that Mormonism is next to Catholicism." She never converted but did become a lasting friend to Jedediah Grant. Incidentally, it was her brother, John B. Floyd, who as Secretary of War in Buchanan's cabinet, is considered by many historians to bear a major responsibility for the United States military expedition sent against Brother Grant's people in the so-called Utah War seventeen years later.[80]

An Old Gentleman (1840)

On their way to an English mission, Brigham Young and George A. Smith were "preaching their way through" to New York. George suffered many illnesses in his youth as well as poor eyesight, and he was suffering on this journey. In fact, by the time they got to Massachusetts, Brigham was even helping his young companion with his meals. At an inn in Stockbridge the young missionary was embarrassed to overhear two other guests. One asked, "Do you know that old gentleman who came in on the stage?" referring to George A., who was only twenty-two. The other guest replied, "No, do you know the young man who waits on him?" referring to Brigham who was thirty-eight.[81]

Who Was William W. Player? (1840)

Not remembering a Methodist preacher who was converted by the Twelve in England in 1840 is certainly understandable—

---

80 Cannon & Woodruff, p. 47.
81 Pusey, p. 39.

they made many converts. But Player should be remembered for a major contribution in Church history. In 1842 the Nauvoo Temple had been under construction for a year and progress was extremely slow and uncertain. What was needed was an expert stone mason. Brother Player, working as a convert among his fellow Englishmen, heard of the need and traveled to Nauvoo and took over as director of stonework on the temple. Without his expertise and personal involvement in every aspect of the Nauvoo Temple stonework, it could be argued that the temple could not have been completed when it was.[82]

A False Doctrine Suppressed? (1840)

With less training to guide them, early Mormon missionaries would sometimes preach their own doctrines. Such was the case some of the Twelve found when they entered their missions in England in 1840. One such incident at a home in Manchester was most embarrassing for George A. Smith. When he entered a room filled with women and girls, one "sister" approached him and apparently speaking for the group said, "We want a kiss of you." He suppressed the inappropriate response and told the group that kissing was not part of his mission. Apparently some local missionaries had been teaching that there was no harm in a "holy kiss" greeting as mentioned in the New Testament. The Twelve put a stop to this practice.[83]

In Only One Year! (1841)

Looking back, the accomplishments of the nine members of the Twelve, after a one-year mission in England, appear impos-

---

82 Smith, George D., *An Intimate Chronicle*, pp. 532-550.
83 Pusey, p. 40.

sible. At the April general conference in Manchester in 1841, they were able to report 7,500 converts; branches established in every major city and town in England; the printing of 5,000 copies of the Book of Mormon, 3,000 hymn books, 2,500 volumes of the Millennial Star, 50,000 tracts; and aiding 1,000 new Saints in emigrating to America.[84] It seems that conducting more than twenty baptisms per day, seven days a week, would have left little time for the raising of money, the actual printing jobs and the numerous sermons preached. After the sufferings of the Saints in Missouri, the Lord knew what was needed.

An Invented Term (1841)

In early Church history, the term "trustee-in-trust," referring to one who has the power to receive, acquire, manage or convey church property, is most familiar—but it seems it is found only among Latter-day Saints. The position was apparently created at a special church conference in January 1841 with Joseph Smith given the title. In his journal for that day he wrote, "Pursuant to public notice, I was unanimously elected sole trustee-in-trust for the Church of Jesus Christ of Latter-day Saints." It is likely it was a corruption of the legal term, "trustee, in trust for . . ."[85] George Miller held the position after Joseph's death and the term has become common among the Saints ever since.

Two Baptisms at Once (1841)

Rebaptism as a means of renewing one's covenant with the Lord was not uncommon in the early days of the Church. Less

---

84 Pusey, p. 43.
85 HC, 4:286.

known, however, is the fact that at times in Nauvoo it was done in conjunction with baptisms for the dead in which each person who was baptized on behalf of another person was at the same time renewing his or her own original covenants of baptism. Such a practice is indicated in a certificate dated July 4, 1841 in which "Catharine Fory renewed her covenant with the Lord, and was baptized in behalf of..."[86]

An Obituary Before Dying (1841)

It's somewhat unusual to read one's obituary while still alive, but that happened to Martin Harris, one of the three witnesses. It may have been a case of name confusion, but in 1841, newspapers throughout the country were reporting the assassination of a Martin Harris in Illinois because he was lecturing against the Latter-day Saints. It made sense because of Harris' apparent break with Mormonism, but it just wasn't true. However, a former acquaintance of Martin and a respected editor, Rochester editor, Alvah Strong, who had worked as a printer in Palmyra, penned a highly respectful memorial for the man he remembered as having "an irreproachable character for probity." Now, Martin had the pleasure of knowing what some people might say of him after his actual death.[87]

Origin of Wards (1841)

The term "ward" used for a subdivision of a geographic entity was in use long before its adoption by the Church. It was first used to define a church subdivision however, in Nauvoo in 1841, to facilitate the building of the temple. Members were

---

86 BYU Studies, Vol. 18, No. 2, p. 229.
87 Anderson, Richard Lloyd, p. 101.

asked to not only pay a tithing but to donate a tenth of their labor to the construction. To better organize the membership in donating every tenth day, the city was divided into ten subdivisions with the donated labor rotating among the divisions every tenth day. Such a division worked so well that the system was kept intact as the Saints moved west and worked equally well for the care of the poor and meeting together as congregations.[88]

The Epitome of Religious Toleration (1841)

No American community has legally provided greater religious toleration to all faiths than the Saints in Nauvoo. A city ordinance not only granted equal privileges to all denominations but stipulated "that any person ridiculing or abusing another on account of his religious belief should on conviction . . . be fined in a sum not exceeding $500 or imprisoned not exceeding six months." By today's inflated exchange rate, the possible fine would be no less than $20,000. There is no record of arrest for violations of this ordinance, but the spirit of toleration in the LDS community was evident in the number of times visiting ministers of other churches were invited to freely speak to the Saints at their public meetings.[89]

Not In Nauvoo (?)

We put a question mark in place of the date because that's the problem with this story. Many years after the event, William Cahoon described how at "about" the age of seventeen he visited the Prophet Joseph as a home teacher—a story we love to repeat on the subject of home teaching. Brother Cahoon

88 Smith, George D., *An Intimate Chronicle*, p. 527.
89 HC, 4:306.

mentions Montrose, Iowa in his story, implying the event took place in Nauvoo. Actually, Brother Cahoon was born November 7, 1813 and thus he was "about" twenty-six when he moved to Nauvoo. Since the revelation on home teaching was received in April 1830, the story of such a visit is possibly true, but the setting had to have been Kirtland since that is where William first met the prophet when he was "about" seventeen or eighteen—but it did not happen in Nauvoo!

The Little Giant Named (1842)

The nickname for Stephen A. Douglas, senator from Illinois and participant in the famous Lincoln-Douglas debates, is well known. Far less known is how he acquired that famous title. The story was taken from the Peoria Transcript and reprinted by the Illinois Historical Society as an important source document on September 13, 1858. The article pointed out that for the sobriquet 'Little Giant', Stephen Douglas "is indebted to Joe Smith, the Mormon Prophet, for the first application of it to him." It went on to say that as a result of Douglas's defense of the Saints, Joseph called him 'Little Giant' for his "unbounded admiration" for him. The Saints lost any "admiration" for the 'Little Giant,' however, when he turned against them as he campaigned for president several years later.[90]

The Real Beginning (1842)

History books like to use the date 1848 as the organized beginning of women's rights when the Seneca Falls convention drew up a declaration enumerating rights deserved, but denied, women. Actually, an organized movement had been

---

90 *Improvement Era*, September 1926, No. 11.

initiated six years earlier at the founding of the Relief Society in Nauvoo. Mormon women have recognized this for years. Sarah M. Kimball, a major participant in the founding of the Society and later president of the Utah Woman's Suffrage Association, declared in 1870 that the "sure foundations of the suffrage cause were deeply and permanently laid on the 17th of March, 1842." The national woman's movement was merely a secular manifestation of what had occurred in Nauvoo in 1842.[91]

Waiting For Emma (1843)

The temple endowments in Nauvoo were revealed to the Prophet Joseph in 1842, but there was at least a year's delay in administering such blessings to the women of Nauvoo. The prophet's wife, Emma, refused to accept the implications of plural marriage associated with those endowments and Joseph wanted her to be the first woman to receive them. It was not until May 1843 that Emma first consented to Joseph taking plural wives, after which she received her own endowments, opening the way for the other sisters. Such endowments, because the temple was not complete, were received in the Red Brick Store. Emma would later recant her decision but by then the other women were receiving their own endowments.[92]

Not Following the Prophet (1843)

While visiting Emma's relatives near Dixon, Illinois in June 1843, the prophet was taken into custody by two deputies with an extradition order from Missouri. Before he could be taken across the river however, he was able to contact Cyrus Walker, an attorney and Whig candidate for Congress in the upcoming

---

91   Madsen, Carol Cornwall, "Emmeline B. Wells: 'Am I Not a Woman and a Sister?" *BYU Studies*, Spring 1982, pp. 172-173.

92   Cook, Lyndon W., Revelations of the Prophet Joseph Smith, p. 294.

election. Upon Joseph's promise to cast his vote for him, Walker, believing Joseph's vote meant the Mormon vote, obtained the prophet's release. In that fall's election, although favoring the Democrats, Joseph kept his promise and voted for Walker. He did tell his people however, that Hyrum had received a revelation to vote for the Democratic candidate, Joseph Hoge, and he never knew Hyrum to have a revelation and fail. The Saints voted for Hyrum's man and Cyrus lost the election.[93]

Joseph the Poet (1843)

In 1843 W. W. Phelps wrote a poem titled "Go With Me." As a reply to Phelps' poem, Joseph published a lengthy poem titled "A Vision" commonly known as "I Will Go." The "vision" refers to a revelation received in Hiram, Ohio, and canonized as the 76th section of the Doctrine & Covenants. This poem, consisting of 78 stanzas, clarified some of the passages in the original revelation, to the satisfaction of many members who had questioned its departure from their traditional concepts of heaven and hell. There is some question as to proof of the authorship; possibly Joseph had the help of Phelps himself, Parley Pratt or someone else. It appears obvious however, that its publication, which included the words "I, Joseph, the prophet" had his approval and quite possibly his authorship.[94]

Seceding From Illinois (1843)

It was a novel idea but not very workable. In December 1843, after the Saints started experiencing the repercussions of their bloc voting in the previous election, they petitioned

---

93 Hill, Marvin S., pp. 129-132.
94 Merrill, Byron R. [et al.], pp. 142-152.

Congress to set Nauvoo aside as a federal district with "all the rights, powers, privileges, and immunities belonging to Territories." In a complete reversal of the stand they later took in Utah, when they objected so vehemently to territorial status in favor of being a state, they were now asking for federal troops. There was a difference however. The Nauvoo Legion would be incorporated as part of the regular forces and they would all be under the command of Lieutenant-general Joseph Smith, Jr. Not surprisingly, the petition made little headway.[95]

The Turning Point in Illinois (1843)

There were a number of reasons for anti-Mormonism in Illinois that made expulsion of the Saints inevitable. The final straw, however, appeared to be political. Proud of their political power, the Saints cast their lot with the Democrats who seemed to promise them the most. The fall election in 1843 saw the Democrats winning Hancock County by over 1,300 votes and the entire state by fewer than six hundred. This not only assured the Mormons of the enmity of all the Whigs, a powerful force in Hancock County but also of the old-time Democrats who saw their political power slip away to Nauvoo. Governor Ford himself later stated that "From this time forth the Whigs generally, and a part of the Democrats, determined upon driving the Mormons out of the state."[96]

Joseph Went to His Room (1843)

To provide Joseph and Emma with some badly needed income, the Mansion House began holding weekly dances during the winter of 1843-44. Joseph was adamantly opposed,

---

95   HC, 6:131.
96   Ford, 2:154.

but Emma insisted. Although the prophet did not publicly speak against dancing, he would register his disapproval of the dances in the Mansion House by going to his room upstairs during the dances and privately telling his friends not to let their daughters attend the dances. To avoid offending the musicians, Joseph did attend one of the dances and even asked one of the players to dance the hornpipe for him. That attendance and his refusal to oppose Emma and stop the dances suggested a tacit approval. As a result the Mansion House parties that winter were a most popular diversion in entertainment starved Nauvoo.[97]

A Plan to Abolish Slavery (1844)

Would the Prophet Joseph's plan for abolishing slavery in his presidential platform in 1844 have prevented the Civil War if attempted? Such a plan had been mentioned by a few abolitionists, but was unique in a national political platform. He suggested slavery be abolished by 1850 by paying slave owners for their slaves from the proceeds of the sale of public lands and that the former owners hire them back as free laborers. "An hour of virtuous liberty on earth is worth a whole eternity of bondage!," he said. Incidentally, he also suggested that additional purchasing funds could be accumulated from the deduction of pay from members of Congress.[98]

Foreshadowing Little Rock (1844)

As the Prophet Joseph began his presidential campaign in 1844, he published his *Views of the Powers and Policy of the Government of the United States*, setting forth his stand on the

---

97 Hicks, p. 75-76.
98 Roberts, CHC, 2:192.

proper role of the federal government and what he would attempt as president. In it he foreshadowed by over a century the role of the federal government in protecting the rights of citizens when a state fails to do so. He said, "Give every man his constitutional freedom and the president full power to send an army to suppress mobs . . ." This was not done until 1957 when Eisenhower used "federal" forces to protect the civil rights of Blacks in Little Rock, Arkansas.[99]

Five Weeks on the River (1844)

Priscilla Mogridge was only twenty when she left her English home to migrate to Nauvoo. Along with 250 other Saints she embarked on the sailing vessel *Fanny* and arrived in New Orleans in February 1844 after a crossing of six weeks. There the Church steamer *Maid of Iowa* met the arrivals as it did so many others to transport them up the Mississippi to Nauvoo. Sister Mogridge described the journey up the river, hindered by mobbings, persecutions, and insults wherever they tied up. At one point, the captain, Dan Jones, ordered the brethren to parade with armed muskets to stop a stoning. When the steamer finally arrived at Nauvoo to be greeted by the Prophet Joseph, they had been on the river for five weeks.[100]

Back To New Jersey (1844)

In late 1844, Rachel Ivins, confused and distraught over rumors of polygamy in Nauvoo, returned to New Jersey. Before the prophet's death, he had sought an interview with her. Believing she would be asked to be his plural wife, she had refused to meet him, outraged at the idea. She soon discovered

---

99   HC, 6:206.
100   Tullidge, pp. 289-291.

however, that it was not easy to abandon the Church she had grown to love. Nine years later she joined with other family members who decided to join the Saints in Utah. There, two years after her arrival, she accepted the principle that had once outraged her and became the seventh wife of a man she had met years earlier when he was a young missionary in New Jersey. Shortly after the birth of her first and only child, her husband died. Rachel spent her remaining years devoted to raising another of the Lord's prophets—Heber J. Grant.[101]

Governor Ford Agreed (1844)

Governor Thomas Ford did not always side with the Hancock County mobs as many Saints are prone to believe. For instance, according to John Taylor, sometime after the Carthage murders, Ford told him that *The Expositor Press* "ought to have been removed, but that it was bad policy to remove it as we did; that if we had only let a mob do it, instead of using the law, we could have done it without difficulty, and no one would have been implicated." History suggests that he was undoubtedly right. Several abolitionist presses had been destroyed previous to *The Expositor*, but always by mobs and it was impossible to charge anyone in such cases.[102]

Hyrum Wanted—Dead! (1844)

On June 13, only two weeks before the Carthage martyrdoms, a mass meeting was held in Carthage to draw up a set of resolutions against the Saints. These resolutions, which led to the martyrdom, appeared more critical of Hyrum Smith than his brother—and specifically because he did "offer a reward for

---

101 Cannon and Whittaker, pp. 23-34.
102 HC, 7:121.

the destruction of the . . . *Warsaw Signal*," and because he "publicly threatened the life of . . . Thos. C. Sharp, the editor of *The Signal*." As a result of such acts, the antis resolved to be ready to "co-operate with our fellow-citizens in this state, Missouri, and Iowa, to exterminate, utterly exterminate, the wicked and abominable Mormon leaders."[103]

Joseph and the Lawrence Sisters (1844)

Two of Joseph's plural wives were sisters, Maria and Sarah Lawrence. Attempting to demonstrate the Prophet's greater feelings for his plural wives than for Emma, Mark Hoffman forged a letter in which Joseph, after his temporary attempt to flee west before changing his mind and making the fatal trip to Carthage, wrote to Maria and Sarah, requesting that they go to Cincinnati and wait "until you hear from me."[104] Evidence does seem to suggest, however, that Emma was more jealous of the Lawrence sisters than any other plural wives which may explain the reason for Emma's trip to Quincy shortly after Joseph's death to legally remove her husband's guardianship of Maria and Sarah.[105] It mattered little—Sarah would marry Heber C. Kimball and Maria would marry Almon Babbitt.

Carthage Jail Not Part of Plan (1844)

According to Governor Ford, Joseph's enemies not only didn't expect him to surrender to authorities after the destruction of *The Expositor*, but they didn't want him to. When the Constable went to Nauvoo to arrest the prophet, he returned at once when told Joseph had fled, and made no effort to determine the truth. As part of the "conspiracy" that Ford said he

---

103 HC, 7:122.

104 Jessee, *The Personal Writings of Joseph Smith*, p. 598.

105 Smith, George D., *An Intimate Chronicle*, p. 139.

later discovered, the antis were afraid of the Mormons submitting to "the protection of the law." This would prevent the antis from "calling out an over-whelming militia force, for marching it to Nauvoo, for probable mutiny when there, and for the extermination of the 'Mormon' race'." Joseph ruined their plans by going to Carthage before the plan could be enacted.[106]

The Lost Letter (1844)

Oliver Cowdery had been out of the Church for seven years when the Prophet Joseph sent him a letter, forgiving him for past wrongs and inviting him back into the fold. Fourteen months later Joseph was spending his last day in the Carthage jail when he received a letter brought to him by Almon W. Babbitt. It was from Oliver. Because of the events that followed, the letter became lost. Was it a response to the invitation? Was it positive and did Oliver change his mind after Joseph's death? Unless the letter shows up we'll never know, but we do know that four years later when he asked for rebaptism, he used the same words Joseph had used in his invitation—yes, he had "eaten husks" enough and now wanted back into the church.[107]

The Assassins Helped (1844)

Only a few days after the Carthage martyrdoms, the badly wounded John Taylor insisted on returning to Nauvoo. Believing he could not stand riding in a wagon or carriage, it was decided to carry him all the way to Nauvoo in a litter. As they neared some woods outside of Carthage, Taylor requested that someone send for some Latter-day Saints living nearby to assist the litter carriers, which was done. As the Mormons

---

106 Ford, 2:179.
107 Smith, Joseph Fielding, *Church History and Modern Revelation*, 4:196-197.

arrived, the original carriers melted away one by one and Taylor felt more at ease. He knew several of them had been members of the original mob that had attacked the jail. A sleigh was soon provided for the rest of Taylor's journey.[108]

A Few Locks of Hair (1844)

It was fairly common in the nineteenth century to save as mementos locks of hair belonging to deceased loved ones. We know that this was the case with the Prophet Joseph Smith. Two years after Joseph's death, Irene Haskell's mother, while crossing Iowa, wrote home to her family. She regretted not having sent "some of Joseph's hair" to her sister: "All that have any here [have it] in their bosom pins, finger rings, etc." The word "all"—plus the number of Saints who claimed to have locks of the prophet's hair—makes one wonder just how much hair was cut from the head of the beloved prophet.[109]

The Doctor Was Also a Liar (1844)

There may be debate over whether Thomas Barnes was a quack doctor, as the early Saints claim, but evidence suggests he was a liar. He was a player in the anti-Mormon mass meetings leading up to the deaths of Joseph and Hyrum and on the day of the Carthage meeting in which the mobbers resolved to "exterminate the wicked and abominable Mormon leaders" he reported to the committee that he had been unsuccessful in helping to serve a writ on the Mormon prophet. He was given a vote of thanks for his services to the anti-Mormons, but years later he denied any involvement, and said he abhorred violence. He was, incidentally, the quack, as Taylor termed

---

108 Roberts, *The Life of John Taylor*, p. 148.
109 Black & Hartley, p. 9.

him, who turned up after the assassinations and removed a musket ball from John Taylor with a dull penknife and a carpenter's compass. He even had the nerve to send a bill for his services that Taylor refused to pay.[110]

Joseph's Tomb (1844)

It is a well-established fact that the Prophet Joseph had prepared a tomb for himself near the Nauvoo Temple. He made reference to it himself and many who knew Joseph spoke of it later. Franklin D. Richards reported in the 1880s that he had visited Nauvoo, sought out the tomb and believed he discovered the vault within a building south of the temple site where it was being used as a wine cellar. Joseph's *History of the Church* records that on May 24th,1845, the remains of his brother William's wife, Caroline "were deposited in the tomb of Joseph."[111] She is apparently the only one we can verify as having been interred in Joseph's tomb. Emma, reportedly, had refused Brigham's request to place Joseph's body in the prepared tomb.

Shocking Rumors (1844)

After Joseph's death, William Clayton gave both advice and assistance to his widow until Emma insisted that all of Joseph's business as Trustee-in-trust should be turned over to her lawyer. When Clayton resisted, Emma said there was nothing with Joseph's name on it that should be secret—she had no secrets herself. William refuted this, saying he knew there were things she did not want the world to know, although he had never told anyone nor intended to. Is it possible Clayton was

---

110 Burton, pp. 630-632.
111 HC, 7:418.

making reference to the rumors that Emma, in reaction to Joseph's plural marriages, had herself encouraged relationships with other men? Although little if any evidence supports these rumors, this may have been Clayton's allusion when he said that day to Emma, "It is still the truth and I shall not deny it."[112]

Relief Society Suspended (1844)

In March 1844, only two years after its organization, it was decided to suspend further meetings of the Relief Society. There are no contemporary records to explain the reason but Eliza Snow explained in 1869 that Emma "gave it up So as not to lead the society in Erro[r]." John Taylor publicly clarified this in 1880 when he said that it was done over concern of Emma's use of the society to preach against plural marriage. Whatever the case, what the leaders saw as a misuse of the organization, prevented the society from functioning as it was designed for the next twenty-three years, until President Young reactivated it in Utah.[113]

An Unbelievable Accusation (1844)

After the death of her husband, relations between Emma and the Twelve deteriorated rapidly. Emma became especially upset as those she had considered her friends sided with the Twelve. William Clayton claimed Emma accused him of spending time in "secret" counsel with the Twelve and said, "it was secret things which had cost Joseph and Hyrum their lives." She went on to say, according to Clayton, "I prophecy that it will cost you and the Twelve your lives as it has done

---

112   Smith, George D., *An Intimate Chronicle*, p.144.
113   Beecher, p. 89.

them." What followed is one of the most unbelievable comments ever made about Emma by a contemporary Saint. He wrote that she repeated it two or three times and in a manner that he understood, "she intended to make it cost us our lives as she had done by President Smith."[114] This referred perhaps to her encouraging Joseph's return from across the river, but such an unbelievable charge seems more revealing of Clayton than Emma.

For The Relief of The Saints (1845)

According to a report in *The Nauvoo Neighbor* on 26 February 1845, a bill had been recently introduced in Congress titled "An Act for the Relief of the People Called Mormons, or Latter Day Saints." This bill, which apparently never came to a vote, provided for a twenty-four mile square tract "in the region known as the Pineries in the Territory of Huron" to be known as the Mormon Reserve. If approved, it would have established a Mormon reservation, similar to those being established for Native Americans. The editor of *The Neighbor,* John Taylor, looked approvingly at the idea but objected to the small size. Nevertheless, suspicious of any federal act designed to "relieve" the Saints of their oppression, the idea was never taken seriously by the Saints whose destination was already determined.[115]

Advice to Islanders (1845)

Substantial Pacific Island immigration wouldn't happen until the twentieth century, but an 1845 letter written by Church leaders in Nauvoo to Addison Pratt serving a mission in

---

114 Smith, George D., *An Intimate Chronicle*, p. 144.
115 Givens, p. 30.

the Sandwich Islands (Hawaii) outlined settlement plans the Twelve intended to follow in 1847. "If any of the brethren of the islands wish to emigrate to the continent," they wrote, they could go to several places along the west coast. The letter informed Pratt of plans to establish settlements in those places, but "the [main] settlement will probably be in the neighborhood of Lake Tampanagos [sic, Utah Lake] as that is represented as a most delightful district and no settlement near there."[116]

Bodies Viewed After Burial (1845)

Seven months after the martyrdom in Carthage, Joseph's and Hyrum's bodies were moved from the basement of the Nauvoo House and reburied under a little outbuilding near the Homestead. On February 1, 1845, Heber C. Kimball recorded in a pocket diary, "At ten o'clock in the evening Elder B. Young and myself went to see Joseph and Hyrum." Heber's daughter, Helen, remembered the incident and her father bringing home a small scrap from each of their burial robes.[117] William and Dimick Huntington, who helped move the bodies, also took some of Joseph's hair. This hair was placed in the head of a cane made from the oak box in which the bodies were returned from Carthage.[118]

Dividing Nauvoo (1845)

After the death of the Prophet Joseph, the state of Illinois rescinded the Nauvoo city charter, thus leaving the Saints without a city government.

116   Christian, Lewis Clark, "Mormon Foreknowledge of the West," *BYU Studies.* Fall 1981, p. 411.

117   Holzapfel & Holzapfel, p. 280.

118   Barnett, Steven G., "The Canes of the Martyrdom." *BYU Studies*, Spring 1981, p. 206 fn.

Governor Ford suggested to Brigham Young that this could be remedied by setting up town governments and applying for town charters. The law, however, limited town corporations to areas of no more than one square mile. The governor said, "I would advise that you incorporate as many towns, one mile square as will cover the city." Since Nauvoo was much larger than a square mile, this would have meant a number of small towns would be established where Nauvoo existed. The Saints decided against the suggestion.[119]

Jail? Not Again (1845)

Bishop George Miller was not a man to be trifled with. In September 1845 he was in Carthage with his wife transacting some official business when he was arrested by constable Michael Barnes and taken before Captain Robert F. Smith, the same justice of the peace who had illegally assigned Joseph and Hyrum to the Carthage jail on charges of treason. The charge against Brother Miller? Treason—a non-bailable offense. Knowing what had happened to his friends on the same charge by the same men, he told the captain there were not enough men in Carthage to put him in jail. He had served in two wars and killed snakes in Illinois but would not go into that jail alive. Esquire Smith took his verbal recognizance for his appearance at a later date and released him.[120]

A Window in the Nineteenth Century (1845)

Not long after the death of the Prophet Joseph, John Greenleaf Whittier, on impulse, visited a Latter-day Saint meeting in Lowell, Massachusetts. Apparently impressed, he

---

119   Berrett & Burton, 2:47.
120   HC, 7:442-443.

wrote a description of the meeting and his appraisal of the Mormons and their prophet. Recognizing that "the reports circulated against them by their unprincipled enemies in the west are in the main destitute of foundation," he judged their fallen leader. "Once in the world's history we were to have a Yankee prophet, and we have had him in Joe Smith... He has in the words of Horne, 'knocked out for himself a window in the wall of the nineteenth century,' whence his rude, bold, good-humored face will peer out upon the generations to come."[121]

Didn't The Attorney General Know? (1845)

In 1845 as the sham trial against the accused assassins of Joseph and Hyrum began, the Attorney-general of Illinois, Josiah Lamborn, asked the Saints to hunt up the witnesses and collect and arrange testimony. Brigham Young found it necessary to remind the Attorney-general, through his representatives, George A. Smith and John Smith, that although the Saints stood ready to "assist in favoring the ends of right," the trial was not "between the Mormons and murderers; but it is between the state and the prisoners or offenders." As the Saints expected, the trial was a sham and the assassins were found not guilty.[122]

They Didn't Wait for Brigham (1845)

Early in 1845, a year before the exodus from Nauvoo, James Emmett led a small group of Saints westward. Like some others, after the death of the Prophet Joseph, he was not willing to accept the advice of Brigham or the Quorum of the Twelve. Destitute and suffering from a shortage of food, along

---

121   Mulder & Mortensen, pp. 158-159.
122   Berrett & Burton, 2:55.

with his followers, Emmett himself finally returned to Nauvoo in August, confessed his faults for leading away many who thought they were acting under the counsel of the Twelve, and asked to be restored to the priesthood. This was done and his movement west was called a mission. His group stayed encamped among the Sioux on the Missouri River about thirty miles above the mouth of the Big Sioux River until the remaining Illinois Saints arrived the following year at Winter Quarters, over a hundred miles south of their encampment.[123]

Lucy's Vision (1845)

Exactly one year from the time of the Carthage martyrdom, Joseph's mother announced that she had received a vision that her only surviving son, William, should lead the Church as president. Brigham Young was willing to have the reported vision read from the stand the next Sunday and let the people judge, but before that could happen, Lucy asked that it not be done—that it was incorrectly recorded and was intended only for her family. Brigham and the Twelve felt no animosity toward Lucy—only toward her rebellious son whom the people shortly rejected even as a patriarch. Lucy apparently recognized the misinterpretation of the "vision" and remained friendly and accepting of Brigham and the Twelve as the rightful leaders.[124]

A Dichotomy Explained (1845)

Many students of Nauvoo history wonder at the phenomenon of thousands of Saints still adding to their homes in Nauvoo in 1845, building shops and public buildings, planting

---

123   Hanson, pp. 93-94.
124   Jessee, *John Taylor's Nauvoo Journal*, pp. 73-75.

gardens and orchards and improving their city, while at the same time constructing wagons to carry them away from these improvements. Parley P. Pratt, aware of such a dichotomy, attempted to explain it when he said, "We do not want to leave a desolate place, to be a reproach to us, but something that will be a monument of our industry and virtue . . . all we leave will be a monument to those who may visit the place of our industry and virtue." Nauvoo Restoration, Inc. has become a prophecy fulfilled.[125]

In the Company of Greats (1845)

Orson Spencer, with two college degrees, was one of the best formally educated leaders of the early Latter-day Saints. In late 1845 he was selected by the Quorum of the Twelve to write a letter to Governor Thomas Ford detailing the grievances of the Saints under Ford's administration. In it he gave the best description of the feelings the Saints had for the non-Mormon Sheriff Backenstos, who had tried so desperately to defend the rights of the Saints. He called him "this valiant man with the firmness and patriotism of Jackson, S. Adams, and P. Henry, [who] had even won a victory that will laurel his brow in the circle of such worthies as Washington, Marion, and Howard, in all time to come."[126]

A Murder In Old Nauvoo (1845)

On the night of June 23rd 1845, a non-Mormon named Irvine Hodge was bludgeoned and stabbed to death in a cornfield between the homes of John Taylor and Brigham Young. He had come to Nauvoo to apparently see Brigham Young

---

125   Black & Hartley, p. 40.
126   Berrett & Burton, 2:105.

about helping two of his brothers who were sentenced to be hung in Burlington on charges of murder. Like most of the gentile community, he believed that his brothers were Mormons, but this being untrue, Brigham declined to get involved. Before Irvine died from the attack, he revealed that he knew his attackers but refused to identify them, other than saying they were from the "river." The brothers were subsequently hung. The mystery is not only who killed Irvine and why but why Irvine refused to identify his attackers.[127]

Fated Companions (1845)

The death of Edmund Durfee at the hands of a mob at Green Plains, Illinois, November 15, 1845, is well known among Latter-day Saint history buffs. Less known is that the death he suffered at the hands of anti-Mormons was a fate he shared with his early missionary companion. In 1832, Durfee had served a mission with Joseph Brackenbury in Chautauqua County, New York. There, in January 1832, shortly after they baptized the Sherman family, Brackenbury was allegedly secretly poisoned by anti-Mormons of that neighborhood. Thirteen years later, his companion was shot down by a mob that was burning out the Saints in Hancock County.[128]

That Will be the Place! (1845)

One of those tantalizingly brief reports in LDS history came from a resolution in the Council of Fifty on September 9, 1845. That afternoon the council met and resolved that "a company of 1,500 men be selected to go to Great Salt Lake Valley and that a committee of five be appointed to gather information

---

127   Jessee, pp. 66-67 & 91.
128   HC, 7:524.

relative to emigration." That the Salt Lake Valley had been selected as the future location of the Saints at this date seems apparent but the lack of details on how it was to be accomplished at that time generates some interesting questions. Why such a large group of men only in the initial move? And were they intended to be settlers or explorers? And just when was the group supposed to make the attempt? And wouldn't such a large exodus of men leave Nauvoo rather defenseless? Whatever the case, the idea was dropped because of the increasing persecutions that fall.[129]

A Return to Nauvoo? (1845)

As late as December 9, 1845, while preparations were well underway for the exodus from Nauvoo, Brigham Young did something that makes us wonder whether he was contemplating a possible return in the distant future. In negotiations with the Catholic Church over the purchase of Church property, Brigham made an offer to lease the temple to them "for a period of from five to thirty-five years, at a reasonable price, the rent to be paid in finishing the unfinished parts of the temple, the wall around the temple block and the block west of the temple and keeping the temple in repair." The offer was not accepted.[130]

A Bit of Deception? (1846)

Although it doesn't explain all the last minute construction and long-term planning in Nauvoo during the final months, Heber C. Kimball explained the last minute finishing of his own home that he lived in only a few months. Speaking from the

---

129 Berrett & Burton, 2:112.
130 Holzapfel & Holzapfel, p. 292.

pulpit of the Tabernacle in Salt Lake City in 1853, he admitted to a bit of deception on his part. "I went to work and built that large house (restored in Nauvoo today) when I knew we should leave in a short time, to excite your feeling with the belief we were going to stay there, that you might build and complete that temple. This course was for your own salvation." How well this deception worked we can't tell, since a large percentage of the Saints were aware of their impending move by this time.[131]

A Delayed Exodus (1846)

It is well known that the Saints began their exodus from Nauvoo on February 4, 1846, in the midst of an extremely frigid winter. Actually, Brigham had intended to leave a day earlier. On February 3rd, after weeks of ordinance work in the temple, he told numerous Saints still waiting at the temple that they would have to wait until more temples were built in the West to receive their blessings, but he was going to get his wagons started and be off. He walked away from the temple, expecting the crowds to disperse but they didn't. Feeling unable to leave so many without such blessings, he returned and resumed his work in the House of the Lord. The exodus for hundreds of Saints would have to wait while Brigham and other authorities continued their temple work.[132]

---

131 Kimball, *Heber C. Kimball*, p. 119.
132 HC, 7:579.

4

The Uprooting
(1846–1847)

Pretended Uncertainty (1846)

The apparent uncertainty about a final destination portrayed at times by Brigham Young in 1846 and 1847 has confused many people. Brigham had a reason for giving such an appearance of ambivalence. He certainly did not want to discourage Mormon Battalion members with the prospect of returning a thousand miles to the Great Basin from their California destination, his goals were more achievable if the federal government was not aware of his exact plans, and if the Great Basin was found unfavorable for settlement, he could simply continue the westward trip without appearing to change his mind. Brigham was certainly not as open or explicit about his communications with the Lord as Joseph had been.[133]

Upper California (1846)

Latter-day Saint critics have challenged the claim that Joseph Smith's prophecy about finding a home in the Great Basin was truly a prophecy since there was so much "speculation" about going to "California" after his death. This is a result of not understanding the word "California" as it was defined in

---

133   Bennett, *Mormons at the Missouri*, p. 290.

1846. Often termed "Upper California," it referred to the upper portion of Mexican territory including such present states as Arizona, New Mexico, California, Nevada, Utah and portions of Wyoming, Oregon and Idaho. Evidence of the Great Basin plans of the pioneer Saints is found in the song they were singing in 1846, called "The Upper California," one line of which went, "It lies between the mountains and the great Pacific Sea," an area that encompasses nearly a third of continental United States.[134]

But Not at Sugar Creek! (1846)

One of the most popular stories among Latter-day Saints tells of the nine babies born at Sugar Creek Camp during the February exodus from Nauvoo in 1846. The story originated with Eliza Snow who said "it was reported that . . ." The story causes us to wonder why husbands would take expectant wives into the wilderness at such a time when it really wasn't necessary. The real story comes from the diary of Jane Johnston who was in the forced exodus of the "poor camp" in September. She described that first night on the Iowa shore: "I was the midwife, and delivered nine babies that night." Sister Snow merely mixed up the dates, which should make us feel better about the intelligence of those Saints who exited in February.[135]

Unready Saints (1846)

The advice sounds familiar. As the Saints were preparing to leave Nauvoo in the spring of 1846, they were counseled to have at least a year's worth of provisions. As the Church leaders organized their camp across the river at Sugar Creek, hundreds

---

134 Roberts, CHC, 3:61.

135 Pearson, Carol Lynn, "'Nine Children Were Born': A Historical Problem from the Sugar Creek Episode," *BYU Studies*. Fall 1981, p. 443.

of families joined them, many of them improperly prepared and who should have stayed in Nauvoo. Historian B. H. Roberts estimated that at least 800 men showed up at Sugar Creek in the last two weeks of February with no more than two week's provisions. Brigham Young and other leaders had provided their extensive families with a full year's provisions as they had been advising their followers, but before they left Sugar Creek, they had fed most of it to those who had not followed the counsel of the church leaders. This caused unnecessary suffering for all.[136]

Half of Your Land (1846)

In January 1846 Samuel Brannan, who would later leave the Church when he settled in California, wrote to Brigham Young from New York with an offer from A. G. Benson, Kendall and Co., an obvious conspiracy of political landsharks. Brannan had already signed a contract with them and wanted Brigham and other Church leaders to do the same. This group of conspiring politicians and "businessmen" would use their considerable influence to prevent the government from interfering with their exodus from Illinois if the Saints would agree to deed over one half of all land they would settle on in the west. Brigham recognized the intrigue but the question is, did Brannan or was he part of the conspiracy?[137]

A Nauvoo Heroine (1846)

When the remaining Saints in Nauvoo became too few to adequately defend their city, the mobs attacked and the resulting conflict in September 1846 became known as the

---

136 Roberts, CHC, 3:41.
137 HC, 7:588-591.

"Battle of Nauvoo." The battle lasted for several days and in the skirmishing, the Saints had both martyrs and heroes, but one of the least known was a heroine—Mary Ann Nickerson. She lived across the river in Iowa and during the battle she made cartridges in her home, delivering them alone in her skiff to the brethren in Nauvoo. She was also able to help refugees escape the mobs by ferrying them back across the river to safety on the Iowa shore. She later became a plural wife to John Tanner in Utah.[138]

Exodus Wives (1846)

Making arrangements to take a family westward from Nauvoo into the wilderness with such crude transportation as existed in the 1840s, was a daunting task. For a man to be responsible for more than one family must have been even more daunting, but such was the case with those living in plural marriages. There were at least 152 men living the doctrine in Nauvoo at the time of the exodus, who were responsible for 587 wives and 734 children. Of this number, seventy-seven wives belonged to Brigham Young and Heber C. Kimball, while the majority had no more than three or four. It is noteworthy, however, to remember that both Brigham and Heber had taken as wives many of the widows and elderly who would have had no one to care for them otherwise.[139]

Independent Sisters (1846)

Mormon women who had shown so much independence in Nauvoo while their husbands were away so much, refused to take a backseat as they started the journey west from Nauvoo.

---

138 Tullidge, p. 433.
139 Smith, George D., "Nauvoo Roots of Mormon Polygamy, 1841-46: A Preliminary Demographic Report," *Dialogue*. Vol. 27, No. 1, pp. 30-34.

Louisa Barnes Pratt has given us an example of this free spirit. "Last evening the ladies met to organize. . . Several solutions were adopted. 1st. Resolved: that when the brethren call on us to attend prayers, get engaged in conversation, and forget what they called us for, that the sisters retire to some convenient place, pray by themselves, and go about their business. 2nd: If the men wish to hold control over women, let them be on the alert. We believe in equal rights."[140]

And Fifteen Minutes More (1846)

As the Saints were crossing the plains of Iowa in the summer of 1846, midwife Patty Sessions became extremely ill. When the doctor said it would be a miracle if she survived, she resigned herself to death and gave orders for her burial, including having "the latitude and longitude taken where I was lain . . . so that I could be found when called for." Brigham, knowing her importance to the Saints, visited her and said, the Saints "must hold onto me as long as I breathed and 15 minutes after I had done breathing." Cheered by theses words and the many prayers and visits of her friends, Patty recovered to live a full forty-six years more.[141]

Black Nauvooans (1846)

There are few references to Blacks in Nauvoo, except for Jane Manning whose family converted in Connecticut and walked to Illinois. She would later walk barefoot across the plains to Utah. Despite the scarcity of references, there were at least twenty Blacks who crossed Iowa with the Saints after the exodus from Nauvoo. In Latter-day Saint journals we find

---

140   Black & Hartley, p. 98
141   Smart, Donna Toland, p. 61.

references to "Black John," Liz Flake, Peter "the Black Boy," Charlotte, "Negro Sam," "Faithful Sam," and so on, as well as hired Black teamsters. There were three Blacks in the 1847 Pioneer Party that broke the trail into the Salt Lake Valley including Green Flake, who drove Brigham Young's wagon.[142]

Just Too Many Snakes (1846)

As the Saints moved across Iowa from Nauvoo, the original plan was to establish one large farm part way across to provide food and quarters for those who would be following. The site selected on Weldon Creek was named Garden Grove, where on April 27, the pioneers started erecting homes, building fences, digging wells and establishing the farm. It was soon discovered however, that the site was not as well timbered or watered as hoped, and to add to their dismay, the place was infested with rattlesnakes. Some of the men were killing as many as eight or more each day. Helen Whitney wrote that she remembered seeing some of the brethren "killing snakes in the grass, where our tents were afterwards pitched." As a result another settlement was established twenty-seven miles northwest which was named Mt. Pisgah.[143]

Whose Idea? (1846)

It sounds ironic that the federal government would request a battalion of Saints to help in the war against Mexico after their failure to give the Mormons help against their persecutors. Actually, the request was made rather reluctantly after Jesse C. Little, Brigham's representative in Washington, had pleaded for such an opportunity, offering as many as two thou-

---

142 Black & Hartley, p. 99.
143 Bennett, Richard, *Mormons at the Missouri*, 1846-1852. pp. 39 & 249.

sand men as a means of gaining money and supplies for the westward journey. President Polk was apprehensive about such a large Mormon army moving west and authorized Colonel Kearney "to receive five hundred of the Mormons into the service so as to conciliate them and prevent them from becoming the enemies of the United States."[144]

The First Saints West (1846)

John Brown, a convert from Mississippi, moved to Nauvoo in 1841, where he served faithfully on the building of the temple and then served a successful mission back through the south. Forced to flee Nauvoo in the 1846 exodus, John returned to Mississippi with a message from the Twelve to the 150 Saints still in Monroe County. Although he was only twenty-six, he was to lead those Saints westward where they would meet the main body in Wyoming on their trip to the Great Basin. Not knowing the main body had stopped at Winter Quarters, Brown and his company, now including some from Tennessee, continued all the way to the present site of Pueblo, Colorado on the Arkansas River where they established quarters. Brown himself would later return eastward to accompany the Pioneer Party in 1847, but he had the honor of leading the first Saints west in 1846.[145]

How Brigham Did It! (1846)

Contrary to popular belief, recruiting volunteers for the Mormon Battalion was not as easy as believed. To encourage enlistment, Brigham gave the Saints three choices: 1) They could enlist. 2) They could start bringing the poor from Nauvoo

---

144   Hanson, p. 116.
145   Sessions, pp. 133-141.

or 3) They could go with a proposed group of volunteers over the mountains. Whatever the case, they would not be able to stay with their families, which was the problem in getting the Battalion volunteers. The day after these choices were offered the Saints, Captain Allen had his battalion complete, although there were more "laundresses" and children than he really wanted.[146]

A Non-Marching Battalion (1846)

Contrary to the beliefs of most Latter-day Saints, the famous Mormon Battalion was not the result of a request by the U. S. Government for volunteers to fight in the Mexican War but a favor granted the Saints for help in moving west. As explained previously, President Polk balked at the number of volunteers the Saints were offering. On June 3rd 1846, he wrote a letter saying he had asked Mr. Little if "the Mormons now on their way to California would be willing, on their arrival in that country, to volunteer and enter the United States Army." Colonel Kearny, who was given the orders, interpreted them to mean accepting the Saints at any time, and thus a non-marching battalion to be recruited in California never occurred.[147]

First Government Offer (1846)

As late as July 1846 Brigham Young was planning on making his "Winter Quarters" on Grand Island in the Platte River in Nebraska, 150 miles west of Council Bluffs. To encourage recruitment of the Mormon Battalion, Captain Allen had promised in the name of the U. S. Government, permission

---

146   Bennett, Richard E., *Mormons at the Missouri, 1846-1852*, p. 62.
147   Black and Hartley, eds., p. 137.

for the Saints to spend the winter of 1846 and 1847 on that 52 mile long island, leading Brigham to comment that this was the first time the federal government had offered to aid the Saints in any way. By the end of July, Brigham, revising his plans, turned down the first offer of aid by the federal government, and chose a site across the Missouri River from the Bluffs, now the site of Florence, Nebraska.[148]

Resistless Bargains (1846)

Because of an early departure from Nauvoo in February 1846, the Saints found themselves on the Iowa prairie with serious shortages of supplies. This necessitated working for Iowans to gain supplies for their continued journey. The eastern Iowa towns of Farmington, Bonaparte, Bentonsport, and others reveal a number of finely built brick buildings that the Saints built in exchange for goods. Iowa historian Edgar Harlan wrote that the Saints "drove resistless bargains for their skill and labor" and that "the spring of 1846 in the Des Moines Valley above Farmington saw more frontier cabin shanties replaced by two story dwellings than has occurred, perhaps, in any life time and area in any western state."[149]

Don't Burn The Temple! (1846)

When the Saints were forced from Nauvoo in 1846, Brigham Young considered it essential that the temple be sold to help pay some of the westward trek expenses. The Kirtland Temple had not been sold because of legal barriers imposed by apostate groups and now, unstable conditions in Nauvoo and the same kind of legal barriers was making the sale of the

---

148   Roberts, CHC, 3:60-90.
149   Bennett, Richard E., *Mormons at the Missouri*, 1846-1852, p. 245.

Nauvoo Temple impossible. Some apparently feared that Brigham, recognizing the futility of selling the Nauvoo Temple, might resort to burning it to keep it from apostate groups. In September 1846, the Strangites wrote in their church newspaper, "All we ask of the Brighamites, is that they will not burn the temple down and lay it to the mob." Such groups must have felt their fear justified when Brigham stated in the Salt Lake Bowery in 1860, "I hoped to see it burned before I left . . . I was glad when I heard of its being destroyed by fire."[150]

Popular Conception Uprooted! (1846)

One of the most prominent misconceptions in Mormon history is belief that most of the pioneer Saints who exited Nauvoo in 1846, spent the following winter at Winter Quarters in Nebraska. Actually the suffering Saints who spent that winter on the western banks of the Missouri River constituted only a minority of the Saints who had been driven from Illinois. Evidence seems to suggest that the population there was approximately 4,000 while the remaining 8,000 were scattered in settlements along the river, at Mt. Pisgah and Garden Grove back in Iowa, in St. Louis (around 1,500), with the Mormon Battalion and small towns in northwestern Missouri and Iowa.[151]

Thomas Kane's Hopes (1846)

Beginning with Thomas Kane's first meeting with the Latter-day Saints at the time of their exodus from Nauvoo in 1846, he worked diligently in their behalf. His long-time friendship and assistance is evidenced by the placing of his

---

150   JD, 8:203.
151   Bennett, Richard E., *Mormons at the Missouri, 1846-1852*, p. 90.

statue in the Utah State Capitol. But he may have begun his friendship with less altruistic motives. As he wrote to his brother in May, 1846: "If on the journey I shall have ingratiated myself with the disaffected Mormon Army [I could] according to the prompting of the occasion be or be not the first U. S. Governor of the new territory of California." When this didn't work out, his acquaintance with the Saints developed into a life-long friendship.[152]

Not Defiling the Camp (1846)

It is rare to find in any journal or diary of pioneers moving west, a description of the disposal of human waste. Hosea Stout, however, recorded in his journal on February 16, 1846, while crossing Iowa, how he "instructed the troop not to defile the camp as was too much the case but remember the law of Moses . . . wherein the Lord would turn away from them . . . if they did not [observe] the proper prescribed rules of cleanliness." Such rules were observed on all western bound wagon trains—men to the right and women to the left, using pits dug by the men. Privacy, such as it was, might be accomplished by having friends stand between users and the wagon train.[153]

The Message To Clayton (1846)

The story of the anthem "All Is Well" by William Clayton and renamed "Come, Come, Ye Saints" is well known in LDS history. While on the Iowa plains Clayton received word that his wife Diantha back in Nauvoo had a son and though his wife was not entirely well, his little son was. After reading the letter containing the information, he retired to his tent and

---

152 Kane, Elizabeth Wood, *Twelve Mormon Homes*, p. ix.
153 Brooks, *On The Mormon Frontier: The Diary of Hosea Stout*, 1:123.

composed the hymn. Less known is the story of the Saint who gave the message to Clayton. His name was Stillman Pond and all would not be well with him. Before he left Winter Quarters for the Salt Lake Valley, he was to suffer the loss of his wife and nine of his ten children. History is silent concerning Brother Pond's thoughts about the message in the hymn that his news inspired.[154]

First City in Nebraska (1846)

The only remaining evidence of the first city established in Nebraska, is a monument dedicated by the Church in a small park in Florence in 1997. Located three miles southwest of the site of Winter Quarters Cemetery and Temple, it was established by an advance pioneer company under the leadership of Alpheus Cutler in August 1846. Cutler was elected mayor of the tent city of Cutler Park, which had a city council, a police department and fire guards and a population of about 2,500. Because of problems with nearby Indians, the city was abandoned and the better-known Winter Quarters was established eastward on the banks of the Missouri River.

Cannibalizing Mrs. Murphy (1846)

Some members of the ill-fated Donner Party that had preceded the Pioneer Party into the Salt Lake Valley by a year but were caught in the Sierra Nevadas by deep snows, survived by resorting to cannibalizing the dead. One of the victims was a Mrs. Murphy, a Mormon widow with five children. Wilford Woodruff claims she was an apostate because she moved from Nauvoo to Warsaw, an anti-Mormon town and went west with

---

154   Black & Hartley, p. 215.

gentiles. A surviving daughter however, denied this—saying her mother hired out to the Donners as a cook in order to reach California, a goal she believed was the destination of the Saints in 1846. The daughter, who left the camp to seek help, believes her mother was killed by some of the survivors. Was it perhaps, because they knew she was still a loyal Mormon?[155]

Winter Quarters Not Wilderness (1846)

There is a common belief that when the Saints set up Winter Quarters (now Omaha, Nebraska) in the fall of 1846, it was wilderness. Actually that area had been an Indian trading site since Lewis and Clark passed there in 1804. There had been a military presence off and on for the past twenty-two years and steamboats had reached there twenty-six years earlier and it was already a point of departure for overlanders to the west coast. There were over eighty inhabited sites upstream and a small village on each bank with regular mail service. It was apparently the difficulties and the lengthy time encountered by the Saints in crossing Iowa that gives the impression of their Missouri River quarters being on the uninhabited frontier.[156]

Heber's Camp (1846)

The number of Saints who abandoned Nauvoo for the hardships of seeking a home in the wilderness has always been impressive, as have the responsibilities faced by the brethren in caring for their own families under such conditions. None were greater however, than those faced by Heber C. Kimball. His camp at Winter Quarters consisted, according to his journal, of

---

155   Tyler, pp. 312-313.
156   Kimball, *Heber C. Kimball*, p. 137.

266 individuals over the age of twelve, 235 wagons, and some 1,600 animals. Of all the women sealed to him, at least twenty-five were at Winter Quarters, although not necessarily in his camp. It is of interest to note that his journal specifies only individuals over the age of twelve. Perhaps the infant mortality rate was so high, he thought it not wise to count those younger than twelve.[157]

D&C 136—Not What It Seems! (1847)

Brigham Young's only canonized revelation to the church, (D&C, 136) concerning the Camp of Israel in their westward trek, was not given by the Lord to show Brigham how to organize the Saints for their journey west. He already knew how to do that, but at the time there was opposition to Brigham's secular leadership by members of the Council of Fifty who felt they had as much authority as the president in making decisions about the journey west. The revelation was in essence a statement on apostolic supremacy and accepted by his loyal followers as such. Dissidents such as George Miller and James Emmett could not accept the revelation and quit the church soon after it was issued in January 1847, but the question of supremacy was settled by this revelation.[158]

Disfellowshipping A Branch (1847)

Counterfeiting on the specie-short American frontier didn't carry quite the stigma that it does today, but it was still a crime and even some Latter-day Saints were caught up in it. Orson Hyde, who had been placed in charge of the Saints still in Iowa on the Pottawattamie lands in 1847, found the problem espe-

---

157 Kimball, *Heber C. Kimball*, p. 143.
158 Bennett, Richard E., *Mormons at the Missouri, 1846-1852*, p. 157.

cially troublesome. Garden Grove, one of the semi-permanent settlements established midway in Iowa to aid the poor during the exodus in 1846, developed such a reputation for this practice and even theft, that Brother Hyde felt it necessary to disfellowship an entire branch—until the guilty ones could be found out.[159]

They Needed the Poor! (1847)

On the advice of Mormon leaders Orson Hyde, Orson Pratt, and John Taylor, the Saints in England sent a 168-foot-long petition, containing 13,000 names to the Queen, requesting the British Government's aid in removing some of England's impoverished masses to America. Victoria did not respond and the Prime Minister, Lord John Russel, apparently expressing the view of most of England's statesmen, opposed the removal of the poor. It is difficult to understand the reason for rejecting such a beneficial suggestion, except to keep the poor in England to provide cheap labor for the booming industrial revolution then underway.[160]

The Dancing Revelation (1847)

Not as well known as Joseph for his revelations, Brigham Young did receive an unusual revelation on 14 January 1847 at Winter Quarters. This was part of the well-known section 136 that is usually associated with the organization of the Saints for the westward movement. Verse 28 however, says, "If thou art merry, praise the Lord with singing, with music, with dancing, and with a prayer of praise and thanksgiving." For the first time dancing was formally sanctioned in the name of the Lord. Nine

---

159   Bennett, Richard E., *Mormons at the Missouri, 1846-1852*, p. 182
160   Larson, *Prelude to the Kingdom: Mormon Desert Conquest*, pp. 101-102.

days later, the prophet called the people together in a newly built hall, arranged them in squares and then prayed that God would accept the evening's offering of dance, setting a pattern, according to one apostle, of how to "dance before the Lord."[161]

World's Largest Log Cabin (1847)

After the return of the pioneer party from the Great Basin to Winter Quarters in 1847 there was a need for calling a conference to approve the reestablishment of the First Presidency. It was now December and a building was needed for such a meeting. Within three weeks of bitterly cold weather, over two hundred men built a huge cottonwood log building, 40 by 60 feet, at Miller's Hollow, later named Kanesville (now Council Bluffs). Described as the biggest log cabin in the world, it was capable of holding between 800 and 1,000 people. Built over a spring, it had to be dismantled in 1849, but it gained the distinction of being the first LDS Tabernacle and multi-ward meeting house built by the Saints.[162]

How to Prevent Gambling (1847)

The notorious Bill Hickman, gunman, friend of Brigham, and later apostate, left Nauvoo with the Saints in 1846 but wintered over in southern Iowa before joining the main body of Saints in Winter Quarters in the fall of 1847. He might have stayed longer in Iowa, where he found it both fun and profitable to race a fast black stallion he owned, urging others to bet against him. Brigham heard about this unsavory habit and warned Hickman against it. To make sure he stopped, he asked Brother Hickman for his horse as a gift for his ten-year-old son

---

161   Hicks, p. 77.

162   Bennett, Richard E., *Mormons at the Missouri, 1846-1852,* p. 212.

Brigham, Jr. Out of friendship and fear of the powers of a prophet of the Lord, Bill surrendered his horse.[163]

And Three Women! (1847)

The makeup of the pioneer train that crossed the plains from Winter Quarters to the Salt Lake Valley in 1847 was planned to have 144 men, representing 12 men from each of the tribes of Israel. But when it started it added three women and two children, which generates the question, "Why were they included?" It seems that the wife of Brigham's younger brother, Lorenzo, suffered from asthma and felt she would die if left behind. Brigham objected but finally agreed and, to give Harriet some female company, took one of his own wives, Clara, who was Harriet's daughter. To add to Brigham's woes, Heber C. Kimball then insisted on including his Norwegian wife, Ellen, and Harriet insisted on taking two of her children. There were no reports of regrets by the end of the journey.[164]

And Other Pioneer Women (1847)

The addition of the three sisters to the Pioneer Camp of 1847 is quite well known. Less known is the fact that six additional females with the Mississippi Saints joined the pioneer group at Fort Laramie and thus nine women entered the Salt Lake Valley with the first Saints. And these were not the first sister pioneers. There had been eleven with Zion's Camp in 1834 and over seventy started west with the Mormon Battalion in 1846, nearly half of them as laundresses and thirty-three being wives of battalion members. And when the main body of Saints started west in the summer of 1847, because of the

---

163   Hilton, p. 19.
164   Knight & Kimball, p. 5.

shortage of men, a major portion of the actual driving of wagons and handling of stock fell to the women in a far greater degree than in any gentile wagon trains.[165]

A Bushel of Corn (1847)

Much has been written about Brigham Young's meeting with Jim Bridger in which the mountain man offered $1,000 for the first bushel of corn grown in the Salt Lake Valley, certain it could never be done. Put into context with his other positive comments about the valley however, it seems he was expressing eagerness for a demonstration rather than doubt as to its possibility. Wilford Woodruff reported that Bridger referred to the valley as a paradise and indicated that if the Saints settled it, he wanted to be with them. George A. Smith reported Bridger as even more enthusiastic, suggesting that in the southern portion of the valley, wheat, corn, and other crops of the best quality were already being raised.[166]

The Real Mormon Trail (1847)

After a century and a half, the few traces of the wagon ruts of the Mormon trail today leave the impression that the trail was really only a narrow rutted trail or road. Actually, the "trail" depended totally on the terrain through which it passed. Where it was necessary to cut the trail, through canyons or at river crossings, it would normally consist of a single trail with wagons following each other. In crossing flat lands such as the prairies of Nebraska or Wyoming however, the "trail" could be up to thousands of yards wide in order to make available more grass for the animals and to keep down the dust. At times the

---

165   Roberts, CHC, 3:289.
166   Pusey, p. 71.

trains would travel as many as five abreast, not only to lessen the dust for those in the rear but to guard against Indian attack.

And Pretty Brunettes (1847)

Unlike most of the perceptions of Indians encountered by westward travelers, the Saints were especially impressed with the Sioux. After their first friendly meeting with that tribe by the Pioneer Party in May 1847, Norton Jacob referred to them as "noble looking fellows" and to some of the women as "pretty brunettes." Lorenzo Young thought them "quite intelligent" and William Clayton, describing their neat and clean clothing and "nice robes artfully ornamented with beads and paintings, said "they will vie with the most tasteful whites" for cleanliness and neatness.[167] As hostilities increased between the Indians and encroaching whites, such descriptions became less and less common.

A Real Sport! (1847)

Lot Smith, known best for his exploits as a Mormon guerrilla fighter in the Utah War of 1857, also made his mark in the Mormon Battalion ten years earlier. One story from that affair may be apocryphal but it certainly typifies Brother Smith. After his arrival in California he halted a bull-fight, telling the Spaniards it was a cowardly and cruel exhibition. Real courage would be to ride the bull instead of killing it, he said. When told it was impossible, Lot immediately leaped onto the neck of one of the bulls and holding it by the horns, rode around the ring. He was shortly thrown but he had demonstrated his point— and his courage.[168]

---

167 Knight and Kimball, p. 115.
168 Kane, Elizabeth Wood, *Twelve Mormon Homes*, pp. 22-23.

Not Trail Blazers (1847)

Although few public schools teach much about Mormon history, most texts include a map of western trails, including the "Mormon Trail" along the northern side of the Platte River. It is a common misconception, according to Stanley Kimball, historian of the Mormon Pioneer Trail Foundation, that the Latter-day Saints blazed this trail to stay clear of gentiles on the more traveled Oregon Trail. Kimball insists there is little evidence the Saints blazed a single mile of the "Mormon Trail" along the Platte or anyplace else. There might be short variants because of high water, cholera, bad weather, and so forth, but they invariably used roads and trails already used by previous travelers.[169]

The Chief Grumbler (1847)

During the pioneer journey of 1847, President Young found it necessary to constantly warn the brethren about grumbling. Finally, in a stroke of humorous genius, he announced that only Henry G. Sherwood, the commissary for the camp, had a legal right to find fault, since he had been elected to the office of "chief grumbler." Whoever had a complaint, Brigham said, must get permission from Sherwood to grumble. Norton Jacob, one of the captains of ten, said this bit of humor with a message had "excellent effect in putting a check on some fractious persons," especially Solomon Chamberlain, who was voted the most even tempered man in the camp—"Invariably cross."[170]

Tame Buffalo (1847)

As the pioneer party made its way across the Plains in 1847, the buffalo were so numerous that President Young had to continually warn the brethren against killing too many because

169 BYU Studies, Vol. 24, No. 3, p. 321fn.
170 Knight & Kimball, p. 51.

the meat was going to waste. Their numbers in some parts of Nebraska were so numerous it was obvious they had not been much hunted and were not yet afraid of humans. Norton Jacob, a journalist in the train, noted they were so tame they "walk near the sides of the wagons. Horsemen have some difficulty driving them from the path ahead. If horsemen chase buffalo, the animals turn around and look at them as soon as the riders stop." Contrary to what history texts tells us, these pioneers reported that even the Indians did not hesitate to waste the plentiful herds, often taking only the hides and choice cuts of meat and leaving much of it to rot on the prairie.[171]

Is This Really the Place? (1847)

The first pioneers into the Salt Lake Valley made camp on Mill Creek and started to irrigate and plow the land on the afternoon of July 23, the day before Brigham entered the valley. This fact has been interpreted as meaning the decision to settle there had been made. Actually, on the 25th, William Clayton noted in his journal that they would search for a better location the following day if Brigham was well enough. He was not and on July 28, Clayton wrote, "The brethren are more and more satisfied that we are already on the right spot." So, was it a prophet's vision remembered by Wilford Woodruff thirty-three years later or Brigham's health in 1847 that decided "that was the place"?[172]

It Begins at the Temple (1847)

Only four days after the Saints entered the Salt Lake Valley, Brigham Young marked the spot for the temple that would not be completed for another forty-six years. Apostle Orson Pratt

---

171   Knight & Kimball, pp. 79-87.
172   Kimball, *Heber C. Kimball*, p. 169.

was then given the job of surveying not only the Temple Block of forty acres, but starting from there, the rest of the city. He established a point on the southeast corner of the square as the base and meridian from which all surveys were to be made. The stone marker that still stands was placed there in 1855 by the surveyor-general of Utah. Not only is every point throughout the city measured from that spot near the temple, but that is also the origin for the survey of the entire Great Basin. In other words, every location in the entire Mormon West has the Salt Lake Temple as its reference point.[173]

Forever Young (1847)

Only sixteen days after the Saints settled in the Salt Lake Valley, the first white child in the Utah Territory was born. Both her parents, John and Catherine Steele had been with the Mormon Battalion and arrived in the valley from California shortly after the arrival of the pioneer party. They named their new daughter Young Elizabeth after Brigham Young and Queen Elizabeth. Although she was born after the arrival of the pioneer party, she was always considered one of the original pioneers until she died at Hurricane in 1938 at age ninety-one. Due to her unusual first name, she was known throughout her life as Young Elizabeth.[174]

Illiterate Fanatics? (1847)

One of the most common charges leveled against the early Saints was that of being illiterate religious fanatics. The most dramatic refutation of this charge is discovered in their first undertakings upon arrival in the Salt Lake Valley. It was not to

---

173 Oman, Richard G., "Exterior Symbolism of the Salt Lake Temple: Reflecting the Faith That Called the Place into Being," *BYU Studies.* Vol. 36, No. 4, p. 29.

174 Tullidge, p. 443.

build chapels, but schoolhouses. Within three months, with their survival depending on seemingly more crucial tasks, the first school was being held in a tent in the Old Fort, with the students sitting on rough logs and practicing their lessons on smooth pieces of wood. Their teacher, Mary Jane Dilworth was using an old camp stool for a desk. Within the next three years, several Salt Lake City wards were constructing schoolhouses, usable on Sundays for church meetings. Chapels would wait until education was taken care of.[175]

A Sister Wife's Love (1847)

While Heber C. Kimball was making the trek to the Salt Lake Valley in 1847, several of his children were ill in Winter Quarters—little David, infant son of Sarah Ann Whitney Kimball and Vilate Kimball's little boy, Solomon. Sarah Ann was still grieving over the loss of her first born and even though Vilate dearly loved her son Solomon, she reasoned that she was still the mother of seven living children. The love between these two wives was such that Vilate prayed that if God required the life of one of the two children, He would take hers and Sarah Ann's would be spared. As it turned out, Vilate's was spared while Sarah Ann's little son died of the cholera.[176]

Begging Missions (1847)

During its history the Mormon Church has sponsored a variety of missions. Perhaps the strangest were those sent out in the winter of 1847-48 to raise funds for the impoverished Saints as they were journeying westward. The idea originated with Col. Thomas Kane, who believed that his fellow Americans

---

175 Bushman, Claudia L., pp. 68-71.
176 Kimball, *Heber C. Kimball* ,p. 177.

who had donated so generously for the Irish Famine Relief and other worthy causes would certainly open their purses for fellow Americans exiled so cruelly from their homes in Illinois. A force of between 100 and 150 men were therefore sent throughout Eastern United States, "begging" for funds or supplies to aid the Saints. The results were less than successful and one can only admire the faith and fortitude of the men who suffered so many rejections and insults as they tried to aid their families and friends.[177]

First Ladies Aid the Saints (1847)

It was the type of Washington dinner that attracts the rich and famous—but it was for the benefit of a despised sect—the Mormons. First reported in the New York Herald, it was picked up and reported in the January 1848 issue of *The Prophet of the Jubilee*, the Welch church periodical. All contributions from the dinner, attended by Washington's mayor and clergy, were donated to the Saints as they were making their way west. Two of the most interesting attendees and contributors were Dolly Madison, former first lady and Mrs. Polk, wife of the then President. Did the latter's sympathy for the Saints have anything to do with her husband agreeing to the Mormons' request for organizing a battalion to help in the move west?

The Generous Mr. Buchanan (1847)

In the summer of 1847, Charles C. Dana and Robert Campbell left Mt. Pisgah for the East Coast to plead for help for the impoverished Saints at Mr. Pisgah. (See Begging Missions) Receiving mixed receptions they even journeyed to

---

177   Bennett, Richard E., *We'll Find the Place*, p. 333.

Washington D. C. and gained audiences with top government officials, including several of the Presidential Cabinet. President Polk listened respectfully and then directed his private secretary to give the two Saints $10. From the Secretary of State, James Buchanan, who would send an army against the Saints ten years later when he gained the Oval Office, they also received ten dollars. One must wonder if President Buchanan ever remembered the time his generosity outshone his political ambitions.[178]

Winter Quarters Deaths (1847)

There were several settlements of Mormon pioneers along both sides of the Missouri River during the winter of 1846 and 1847 and the dead were buried in scattered locations, many now lost. The largest settlement was Winter Quarter, now the site of Omaha, Nebraska, for which there are better burial records. Noting the census of December 1846 and the sexton's list of burials both there and in Cutler's Park before the move to Winter Quarters, it is possible to arrive at a fairly conservative death rate of approximately 82 per thousand. This is almost identical to the 82.5 figure for all the Saints scattered from Garden Grove to Winter Quarters, a figure arrived at by Richard Bennett who spent several years researching such deaths. That death rate was more than four times the national average.[179]

Transcontinental Railroad Pioneers (1847)

Few historians have ever made a connection between the Pioneer Party's trek to the Salt Lake Valley in 1847 and the Transcontinental Railroad. George A. Smith, a member of that

---

178   Bennett, Richard E., *We'll Find the Place*, p. 304.
179   Beecher, pp. 90 & 160.

original party however, said years later that such a railroad was often a matter of conversation in camp and as they traveled, "every place we found that it seemed difficult for laying the rails we searched out a way for the road to go round or through it." Brigham Young corroborated this when he said, "I do not think we traveled one day from the Missouri river here, but what we looked for a track where the rails could be laid with success, for a railroad through this territory to go to the Pacific ocean."[180]

Signed by God (1847)

When Brigham Young refused to change his settlement plans and take the Saints to California as Sam Brannan advised, Brannan became angry and decided to seek revenge. He did this by pretending to the Saints in California that he was Brigham's agent and responsible for the collecting of tithes. Using such money for personal investments he was soon one of the wealthiest citizens in the state. When Brigham learned of his apostasy he sent Amasa Lyman and Charles C. Rich to ask for the tithes he had fraudulently collected. Brannan's reply: "I'll give up the Lord's money when he [Brigham Young] sends me a receipt signed by the Lord, and no sooner." Brannan died a pauper in 1889.[181]

Who's In Charge? (1847)

In December 1847 Brigham was finally sustained as President of the Church. He overcame the objections of Quorum members such as Orson and Parley Pratt and John Taylor who felt such a move would diminish their roles in the

---

180 CHC, 5:247-248.
181 VanWagoner & Walker, p. 22.

Quorum of the Twelve. But it was essential. Members such as the Pratts and Taylor were teaching that at any time in the absence of senior member Young, the next senior member had comparable authority and could override Brigham's orders. Meeting at Kanesville on December 5, 1847, Heber and Brigham were able to put the minds of the Twelve at ease on the question of the power that the two senior members seemed to have. Heber said "I have all the power I can handle" and after a thorough discussion Brigham was unanimously confirmed president with Heber his first counselor.[182]

---

182   BYU Studies, Vol. 18, No. 3, p. 403.

5

Asylum at last
(1848–1852)

A Day Off Saves Time (1848)

Crossing the Plains in 1848 with Brigham Young's second train, Louisa Barnes Pratt reported in her autobiography that it was the custom to not travel on the Sabbath. The President said, "Write it in your daybook when you travel on Sunday, then notice your success through the week and you will find more time lost through accidents than you had gained by traveling on the day appointed for rest." This was true apparently even for gentiles. A non-Mormon guide with some gold seekers later remarked that resting every seventh day "would get you to California 20 days sooner." A secular reason would suggest that a periodic day of rest kept the cattle in good condition.[183]

Saved By An Umbrella (1848)

One of the few skirmishes between the Saints and Indians during the Mormon Trail era occurred as the Heber Kimball train approached the confluence of the Elkhorn and Platte Rivers on June 6, 1848. Two of the Saints were badly wounded and three or four members of the attacking Omaha or Ottoe tribes were killed. After the skirmish, the Indians found Dr.

---

183 Knight & Kimball, p. 48.

Jesse Brailey alone on the east side of the Elkhorn and chased him. When one of the attackers aimed his rifle at the doctor, the unarmed man raised his umbrella and aimed it at the Indian, causing him to turn and flee into some nearby woods. The lucky physician quickly found his way safely to the main encampment across the river before the Indians could discover the doctor was unarmed.[184]

Variety of Animals (1848)

A variety of animals accompanied the pioneers on the westward trails—horses, mules, oxen, cows, sheep, pigs, and so forth. What is not as well known or thought of is the variety of livestock you would not expect to see with the wagon trains. The train led west in 1848 by Allen Taylor included nineteen cats, thirty-one dogs, eight geese, six doves, and one crow. Lorenzo Snow's train that year included two beehives, while another train, for some strange reason, was carrying seven squirrels. With proper care, most of these could very well survive the journey, but one must wonder about the care that had to be taken with bees.

Freedom In Tennessee Or Utah? (1848)

In May 1848, a group of converts from the state of Mississippi reached Winter Quarters on their way to the Salt Lake Valley. The group was composed of 56 white persons and 34 Blacks, including a fairly wealthy slave-holding clan named the Bankheads. As they crossed Tennessee, the brothers John and George offered their slaves the choice of being set free or continuing on with them to Utah. Aware that slavery, although

---

184 *Mormon Historical Studies*, Vol. 1, No. 1, Spring 2000. p. 44.

discouraged by Church leaders, was still legal in Utah, eleven of the slaves chose to go west with their masters.[185] At the end of the Civil War, the Bankheads helped each of their former slaves take up a homestead in the valley.[186]

Not-exceeding Thirty-nine Lashes (1848)

In the absence of jails during their temporary residence on the Missouri River during the trek west and during the earliest years in Utah the Mormons found it necessary to impose corporal punishment to deter criminal behavior. In January 1848, the high council in Iowa ruled that any Saint residing on Pottawattamie Lands and caught stealing from another Saint would pay the victim four times the value of the goods or receive "not exceeding thirty-nine lashes." If caught stealing from a gentile, they would repay the value of the goods and also receive the lashing—an interesting distinction being made. During that same year, a lashing was administered on the trail west. Heber Kimball's nephew Carlos Murray was given fifteen lashes for stealing cattle from some non-Mormons.[187]

Stretched Out (1848)

All pioneer wagon trains did not necessarily travel in a neat, compact line as seen in movies. On August 26, 1848, only two days west of the last crossing of the Sweetwater River, Heber C. Kimball's train found itself stretched out no less than 24 miles from the front to the rear of the company, forcing Heber to send some of the ox teams back to aid those in the rear. The reason, according to Kimball writing to Saints back on the Missouri, was the heavy cattle losses brought about by

---

185 *Mormon Historical Studies*, Vol. 1, No. 1, p. 48.
186 Carter, Kate B., p. 21.
187 Kimball, *Heber C. Kimball*, p. 145.

the scarcity of grass, the difficult labor for the oxen and their "inhaling so much of the alkali by breathing, eating and drinking." Within a few days, Heber's and Brigham Young's trains, now traveling together, were aided by reserve oxen sent from the valley.[188]

A Sting Operation (1848)

Hosea Stout, the loyal and effective police chief whom Brigham had left to maintain order at Winter Quarters while he was on the Pioneer trek west, had his hands full in the winter of 1847-1848. Suspecting some individuals of setting up a gambling table, Hosea and some fellow officers set up a sting operation, as he recorded in his journal: "Several of us went into a drinking spree with some who were concerned in it. They soon got high enough to develop their plans and thus we learned all about it."[189] Knowing Stout's diligence in uncovering illegal liquor, he probably also charged them with that.

Emma's Temporal Loss (1848)

Emma and her second husband, Lewis Bidamon, profited nicely from sightseeing tourists at their Mansion House hotel after the completion of the Nauvoo Temple. Emma, however, who married Lewis in a Methodist ceremony, never participated in any Nauvoo Temple ordinances after its completion in 1845. She must have greatly regretted its loss by arson in 1848, however, as certainly her husband did. He stated that the diminished importance of Nauvoo as a result of the temple being burned resulted in their hotel doing only "one-fourth the custom [business] it previously had."[190] On the night it burned,

---

188 *Mormon Historical Studies*, Vol. 1, No. 1, p. 54.
189 Brooks, *On The Mormon Frontier*, 1:294.
190 Berrett & Burton, 2:87.

he had been one of the most active participants in the futile attempt to extinguish the fire.

Idling Away Time (1848)

Like most early Mormon communities, the Church made and enforced ordinances normally left up to civil authorities. Such was the case with five provisional ordinances passed by the Salt Lake Valley High Council that went into effect on January 1, 1848. Four of the ordinances were typical but not the first which was designed to prevent any person from "idling away his or her time." Such persons would have their land taken away by the council and managed so that the slothful one's family would not suffer. A charge of managing such a one's affairs would then be made against the property. With almost universal ownership of property, such a law could be most effective.[191]

Paper—Not Gold! (1848)

When the Saints arrived in the Salt Lake Valley in 1847, it was reported that "the only money in Utah" to care for the needs of 1,700 persons was "about $50" brought by Brigham Young. The situation improved somewhat in the fall of 1848 when Battalion members returning from California brought several thousand dollars worth of gold dust. With the people pleading for a medium of exchange, a meeting was called in December at which time Brigham offered gold dust done up in packages of from one to twenty dollars. The people didn't want gold dust—they wanted specie or if that wasn't possible, paper money. In January, the municipal council started issuing bills done by hand on plain white paper, which was acceptable.[192]

---

191   Anderson, Nels, p. 85.
192   Arrington, *Great Basin Kingdom*, pp. 56 & 438fn.

Zion's Fertility (1848)

In an effort to attract more Saints to the Salt Lake Valley, pioneers often commented on the fertility of the soil and the abundant crops. Parley P. Pratt had one of his letters published in *The Millennial Star* in which he mentioned a man who planted only eleven pounds of wheat in the fall of 1847 and reaped twenty-two bushels. He mentioned barley that came up from the roots of the previous crop and four times the quantity. A critic, referring to Pratt's comments about such crops, thought he might have been thinking about babies. There were 248 born the first year in the valley.[193]

First Settler in Utah (1848)

He was not a Latter-day Saint, but a fur trapper from Connecticut named Miles Goodyear. He had laid claim to approximately 300 square miles of present-day Weber County and much of what is now Davis County, including the present site of Ogden. The original name for the little settlement established there was Brownsville after Captain James Brown, the leader of the first settlers. Being a prime location, Brigham Young sent Brown of the Mormon Battalion to purchase the claim with Battalion funds—the first purchase of land to be made by the Saints in Utah. In November 1848, the deed was transferred for a price of $1,950. The Goodyear cabin, built two years before the arrival of the Saints, has been restored and is now on the grounds of the Ogden Temple.[194]

Battalion Funds (1848)

Most of the government pay for the soldiers in the Mormon

---

193   Anderson, Nels, p. 81.
194   Anderson, Nels, pp. 59 & 71.

Battalion was sent home, but not necessarily for the use of the families. Much of it was for the general use of the Church in moving the Saints west and settling them in Utah. Counting the soldiers' pay at $7.00 per month for privates to $50.00 for captains, plus weapons, clothing and other allotments, it has been estimated that the amount received from the government was between fifty and seventy-five thousand dollars. The current value of such an amount would be no less than three million dollars. Incidentally, the cost of the Mormon Battalion monument in Salt Lake City was at least twice what the entire battalion received in pay.[195]

The Fifteen Shooter (1849)

The Frontier Guardian, a newspaper published by the Saints at Kanesville, Iowa, carried an ad in September 1849 by Jonathan Browning for improved firearms including "slide guns, from 5 to 25 shooters."[196] Browning was making these slide guns, one of the first repeating rifles, back in Nauvoo, and it was such a gun that Porter Rockwell used to kill the anti-Mormon, Frank Worrell, who was pursuing Sheriff Backenstos in 1845 on the river road south of Nauvoo. It was also a fifteen-shooter that Heber Kimball borrowed from Howard Egan to kill a buffalo during the pioneer trek in May, 1847.[197] The invention of the metallic cartridge ended the chance of these simple, but effective cap-lock rifles being mass-produced.

No Business Center (1849)

In July 1849, only two years after the Saints entered the Salt Lake Valley, a correspondent for *The New York Tribune*

---

195   Anderson, Nels, p. 81.
196   BYU Studies, Vol. 19, No. 1, p. 207.
197   Clayton, p. 118.

visited the city and described his impression. Although finding a city "extending over several square miles" he was surprised to find no business center of hotels or stores. On inquiry he discovered the reason: "There were no hotels, because there had been no travel; no barbers' shops, because every one chose to shave himself, and no one had time to shave his neighbour; no stores, because they had no goods to sell nor to traffic; no centre of business, because all were too busy to make a center."[198] This was all to quickly change with the coming of the gold seekers that very year.

Winter Saints (1849)

Starting primarily with the gold rush of 1849, many California-bound immigrants reached Salt Lake City late in the season and decided to winter over. Many were truly converted and stayed but others discovered the advantage of "converting" as a means of receiving help from the Saints, finding easy pickings for their thieving ways or even marrying young LDS women only to leave them in the spring for the gold fields. In fact, the first jury trial in the Salt Lake Valley, held in January 1851, was for some "winter Saints" who were sentenced to hard labor for theft. After serving part of their sentences, most of them were pardoned and sent on to California.[199]

Celebrating on Empty Stomachs? (1849)

The Saints in the nineteenth century were always sensitive to the charge of being unpatriotic. Perhaps this was the reason they felt compelled in an 1849 issue of *The Frontier Guardian* (a Church paper published in Council Bluffs) to explain why

198 *Millennial Star*, Nov. 15, 1849, p. 338.
199 Roberts, CHC, 3:343.

they did not celebrate Independence Day in Salt Lake City that year. "Our people celebrated the 24th of July instead of the 4th for two reasons," one of course being the day the Saints entered the valley. "The other was, they had little or no bread, or flour to make cakes, &c., that early, and not wishing to celebrate on empty stomachs, they postponed it till their harvest came in."[200]

Desefornia or Caliret? (1849)

As early as 1849, Mormon leaders were applying for statehood for Deseret. In July, Almon Babbitt left for Washington with a memorial requesting statehood. Before Congress had a chance to ignore the memorial, which they did, General John Wilson, the newly appointed Indian Agent arrived in Salt Lake City with a special message from President Zachary Taylor. He carried a presidential proposal that the Californians on the coast join with the "inland Californians", i.e. the Saints in the Salt Lake Valley, who weren't numerous enough for statehood, and petition for statehood as one state. They could agree to divide later when they were more populated. The Californians rejected the proposal, offended at the thought.[201]

European Size! (1849)

By January 1849, after less than two years in the Salt Lake Valley, the Saints had drawn up a constitution and drafted a petition for statehood. It would be nearly half a century before statehood would be realized, but at that time, if admitted, the new state of Deseret would have been as large as most of Europe. Stretching 1,000 miles north and south and nearly 800 miles from east to west, it would have included not only a

200 *Millennial Star*, Nov. 15, 1849, p. 340.
201 Anderson, Nels, pp. 91-92.

seaport (at San Diego) but would have encompassed an area the size of today's France, Germany, Italy, Belgium and Holland combined. In spite of the advantages of living their religion in a sovereign nation, the Mormon leaders had no desire to establish a separate country.[202]

Catching Fish by Hand (1849)

Writing to the English Saints on July 8, 1849, Parley P. Pratt described the beauties and bounties of Utah. He wrote, "I was at the Utah Lake last week, and of all the fisheries I ever saw, that exceeds all. I saw thousands caught by hand, both by Indians and whites. I could buy a hundred, which would each weigh a pound, for a piece of tobacco as large as my finger. They simply put their hand into the stream, and throw them out as fast as they can pick them up. Five thousand barrels of fish might be secured there annually, just as well as less.[203]

A Kidnapping Mystery (1849)

In the very first government established by the Utah Saints in 1849, Heber C. Kimball was chosen as chief justice. With the law-abiding Saints under church control, there was actually very little for the legally unqualified Kimball to do. In his one year in that position, before being replaced by Daniel Wells, only one known case was brought before Heber. According to the Journal history for April 11 of that year, he dealt with the abduction of Orrin Porter Rockwell's daughter by two men. "Judge Heber C. Kimball issued his first warrant to the marshal, for the arrest of those two men, on charges of kidnapping." History appears to be silent regarding the outcome of this case.[204]

---

202 Kimball, Stanley, p. 197.
203 *Millennial Star*, Nov. 15, 1849, p. 3434.
204 Schindler, p. 190.

Ideas Start Small (1849)

The Perpetual Emigrating Fund, launched in 1849 and before it was put out of business by the United States Government in 1887, was responsible for bringing nearly 30,000 immigrants to Utah. It's original purpose, however, was not intended to be so ambitious. After the initial move by Young and the leaders to Utah in 1847, thousands of Saints, impoverished after their expulsion from Nauvoo, remained in Iowa. The fund was designed to remove these Saints to Utah before they could become permanent residents of Iowa or apostatize. This was done so successfully in the next three years, that the P.E.F. was expanded to bring other impoverished Saints from the British Isles and Europe.[205]

A Gold Mining Mission (1849)

The presence of some Latter-day Saints at Sutter's Mill when gold was discovered in 1849 is quite well known. Equally known is Brigham's admonition to the Saints to avoid the "fever" and stay and build up the Lord's Kingdom in the Great Basin and most of the Saints did. Less known however, is the fact that gold and other specie were very scarce in the Salt Lake Valley and when the Salt Lake Mint was opened in 1849, there was a decided shortage of gold to supply it. The ever-practical Brigham therefore permitted leaders to call Latter-day Saints to California in 1849 on missions to work the gold fields—not for their own aggrandizement but to enrich the Church. Some gold was brought back but in general it was not a profitable venture—proving Brigham's initial advice that it would be more profitable to stay in the valley and build up the kingdom.[206]

---

205 Larson, *Prelude to the Kingdom*, p. 106.
206 BYU Studies, Vols. 1-2, 1959-1960, pp. 19-32.

As Good As Gold (1849)

One of the darkest moments in Church History was the failure of the Kirtland Safety Society in 1837 and the devaluing of its bank notes, causing financial distress for the Church and many of its members. This resulted in many blaming the Prophet Joseph for the failure and apostatizing from the Church, resulting in the exodus of the faithful to Missouri. Later, in response to a shortage of money in Utah in 1849, Brigham arranged to have the Kirtland notes, which many had saved, brought out and placed on a par with gold. This helped solve the money crisis and at the same time fulfilled a prophecy of Joseph's that the notes would some day be as good as gold.[207]

A Thousand Burned Wagons (1849)

Writing from the Platte River area in August 1849, a correspondent for *The St. Louis Republican* described the waste and devastation along the trail west. From Fort Laramie, after the first fifty miles, he said "I have counted about one thousand wagons that have been burnt or otherwise disposed of on the road." Unlike the Saints who did all they could to aid those following, he said these gentile wagons were fired to prevent them "from being serviceable to anybody else." In about twenty miles along the Platte, he saw valuable property thrown away that he valued at fifty thousand dollars, in addition to five hundred dead oxen.[208]

The Bowery "Theater" (1850)

Latter-day Saints tend to think of the historic bowery in Salt Lake City as associated only with religious services.

---

207 Anderson, Nels, p. 86.
208 *Millennial Star*, Nov. 15, 1849, p. 365.

Actually three successively larger boweries were built, starting in 1847 but each was referred to as "the" bowery. It was one of these boweries that became the first "theater" in the inter-mountain west, if not in the entire west. Only three years after the construction of the first one, plays and concerts were being held there—the first play being "Robert Macaire" or the "Two Murderers." On July 4, 1850, a concert was held with admission twenty-five cents. Plays and concerts were held in the Bowery until 1853 when the Social Hall was completed which was the first true theater and concert hall in the far west.

It Escaped Their Attention (1850)

At the height of Mormon persecution in the mid-nineteenth century, a major charge leveled at the Saints was the inferior intelligence and gullibility of its members. Perhaps two facts coming out of the year 1850 either escaped the attention of the critics or they chose to ignore them. That was the year that Deseret University (later the University of Utah) was chartered and the first students enrolled. That university had the distinction of being the first such institution west of the Mississippi River. The other fact was revealed in the census taken in 1850 that perhaps highlights the founding of that early Latter-day Saint university. The census disclosed that the average illiteracy rate in the United States was 4.92 while Utah's was only 0.25, the lowest of the states and territories cited.[209]

He Was the Tithe! (1850)

One of the best-known pioneer Blacks in the early Church was Green Flake, a slave of James and Agnes Flake who joined

---

209 Berrett & Burton, 3:329.

the Church in North Carolina in the winter of 1843-44. After migrating to Nauvoo, the Flakes joined the exodus west. Their servant, (the Flake slaves had been offered their freedom but three chose to stay with the family) Green Flake, was selected to accompany the Pioneer Party to the valley in 1847. When his owner died in 1850, his wife joined a group of settlers to San Bernadino. Before leaving Utah, however, she wanted to settle her tithing account and offered Green as tithing. Brigham and Heber Kimball made brief use of his labor before he moved to Union as a free man and loyal Saint.[210]

Enemies Fulfill Prophesy (1850)

The name selected by the Mormon pioneers for their new western home was "Deseret," meaning "honey bee," but when Congress gave them territorial status, they called it Utah. We know that such avowed enemies as Thomas Hart Benton was in back of the name change, but whether it was intended as an insult by naming it after a rather lowly tribe of Indians, the Utes, is uncertain. Whatever the case, the name "Utah" fulfilled a Biblical prophesy that Zion would be established in the tops of the mountains. Utah, as it was discovered, is a corruption of the word "Eutaw," which means "in the tops of the mountains" and that the name "Utes" means "high-up Indians."[211] It seems the anti-Mormons just couldn't win.

Bulletproof Rooms (1850)

When Sidney Rigdon was excommunicated in 1844 he returned to Pittsburgh, giving up connection with his Church. In 1850, he moved to Friendship, New York, into the home of his son-in-law, George Robinson. Robinson, who had also

---

210   VanWagoner & Walker, pp. 87-88.
211   Whipple, Maurine, *This is the Place: Utah*, p. 56.

become disaffected from the Church in Nauvoo, became founder of the First National Bank in Friendship. Stories circulated about his fears that apparently prompted him to put bars on the windows of his home and build a bullet proof room in the bank and his home. Stories also suggested the source of his wealth may have been money stolen from the Church, and if true may account partially for the suspicions the Prophet Joseph had of Sidney and his son-in-law in Nauvoo.[212]

Taylor Discusses Communism (1850)

John Taylor arrived in France in 1850 on what would prove to be a somewhat unsuccessful mission. He did however have an interesting meeting with a M. Krolokoski, a disciple of M. Fourier and a member of the same communistic society that had established the Icarians at Nauvoo under Cabet after the exodus of the Saints. When Krolokoski indicated skepticism of the prospects for success for Taylor's religion, Brother Taylor compared the free enterprise successes of the Saints in Utah by that date with the failure of the French Icarians and their philosophy in Nauvoo. He concluded by asking, "Now, which is the best, our religion, or your philosophy?" Krolokoski replied, "Well, I cannot say anything."[213]

An Unknown Sacrifice (1850)

In September 1850, Lorenzo Snow with three companions ascended a mountain in Italy and there organized the Church in that land. Driven by the Spirit and the intense interest in what had been accomplished, and without realizing the weight of his covenant, he told the Lord that he knew of no sacrifice he

---

212 Rollmann, Hans, "The Early Baptist Career of Sidney Rigdon in Warren, Ohio," *BYU Studies*. Winter 1981, p. 38fn.

213 JD, 5:237-238.

was not willing to offer if the Lord would favor their mission. As his sister, Eliza, later determined, at that very time back in Utah, "the Lord removed, by the hand of death, from my brother's family circle, one of the loveliest of women," Lorenzo's wife Charlotte. His name was on her lips as she passed away. We have no history of any reaction Lorenzo might have made later about his covenant with the Lord.[214]

The "Parents' School" (1850)

It's difficult to imagine the University of Utah having its beginning in a single room in a private home but that's how it began. Although incorporated in 1850 as University of the State of Deseret, it was commonly called the "Parents' School" when it opened in the home of John and Julia Ives Pack in November of that year. It went by that name because it was intended not only as an academic institution but to train the heads of families. Classes were taught by a Doctor Collins in the parlor of the home while in a room across the hall was the first mercantile store opened in Utah. Tuition was eight dollars per quarter, but produce was acceptable as was the case in almost all business conducted in the valley.[215]

Honoring Fillmore (1851)

Utah's Territorial Capital was established 140 miles south of Salt Lake City in 1851 because of its central location. The community was named Fillmore and the county Millard, after the President of the United States, but not just because he was president when Utah gained its Territorial status. Fillmore was in office at the time of the well-known "runaway officials" inci-

---

214 Smith, Eliza Snow, p. 283.
215 Spencer and Harmer, p. 132.

dent but unlike President Buchanan who came later, he with-
stood all pressures to support the federal officials and showed
an objective friendliness when appointing the successors to the
"runaways". He also supported federal legislation that would
cause such officials, who absented themselves without cause, to
forfeit their pay.[216]

Lamanism (1851)

When he was excommunicated in 1851, it was difficult to
understand exactly what had happened to Alpheus Cutler. He
had stayed with Brigham after Joseph's death but when
Brigham returned to Winter Quarters after his pioneer trek to
Utah in 1847, Brother Cutler had become disaffected. Not
willing to go west, he had become convinced that God had a
mission for him—to reclaim Jackson County. And if he couldn't
enlist the help of all the Saints (fewer than three hundred eventually followed him), he would turn to the Lamanites—hence
"Lamanism." Not very successful in inciting the Indians, his
group, better known as the Cutlerites, withered away, with
most of his followers eventually joining the Reorganized
Church.[217]

Secret Weapons (1851)

Only three members of the powerful Council of Fifty were
non-Mormons. One of these was Uriah Brown, a confident of
the Prophet Joseph. He was dropped from the council after the
death of Joseph but in a letter to Brigham Young in 1845 he
indicated that Joseph had been interested in Brown's invention
of a weapon that could be used to defend Nauvoo. He was now

---

216   Hansen, pp. 163-164.
217   Bennett, *Mormons at the Missouri*, p. 226.

willing to sell it for a "just & equitable sum." There is no record of Young's response, if any, but in 1851, Brown was in Salt Lake City seeking re-admittance to the council and with another offer to sell the Saints his "invention of liquid fire to destroy an army or navy." The council tabled the matter, leaving no record of the existence of such a weapon.[218]

He Had To Kill Him (1851)

It was a sad ending to a close friendship. Howard Egan, a close friend and guard for the Prophet Joseph, and James Monroe, a schoolteacher to Joseph's children, were close friends in Nauvoo and carried that friendship out to Utah. In 1851, upon returning from a trip to California, Egan discovered his wife had willingly had a child by his friend James. Seeking the seducer out, he shot and killed him in front of witnesses and was charged with murder. George A. Smith defended Brother Egan in Utah's first murder trial, telling the jury that the deed was a principle of common law dating back centuries and if Egan had not fulfilled "the requirements of justice" he would have been "an accessory to the crimes of that creature." The jury returned within fifteen minutes with a not guilty verdict.[219]

All But Two (1851)

William Howell's missionary story of a mass conversion is somewhat unique. Known as the first missionary to France, that was not where he made his mark. It was while he was returning home from the British Isles in 1851. He was in charge of the emigrating company on the ship Olympus departing

---

218 BYU Studies, Vol. 20, No. 2, p. 181 & HC, 5:246.
219 Brooks, *On The Mormon Frontier*, 2:404-407.

from Liverpool with 250 Saints. There were fifty-two non-Mormons and crew members. With the example and probable help of fellow Saints, there were twenty-one baptisms (from a jerry-rigged platform beside the ship) while crossing the Atlantic. Reaching New Orleans, twenty-nine of the remaining thirty-one non-members were baptized and joined the journey to Utah. With only two not choosing baptism, history doesn't record who remained to man the ship.[220]

Abandoning the Mormon Trail? (1851)

In April 1851, the First Presidency announced in the Fifth General Epistle that English Saints would no longer use the Mormon Trail, but plans were to route them across Central America and up the west coast to San Bernardino, saving "three thousand miles of inland navigation through a most sickly climate and country." Discovering after a brief investigation, however, that the costs of transportation between Liverpool and the West Coast were prohibitive, the presidency, in the Sixth General Epistle in September, announced the restoration of emigration over the old route, which would be used for the next eighteen years.[221]

Do You Get Drunk? (1851)

It is commonly believed that the Word of Wisdom was not a commandment until made so by Brigham Young in 1851 at a general conference. Ten years later however, Brigham himself publicly alluded to the fact that he had only recently overcome habits contrary to the Word of Wisdom. It is especially interesting that in 1856, in the early stages of the Mormon

---

220 Cannon & Whittaker, p. 74.
221 Larson, *Prelude to the Kingdom*, p. 157.

Reformation, a catechism of thirteen questions was introduced by Brigham, outlining the requirements of a sinless life. In addition to the obvious questions on adultery, theft, murder, etc., it contained only one on the Word of Wisdom. No. 5 asked, "Do you get drunk?"[222] The Word of Wisdom was not made a requirement for temple admission until 1928.

But Luther Endorsed Plural Marriage (1852)

When plural marriage was publicly announced by the Saints in 1852, a storm of protest descended upon their heads, largely by Protestant ministers. Little, if anything, was said about the founder of Protestantism, Martin Luther, who gave Prince Philip of Hesse a dispensation to take a second wife, arguing that polygamy was sanctioned by Mosaic Law and was not banned by the New Testament. In 1531 he had advised Henry VIII of England to "take another queen in accordance with the examples of the patriarchs of old who had two wives at the same time."[223] One must wonder where Luther, the founder of Protestantism, would have stood on the Mormon question in nineteenth century America.

---

222 Campbell, pp. 176 & 192.
223 Smith, George D., "Nauvoo Roots of Mormon Polygamy, 1841-46: A Preliminary Demographic Report," *Dialogue*. Vol. 27, No. 1, p. 2.

6

The End of Discretion
(1852–1857)

Fifty-two Teams (1852)

All of the enterprises started by the Saints in early Utah were not successful. One of the most notable failures was the Deseret Manufacturing Company organized in 1852 to refine sugar from sugar beets. John Taylor, on a mission in Europe, was given the job of buying the necessary machinery from a firm in Liverpool at a cost of $12,500. Transporting the machinery from Council Bluffs to Salt Lake City required fifty-two teams. Repeated failures by the quarter million dollar company, partially the result of some vital missing machinery, resulted in a takeover by the Church, but the firm still folded from failure to produce the desired quality sugar. The Church was able to produce sugar, however, from a factory established on Canyon Creek in the Sugar House Ward.[224]

Saved by Slavery (1852)

In 1852 an act was passed by the Territorial Legislature and signed by Brigham Young, legalizing Indian slavery in the Utah Territory, but it was not what it seemed. It sole purpose was to induce the Saints to buy children who would otherwise be

---

224 Roberts, *Life of John Taylor*, p. 240.

starved, tortured, abandoned or killed either by their own people or other tribes. Such inhumane practices were so common among the Utah Indians that the Saints believed the only humane solution was to buy the children. The purchasers had to be approved by the Church leaders and had to promise to feed, clothe, and educate the children. They must also be treated as indentured servants and freed after a period of servitude. Even non-Mormons found little to criticize in the practice.[225]

Some Animals Survived (1852)

Interest in deaths during the treks westward logically focuses on the pioneers, usually overlooking the uncounted deaths of animals. Not subject to human disease, one might wonder why so many animals died, which they did by the thousands. Statistics reported from Ft. Kearney during the summer of 1852 help explain. From May 1 to October 6, pioneers passed by with 74,538 cattle (oxen and milk cows), 7,800 horses, 5,000 mules plus uncounted numbers of sheep and beef cattle. Unable to carry animal feed in the limited space in their wagons, animals were forced to browse for their sustenance. With so many feeding along the limited confines of the trail, we can only marvel that enough survived to carry the pioneers through.[226]

She Didn't Wait To Be Asked (1852)

When Emmeline was left a widow upon the death of Newel K. Whitney in 1850, like many other widows, she was left to her own resources to support herself and two daughters. Some

---

225 Burton, p. 269.
226 Anderson, Nels, pp. 108-109 fn.

might have waited for another proposal, but not Emmeline. She remembered Newel's friendship with Daniel Wells and although he had six wives she wrote to him as a "True Friend" asking him to "consider the lonely state" of a friend's widow. When she mentioned that she had hoped to be "united with a being noble as thyself," he couldn't resist. Whether from a feeling of obligation or real feelings, he asked her to be his seventh wife. Emmeline received her security and three children from this marriage, but also a loneliness that prompted her to spend her remaining years as a leading proponent of women's rights.[227]

Who Is Your Mother? (1852)

Plural marriage was first publicly announced in 1852 in Utah but had been practiced for several years, with many children resulting from these marriages. Young children of these marriages could tell you who their father was but how did they verbally identify their mother? A child of Brother Brown, for instance would be young brother or sister Brown, but from which mother? If the child's mother was Mary Ellsworth Brown, the child would be young brother or sister Ellsworth Brown or if the child of Ellen Horton Brown, the child would be young brother or sister Horton Brown—thus identifying both his or her mother and father.[228]

An Adobe Temple? (1852)

When Brigham selected the spot for the Salt Lake Temple in 1847, no one had any idea what material would be used for the construction. In fact, as late as 1854, adobe was a major

---

227 Cannon & Whittaker, p. 309.
228 Burton, pp. 250-251.

consideration. At the October Conference in 1852, discussion included suggestions for oolite (a relatively soft limestone), red sandstone from the hills nearby, and of course, adobe. It was not until years after the 1857 temporary "move" south that the material was decided upon. And then, with the discovery of granite in the cottonwood canyons southeast of Salt Lake City, quarrying operations began in 1860. Actually, "quarrying" was little used since the canyons were filled with erratics, colossal granite boulders dislodged and transported into the canyons by natural forces eons ago.[229]

The Longest County (1852)

The city of St. George in southwestern Utah is the largest municipality in Washington County. When the county was established in 1852 however, there was only the little town of Harmony on Ash Creek. To make up for the lack of population, the county was extended east and west to take in more area and population. Since the intended state of Deseret included all of present-day Nevada, the county extended from California on the west all the way east to the state of Kansas. At that time it was the longest political subdivision in the United States, stretching over 800 miles from east to west, but it was only 50 miles wide.

At Least Harmless (1852)

Early Mormon "State-of-the-Union" messages were called General Epistles. The seventh one was issued in April 1852, listing numerous accomplishments and exhortations. One was a warning to avoid the 'heroic' type of medical treatments such

---

229 Berrett & Burton, 3:155-156.

as calomel, arsenic, and other opiates—"poisonous medicines, which God never ordained for the use of men." Following the advice of their leaders, most Saints adopted the more natural herbal type of medicine, referred to in the nineteenth century as Thomsonian, after Dr. Samuel Thomson who issued licenses and manuals to practitioners. Levi and Willard Richards, Frederick G. Williams, Priddy Meeks and Calvin Pendleton were Thomsonians. Such methods were more successful because they actually did less harm than traditional methods.[230]

A Newfangled Device (1852)

Utah Saints were frustrated over their inability to counteract the vicious rumors that circulated about them in the nineteenth century. President Young characterized this frustration in a letter to John Bernhisel, his representative in Washington in 1852, when he bitterly asked, if to stem the tide of such untruths, perhaps a newfangled device could be found? "I wish you would just step into the patent office," he wrote, "and see if you cannot find some kind of machine or yankee contrivance [to combat the rumors] approximating as near a perpetual motion as possible, and put it connection with the telegraph wire, and let it roll."[231] Brigham would not see the end of those falsehoods in his lifetime.

It Took Seventeen Years (1852)

Although no mention was made of it at the joining of the rails at Promontory Point in 1869, it was the Latter-day Saints who first petitioned Congress for the construction of the transcontinental railroad. On the 3rd of March, 1852, only five

---

230 Bushman, Claudia L., pp. 45, 62-63.
231 Walker, Ronald W., "President Young Writes Jefferson Davis about the Gunnison Massacre Affair," *BYU Studies*, Vol. 35, No. 1, p. 161fn.

years after arriving in the Salt Lake Valley, the legislative assembly of the territory, composed exclusively of Mormons, petitioned the Congress of the United States to provide a national central railroad connecting the east and west coasts. Perhaps not recognizing the importance of the event after seventeen years or because he was not specifically invited, Brigham was visiting southern Utah on May 10 when the rails were joined.[232]

The Longest Letter (1852)

The early Saints appeared to thrive on establishing records—if not in setting up long counties or large families, then in writing long letters. In response to the charges leveled by the "run-away" federal officials in 1851, President Young compiled a letter in June 1852, refuting the charges. The letter, composed with the aid of secretaries was ninety-two pages long and was entitled "Beating Against the Air." Much of the lengthy missal, a copy of which was sent to President Fillmore, was a review of Mormon history, but the often overlooked and the most interesting part was on page 7 in which Brigham stated it was well known that polygamy was practiced by the Latter-day Saints. This was three months before the "official" announcement that most Mormons believe was the first "public" admission.[233]

A Fatal Barter (1853)

It was Mormon policy to avoid conflict with the Indians whenever possible, but one time an act of kindness caused fatal consequences. It took place at the James Ivie home in

---

232 CHC, 5:243-245.
233 Campbell, pp. 219-220.

Springville, fifty miles south of Salt Lake City on July 17, 1853. A trade by Mrs. Ivie of three pints of flour for three large trout to a Ute woman, brought the squaw a beating by her husband for making a bad trade. When James Ivie attempted to protect the Ute woman, he was attacked by her husband and another brave. In the conflict, one of the Indians died from a fractured skull. When the Ute Chief Walker heard of the death, he precipitated a ten-month war resulting in the deaths of dozens of Mormon settlers and Indians and the abandonment of numerous settlements in Southern Utah—all because of three trout and three pints of flour.[234]

A Brilliant Experiment Fails (1853)

Although suggested many times, reformation of the English language has never been successful. As foreign members joined the Church in the early years, Brigham Young understood the need for an easier language than English. Beginning in 1850, work was started and the Deseret Language was completed by 1853, devised primarily by George E. Watt, an expert in Pitman shorthand. In fact the sounds and structure were borrowed from a Pitman shorthand primer, although the 38 letter designs are still a mystery. It is entirely phonetic and theoretically a far easier written language to learn than English. Four books were printed, including two school readers, part of the Book of Mormon and a complete Book of Mormon but the experiment never caught on and the project was abandoned in 1869.[235]

---

234 Schindler, pp. 203-204.
235 Kimball, Stanley, p. 203.

If a White Man Steals (1853)

When Captain John Gunnison's government surveying party was massacred in Utah in 1853, it was popular in the eastern press to blame the Mormons. Although the Saints had nothing to do with the killings, they were reluctant to help in the search for the Indians involved, knowing the natives had done the act in typical revenge for a previous and needless killing of one of their own people. Brigham simply did not favor the idea of hunting down and killing Indians as the gentiles and army troops did so ruthlessly. He once said, "If a white man steals, shoot him. If an Indian steals teach him better."[236]

A Leap-Year Invitation (1853)

One of the most popular places of entertainment before the completion of the Salt Lake Theater was the Social Hall that opened in 1853. And some of the most popular events held there were the leap-year parties. When seventeen-year-old Belle Park, a daughter of Brigham Young's overseer, heard one year that the party committee had selected the actress Nellie Colebrook to be the prophet's escort, Belle hurried to Brigham's office with her own invitation. Amused, the president not only accepted, to the later indignation of the committee, but since the young lady had no carriage herself, Brigham called for her in his own carriage, taking her parents along also.[237]

Gentiles Support Mormon Immigration (1853)

Most of the gentile travelers on the Oregon and California trails were unaware of it, but they were supporting the immi-

---

236 Anderson, Nels, p. 146.
237 Spencer and Harmer, p. 166.

gration of Mormons into the United States in the nineteenth century. With a talent for turning any business opportunity into a profitable enterprise, the Mormon pioneers established ferries at such major river crossings as the Green and Bear Rivers and were charging three to six dollars per vehicle. In 1853, the Utah territorial legislature allocated ten percent of all the ferry proceeds to be paid to the Perpetual Immigrating Company. If the gentiles had known, we can be sure they would have sought other means of crossing the rivers.[238]

Refusing Counsel (1853)

The consequences of not following the counsel of the prophet is well illustrated in the well-known Walker War of 1853. After the war ended with the loss of numerous lives—both Indian and settler—George A. Smith reported: "If the counsel of President Young had been observed, not one of the Saints would have lost their lives by an Indian." At the very beginning of depredations, Brigham had advised the Saints in all outlying towns to send their livestock to the Salt Lake Valley for safekeeping and to "fort up." Evidence tends to support Smith's observation. One historian points out that "offensive action taken or provoked by individual settlers in the first instance and by militia units in defiance of orders (Young's) was at the root of every death of that war—white and Indian."[239]

A Woman's Place (1853)

Although Brigham believed a woman's place was not just in the home but also in the business and professional world, there was one place he didn't believe she should be—in the harvest

---

238 Arrington, *Great Basin Kingdom*, pp. 105-106.
239 Christy, Howard A., "'What Virtue There Is in Stone' and Other Pungent Talk on the Early Utah Frontier," *Utah Historical Quarterly*. Summer 1991, pp. 310-317.

fields. "I think this is very unbecoming," he said, "this hard, laborious work belongs to men." There was one exception. In 1853, a year beset with Indian conflicts, requiring the absence of so many men from the farms, he asked the women to help in the fields. At the time he said, "I never asked this of them before," and he never did again. He did, however, suggest that when they went to the fields, they "carry a good butcher knife in your belt, that if an Indian should come upon you, supposing you to be unarmed, you would be sure to kill him . . ."[240]

Who Planned the Party? (1854)

Possibly apocryphal, this story first appeared in *The Mormon Prophet and His Harem* by Mrs. C. V. Waite. In early 1854, Dr. Bernhisel, Utah's delegate in Congress, informed Governor Young that the President was replacing him with a Colonel E. J. Steptoe. The colonel arrived in Utah with his military, supposedly to track down the Indian killers of Captain Gunnison. When Brigham paid him a social call on Christmas day he found a "wild" party with several Mormon women present. Brigham rebuked them, sending them home. Whether Brigham had "arranged" for the presence of the women is questionable but a few days later a shamed Steptoe signed a petition asking for Governor Young's reappointment, which was granted.[241]

Everybody Dances (1854)

"Mormons love dancing. Almost every third man is a fiddler, and every one must learn to dance... In the winter of 1854-55, there were dancing schools in almost every one of the

---

240 Beecher, Maureen Ursenbach, "Women's Work on the Mormon Frontier," *Utah Historical Quarterly.* Summer 1981, p. 282.
241 Anderson, Nels, pp. 147-148.

nineteen [ward] schoolhouses." These are the words of apostate, John Hyde. Other early day observers such as Captain
Stansbury, U.S. Army surveyor of the Salt Lake Valley, wrote
that Mormon social gatherings, "patronized by the presence of
prophets and apostles" would open with prayer followed by
"the most sprightly dancing in which all will join with hearty
good will from the highest dignitary to the humblest individual." British traveler and author Sir Richard Burton noted
that in Salt Lake City "dancing seems to be an edifying exercise.
The prophet dances, the apostles dance, the bishops dance."[242]

Gunpowder vs. Whiskey (1854)

The Saints in early Utah had weapons, but lacked a source
of gunpowder. In 854, Brigham hired a Swiss chemist,
Frederick Loba, to establish a powder mill. Sulfur was available
at Cove Creek and charcoal could easily be made. A lacking
ingredient was saltpeter, which Loba solved by digging a large
cellar on the site of present Fort Douglas, but saltpeter takes
some time to form. While waiting for this, Loba bought a
molasses works where he was able to turn sugar into alcohol.
Whiskey seemed more profitable to Loba than powder and
Brigham, irate over the slow manufacture of gunpowder, fired
him. This was the last attempt at the manufacture of that vital
product before the Utah War.[243]

A Real Test of Faith—Property! (1854)

When tithing funds failed to materialize in the early years
in Utah, the Church authorities decided to reestablish the law

---

242 Heinerman, Joseph, "The Mormon Meetinghouse: Reflections of Pioneer
     Religious and Social Life in Salt Lake City," *Utah Historical Quarterly*,
     Fall 1982, p. 341.
243 Gibson, Harry W., "Frontier Arms of the Mormons," Utah Historical
     Quarterly, Winter 1974, p. 21.

of consecration that had been briefly attempted on a small scale in Kirtland. This meant deeding over to the Church all private property and then being assigned an inheritance according to need. During the years 1855 and 1856 about forty percent of the seven thousand families in the territory deeded over all their property, including Brigham Young whose property was valued at $199,625. This seemed to increase the willingness of the members to donate only a tenth of their increase and the Church never had to assume control over any of the properties consecrated.[244]

Asking the "Mormonites" (1854)

A correspondent of the Cambridge Independent Press reported the appearance before a committee of Parliament of Samuel W. Richards, the "supreme authority in England of the Mormonites" at the request of the House of Commons in 1854. He was summoned by the committee so that the British Government might learn the "system of aiding emigration" used by the Mormons. Referring to the "2,600 Mormonite emigrants" who leave Liverpool during the first three months of every year, the reporter continued, the Mormons could "teach Christian ship owners how to send poor people decently, cheaply, and healthfully across the Atlantic." The committee concluded that the "Mormon ship is a family under strong and accepted discipline, with every provision for comfort, decorum and internal peace."[245]

---

244 Arrington, *The Great Basin Kingdom*, p. 146.
245 Larson, *Prelude to the Kingdom*, pp. 132-133.

Tripping the "Light Fantastic Toe" (1854)

S. N. Cawalks, an artist with Fremont's expedition in 1854, was invited by Brigham Young to a Social Hall ball in Salt Lake City. He later wrote: "A larger collection of fairer and more beautiful women I never saw in one room. All of them were dressed in white muslin, some with pink and others with blue sashes. Flowers were the only ornaments in the hair... At the invitation of Governor Young, I opened the ball with one of his wives. The governor, with a beautiful partner, stood vis-a-vis. An old fashioned cotillion was danced with much grace by the ladies, and the governor acquitted himself very well to the "light fantastic toe" (an energetic dance with much swaying and dipping). Cawalks later accompanied his partner to Brigham's supper table.[246]

And If You Believe That! (1855)

The 1855 trial at Fillmore of eight Indians was a farce but the army and federal officials insisted. Two years earlier, Lieutenant John Gunnison, leader of a topographical surveying party, and seven companions were massacred by some Pahvant Indians. The chief, Kanosh, was finally pressured to turn over the guilty ones to the army. He surrendered a squaw, an old blind fellow, a mentally deranged one, an outsider, an old sick man and three boys, ages ten to thirteen. The military and federal judge insisted on charging them with first-degree murder but the Mormon jury found only three adult males guilty of manslaughter and they mysteriously "escaped" from prison later. The Saints didn't endorse the Gunnison killings but neither did they endorse killing innocent Indians.[247]

---

246 Cawalks, pp. 156-157.
247 Dees, Harry C., George W. Bean, Early Mormon Explorer, *BYU Studies*, Vol. 12, No. 2, p. 155.

Converting the Saints (1855)

One of the more successful, though short-lived, newspapers started by the Church was *The Mormon*, which began operations in New York City in 1855 under the editorship of John Taylor. While in New York, Taylor was witness to many plans to overthrow his church but one of the more interesting was by the American Bible Society. They proposed to flood the Utah Territory with Bibles, thinking that would convert the "Godless" Mormons. Upon hearing of the plan, Taylor visited their offices and offered his help, asking only that the Bibles be well bound. He followed this visit up with an article in *The Mormon*, describing his own well-worn Bible and urging the Society to do as they proposed.[248]

In One Ear and Out the Other (1855)

Chief Walker, of the Ute Indians, notorious for his fomenting of the Walker War against the Mormons, died in 1855. His brother Arapeen, who had also participated in that war, took his brother's place as chief, but claimed shortly thereafter to have received a vision from his dead sibling urging him to make peace with the Saints. He not only did this, but was baptized and ordained to the priesthood. He is remembered for saying that the words of Brigham Young "entered his ears, sank into his heart, and stayed there," while the words of Mr. Forney, who took Brigham's place as federal Indian agent, was "mere bawling, it would go in at one ear and out at the other."[249]

---

248 Roberts, *Life o John Taylor*, p. 258.
249 CHC, 5:141.

A Sizable Consecration (1855)

Not long after the law of consecration was reestablished in 1854, Arapeen, chief of the Ute Indians, joined the Church. Following the example of many of his white brethren, Arapeen (Arropine) conveyed by signed document his total holdings that included all of the Ute tribal holdings as well as his own— amounting to over $155,000, to Brigham Young as trustee-in-trust of the Mormon Church. The reestablished law of consecration was intended primarily as a method of making the law of tithing appear a lighter burden. It worked and none of the consecrated property was ever formally transferred to the Church, including that sizable portion of Sanpete County owned by the Ute Indians.[250]

Best Mormon Speakers (1855)

The well-known French botanist, Jules Remy, along with a scholar companion, visited Salt Lake City in 1855, where they attended one of the sessions of the October General Conference. In 1860, an English edition of *A Journey to Great Salt Lake City* by Remy and Benchley appeared in print, describing their impressions of the Latter-day Saints as well as their evaluation of the speakers they heard. "The two brothers Pratt, Orson and Parley, are beyond dispute the best, and we should say, the only orators that we heard; what with their easy elocution, their agreeable delivery, purity of language... they possess whatever is requisite for real rhetorical excellence." They judged President Young, with his "kind of natural eloquence" the next best.[251]

---

250 Fox, *Improvement Era*, February, 1944, No. 2.
251 Mulder & Mortensen, p. 280.

A Boy Apostle (1855)

Brigham Young was often accused of wanting his son Brigham Jr. to secede him as president of the Church. Although there is little evidence, it is reasonable to assume that he expected a son to eventually be president. Since seniority to that position was based on ordination as an apostle and not admission into the Quorum of the Twelve, Brigham may have had that in mind when he ordained his son John W. as a apostle on November 22, 1855. The boy had been born October 1, 1844, and was only eleven years old at the time, making him the youngest ever to be ordained an apostle. Although Brigham confirmed the ordination when John was nineteen, he was never admitted into the quorum.[252]

And Boy Husbands? (1855)

The drive to populate Zion was not limited to merely the concept of plural marriage—but also early marriage. Brigham's counselor, Heber C. Kimball was an outspoken advocate of early marriage. In 1855 he asked all young men to take "wives of the daughters of Zion, and come up and receive your endowments and sealings, that you may raise up a holy seed unto the God of Abraham." Although there is no evidence he went as far as encouraging marriage at fourteen, it was possible to receive one's endowments at that age. He was also known for telling young men to get married and do their courting afterward. The money spent in courting, he said, could go far toward outfitting a new home.[253]

---

252 Jenson, *Church Chronology*, p. xxviii.
253 Kimball, Stanley, p. 200.

In Advance of His Time Again (1855)

Former Boston mayor, Josiah Quincy referred to Ralph Waldo Emerson's 1855 proposal to free slaves by indemnifying the owners with money from the sale of public property as a solution "worthy a Christian statesman." But he went on to say, "What shall I say of the ... religious leader who had committed himself ... to the same course in 1844? If the atmosphere of men's opinions was stirred by such a proposition when war-clouds were discernible in the sky, was it not a statesmanlike word eleven years earlier, when the heavens looked tranquil and beneficent?" Quincy was referring of course to the Mormon Prophet who had made the same proposal shortly before his martyrdom when he was a candidate for president.[254]

How Towns Do Change (1855)

As we visit Las Vegas today, it is hard to visualize its original purpose. Although it served in its first years as a resting place for travelers on the Mormon Corridor between Salt Lake and California, its original purpose was religious. In 1855 thirty missionaries and their families were called to settle near a small spring in the middle of the Nevada desert and take the Restored Gospel to the nearby Indians. There they built an adobe fort and began their missionary work. In that very first year, they baptized sixty-four Indians, including Chief Owntump of the Paiutes. Unfortunately, the original settlers were called home during the federal invasion of Utah in 1857 and the town never fulfilled its original purpose.[255]

---

254 Quincy, Josiah, pp. 397-398.
255 Ludlow, *Encyclopedia of Mormonism*, 3:1006-1007.

Brother Sheets Had No Idea (1856)

When a brother is called as bishop today, he knows he will probably be released in a customary five years. In the early history of the Church, bishops were likely to serve longer than five years, but Elijah Sheets, called to serve as bishop of the Salt Lake City Eighth Ward in 1856, had no idea he would still be serving in that same position in the twentieth century. By the time he was released in 1904, he had become unique in a number of ways. He continued as bishop of the Eighth Ward even when serving a full-time mission to Pennsylvania in 1869 and 1870, he continued to serve while imprisoned for polygamy in the 1880s, he was the last "traveling bishop" in the church while still looking after the Eighth Ward, and when he was finally released he was not even residing in that ward.[256]

Unlike the Gentiles (1856)

Anxious to be admitted as a state, leaders in Utah called a constitutional convention in 1856, strengthening their hand with a census taken the same year. Although it is believed the totals may have been exaggerated in order to impress Congress, they showed 39,058 females to 37,277 males. This was a typical sex ratio on all the Mormon wagon trains headed for Utah. In 1850, in contrast, a St. Louis newspaper reported on the migration that passed Fort Kearny during that summer—primarily gentiles. The ratio on those wagon trains was 39,505 men to only 2,426 women. This is a dramatic example of the settlement objectives of the Mormons versus the gentiles headed for California and Oregon at that time. It could also serve as an argument for the need for plural marriage in Utah.[257]

---

256 Cannon & Whittaker, pp. 255-257.
257 Anderson, Nels, pp. 95 & 141.

Origin of Fast Offerings (1856)

The "Great Hunger" in the winter of 1856-57 resulted from a drought the previous summer and an early and harsh winter. It caused widespread hunger and suffering similar to that in the winter of 1848-49. One step taken by the Church was most logical—advice to ration the little food available. The other step taken was inspiration and is still with us today. Since the early 1830s, members were asked to fast every Thursday to lead the mind closer to God. Now the Church suggested that members donate the food they saved as a result of the fasting to the Bishop for distribution to the poor. These became known as "fast offerings" and the practice, changed to Sundays, has become a basic practice and belief of the church.[258]

Solution to Loitering (1856)

Observing trials, or "courthouse loitering," has always been an entertaining tradition in American life, but Brigham decided it was not for the Saints. When judges and courts made their appearance in Utah, many Saints adopted the practice despite warnings by church leaders. In 1856, Brigham found a solution. He sent Thomas Bullock to take down the names of all such "idlers" and assigned Heber C. Kimball the task of making mission assignments for them. Thirty, with their families were assigned to the Rio Virgin to raise cotton, forty-eight to the Green River area to make farms and build mills, thirty-five or forty to the Salmon River and eight to the West Indies. "These are all good men," Heber pointed out, "but they need to learn a lesson."[259]

---

258 Arrington, *Great Basin Kingdom*, p. 153.
259 Spencer and Harmer, p. 255.

Greased Feathers (1856)

Brigham overlooked few chances to denounce or challenge the antagonists of the Latter-day Saints—and he usually had a colorful way of doing it. During the Mormon Reformation of 1856, he made a speech, including a challenge to those who would come against the Saints as they did the following year when President Buchanan sent the army against the Saints. "They can begin any game they please, and we will be on hand to beat them at anything they have a mind to begin. They may make sharp their two-edged swords, and I will turn out the elders of Israel with greased feathers and whip them to death."[260]

Negro Dan Loses (1856)

That the vast majority of the Saints opposed slavery is well known, but slavery still existed in Utah. In June 1856, the territory brought charges of kidnapping against William Camp and three friends who recaptured a runaway slave named Negro Dan, who belonged to Camp. The four were acquitted in spite of "a great excitement" against them. Hosea Stout, attorney for the defendants, said he was "surprised to see those latent feelings aroused in our midst which are making so much disturbance in the states."[261] What is surprising is that Stout, who knew the Mormon opposition to slavery, was surprised. Although history is silent as to Dan's fate, it may have been those "latent feelings" against returning a man to slavery that kept the Mormon leaders from being too outspoken later in defense of the south.

---

260 Anderson, Nels, p. 189.
261 Brooks, *On the Mormon Frontier*, 2:597.

Handcarts East (1857)

Because of the criticism engendered by the tragedy of the Willie and Martin Handcarts companies caught in the snows of Wyoming in 1856, Church leaders decided on a demonstration to allay doubts about the method. In April 1857, seventy-five missionaries left Salt Lake City, headed east with 25 handcarts, each loaded with 300 pounds. The 1,031 mile trip to Florence took only 48 days with all the men arriving in good condition. It was estimated that by adding women and children, the trip should not take over seventy days. Actually most handcart companies (there were ten) required at least eighty days. Only five more handcart companies made the trip after this demonstration.[262]

Lincoln and Polygamy (1857)

The Latter-day Saints had good reason perhaps to like Abraham Lincoln even before he, as President, enacted his three-word policy of "Let them alone." In a rebuttal to a previous speech by Stephen A. Douglas, who appeared to support the extension of slavery under the guise of popular sovereignty, Lincoln addressed a large crowd in Springfield, Illinois in 1857. "There is nothing," he said, "in the United States Constitution or law against polygamy; and why is it not a part of the Judge's 'sacred right of self-government' for that people to have it, or rather to keep it, if they choose?" This did not mean Lincoln supported polygamy but merely that if popular sovereignty was desirable, the people in Utah should decide the issue.[263]

---

262 Anderson, Nels, p. 164fn.
263 Hubbard, George U., "Abraham Lincoln As Seen By the Mormons," *Utah Historical Quarterly*. Spring 1963, p. 96.

7

The End of Autonomy
(1857–1861)

It Wasn't Yet Ten Years! (1857)

The Saints celebrate July 24th as Pioneer Day, the day Brigham entered the Salt Lake Valley in 1847. That day also traditionally marks the first report of the approaching U. S. Army in 1857, conveniently making it exactly ten years which is what Brigham had prophesied the Saints needed to meet any external threats such as were now looming. Actually, Brigham recorded in his own journal a month earlier on June 26, "Spent the forenoon with Brother Hickman who arrived yesterday from the States." Hickman carrying mail, and with two friends, traveled almost non-stop from Fort Laramie with news of the intended invasion. According to Hickman, Brigham laughed at the warning.[264]

An Incredible Journey (1857)

One of the first Saints to learn of the United States army headed for Utah in 1857, was Abraham O. Smoot, on his way west from Kansan City. East of Fort Laramie, his party met Porter Rockwell headed east with mail. Porter then returned to Fort Laramie with Smoot's party, where it was decided that the

---

264 Hilton, p. 65.

Utah Saints must be warned of the approaching army. On the evening of July 18th, Rockwell, Smoot and Judson Stoddard left Laramie in a light spring wagon. On the evening of July 23rd, they arrived in Salt Lake City, having covered 413 miles in five days—a journey that by wagon train normally required no less than five weeks.[265] The next day Brigham was informed and this time he believed the report.

No Arms Allowed (1857)

President Buchanan had not only not investigated the charges against the Saints before sending his army to Utah but he had not even told Governor Young that he was being relieved of his office as governor. Thus when Brigham was notified that the army had entered Utah Territory, he sent a message to "The Officer now commanding the forces invading Utah Territory." Noting he had not been relieved as governor of the territory, he enclosed his proclamation forbidding all armed forces from entering Utah and ordering the invaders to retire out of it. If they could not do this before spring they must turn over their arms to the territorial quartermaster. He just wanted to be on record for demonstrating proper authority.[266]

Foreigners vs. Foreigners (1857)

The army sent by President Buchanan against the Saints in 1857 was ill-prepared in more ways than one—many of the units having only recently been filled by recruits and many with absent officers. One officer who was present, complained about the ranks of his own artillery unit, saying it was filled mainly with "ignorant foreigners." His opinion was that since the

265 Hilton, p. 65.
266 Coakley, p. 203.

Mormons were also mostly recent immigrants, "we exhibit to the sun the ridiculous spectacle of an army of foreigners led by American officers going to attack a set of foreigners on American soil."[267]

He Would Not Fight the Saints (1857)

The army that was sent against the Saints in 1857 was not entirely devoid of integrity and good will. Captain Stewart Van Vliet, who had previously met the Mormons in Winter Quarters, arrived in Salt Lake City in advance of the American army to secure food and forage. He was politely received by Brigham Young but refused supplies. Nevertheless, he was so impressed by what he observed that he stated "This people has been lied about the worst of any people I ever saw." Promising to work for a peaceful and just end to the conflict, he told Brigham that "If our government pushes this matter to the extent of making war upon you, I will withdraw from the army."[268]

A Depraved Army (1857)

If the Saints feared the invading U. S. Army in 1857, it was not a fear of their prowess, but of their depravity. Historian Norman Furniss described the troops as "drawn from" less-stable elements of society who joined the army only because of their desperate poverty. Furness described them as "exceedingly stupid" and "so depraved that they would sell their last article of clothing for liquor." Furniss, a non-Mormon, believed the Mormon leaders had good reason to fear the impact of such people on the Saints. This certainly explains the reason for the

---

267 Coakley, p. 201
268 Nibley, *Brigham Young: The Man and His Work*, pp. 295-297.

Saints' insistence on the army encamping so far away from Salt Lake City. Camp Floyd was established forty miles away.[269]

Getting Them Out of Kansas (1857)

Historians are still debating the reason Buchanan sent the army to Utah without a more thorough investigation of the charges made by federal territorial officials. One of the theories given credibility in some circles is that the president needed to get the military removed from Kansas to lessen the potential conflict between the troops stationed there and the civilian groups fighting over the issue of slavery. Reducing the heat in Kansas while turning the nation's attention on the unpopular Mormons seemed an obvious solution to a less than competent President who seemed overwhelmed by the Kansas problem and easily persuaded to follow public opinion. On the other hand, this may be giving too much credit to a leader not known for such political deviousness.

The Definition Changed Perhaps (1857)

The military expedition sent against Utah in 1857 eventually ended up being commanded by Colonel Albert Sidney Johnston. In a letter to a Major McDowell, assistant adjutant general, in November of that year, Colonel Johnston described the burning of the supply trains by the Saints as an act of war and "evidence of this treason" against the United States and of the "necessity of a conquest of these traitorous people." Four years later he would resign from the United States army to take up arms against his former country as an officer in the Confederate Army. On April 6, 1862, he would be killed at

---

269 Campbell, p. 241 fn.

Shiloh, on the very date marking the birth of the "traitorous" Church against which he had once led a United States Army.[270]

A Disastrous Advance (1857)

The Utah Expedition of 1857 did not all travel as one compact army. Phillip St. George Cooke's 2nd dragoons accompanied by supply trains and the civil officers appointed for the territory did not arrive at Colonel A. S. Johnston's encampment near Fort Bridger until November 19th. The trek westward across the grassless and frozen prairie took a terrible toll on the soldiers, but especially on the animals of the Expedition. Cooke reported to Johnston that the dead and frozen animals and abandoned and shattered property that blocked the trail marked, "perhaps, beyond example in history, the steps of an advancing army with the horrors of a disastrous retreat." Meanwhile the Saints, still secure in their mountain vastness, spent what was spoken of as one of "the gayest winters ever known in Utah."[271]

Yawgawts Lee (1857)

Yawgawts (Yauguts) is a Ute word which John D. Lee, in his diaries, claims the Indians gave him. He mentions it for the first time in July 1871, describing a meeting with some natives near Panguitch Lake. "When they heard My Name (Yawgawts) which means a Man of tender passions . . ."[272] This translation certainly sound much better than the translation ascribed by most historians to the word, which is "crybaby," a Ute word bestowed on Brother Lee for his show of emotion at the killing of women and children during the massacre at Mountain

---

270 Roberts, CHC, 4:311.
271 CHC, 4:300-301.
272 Cleland & Brooks, 2:165.

Meadows.[273] It seems ironic that the only participant demonstrating such emotion that we know of, is the only one executed for his part in the massacre.

Cutting the Thread (1857)

Although the Saints, by 1857, had been enjoying their autonomy in the Great Basin, they seemed to have had no desire to declare total independence from the United States. But with news of the intended invasion by Johnston's army in July of that year, Brigham was apparently playing with the idea. Only a week after being informed of the approaching Expeditionary Army, he spoke about the possibility in the Bowery. "The time must come when this kingdom must be free and independent from all other kingdoms. Are you prepared to have the thread cut today?... We will wait a little while to see; but I shall take a hostile movement by our enemies as an evidence that it is time for the thread to be cut."[274]

Scattering the Army (1857)

A number of reasons have been given for "Buchanan's Blunder" in sending a major portion of the U. S. Armed Forces to Utah in 1857 when in fact there was no rebellion. One of the most intriguing is that John B. Floyd, an active secessionist and Secretary of War in the Buchanan cabinet had a method in his madness. Although not a friend of the Mormons, he had more sinister motives. Sending a major portion of the armed forces to the far west would leave government forts and arsenals unprotected in the South. Demonstrating a lack of personal integrity, as would later be proven, he could also benefit from

---

273 Schindler, p. 302 fn.
274 JD, 5:98-99.

supply contract kick-backs. He was asked to resign from the cabinet when his lack of integrity became public.[275]

You Don't Fight Fair! (1857)

The military commander of the Utah Expedition, before Albert Sidney Johnston arrived to take over, was Colonel Alexander who had underrated the Mormon resistance. He was shocked to learn of the Saints burning three of his supply trains. On October 12th, he sent a letter to Brigham Young: "You have resorted to open warfare, and of a kind, permit me to say, far beneath the usages of civilized warfare, and only resorted to by those who are conscious of inability to resist by more honorable means." That letter must have provided no end of amusement for the Saints whose ancestors had fought in a similar manner against the British.[276]

It Could Have Been Much Worse (1857)

In August 1857, command of the Expeditionary Force against Utah was given to Col. Albert Sidney Johnston. But the following spring, General William Harney was given command of the newly formed Department of Utah and thus placed over Johnston. He was on his way west to take command when informed a peaceful settlement had been reached with the Saints. It might have been disastrous otherwise. Harney was known as "squaw killer" Harney for his ruthless conduct of war against his enemies. He had already stated his solution for solving the Utah problem— "Capture Brigham Young and the twelve apostles, and execute them in a summary manner and winter in the temple of the Latter-day Saints." Fortunately, the 'war' ended before the "squaw killer" arrived.[277]

275 Roberts, *Life of John Taylor*, p. 269.
276 Anderson, Nels, p. 176.
277 Lecheminant, Wilford Hill, "A Crisis Averted?" *Utah Historical Quarterly*. Winter 1983, pp. 30-31..

A Well-Armed Militia (1857)

Although never given the chance to demonstrate their effectiveness in a stand-up fight with the United States army in 1857, the Saints might have been a force to contend with. The Nauvoo Legion, the name by which Mormon militia still went in Utah, numbered sixty-one hundred men by 1857. Their arms were impressive. In addition to nearly 2000 muskets and rifles supplied by the federal government to them as a territory, there were over 2,500 rifles and muskets in private hands, over 350 pistols and revolvers as well as seven cannons. By the spring of 1858, numerous other weapons were being brought in or sent in by Saints from around the country. A war by the Saints could never have been decisively won, but it would have been costly for the U. S. Army.[278]

Colonel Kane the Peace Lover! (1857)

Colonel Thomas Kane, a close friend of the Saints and a lover of peace, and largely responsible for a peaceful ending to the "Utah War," was not one to take an insult lightly. Because he might be ending a war that the army looked forward to, he was not warmly welcomed by Col. A. S. Johnston and his soldiers at their camp east of Salt Lake City in the winter of 1857. When an orderly, sent to invite Kane to a courtesy meal with Johnston, placed him under arrest, Kane considered it an insult and challenged Johnston to a duel. It blew over upon discovering it was the orderly's fault—whether malicious or a misinterpretation of orders we don't know. Such a duel could have made a drastic change in the outcome of the "war" however.[279]

---

278 Gibson, Harry W., "Frontier Arms of the Mormons," *Utah Historical Quarterly*. Winter 1974, pp. 14-20.
279 Roberts, CHC, 4:355.

Rejecting the Judge's Offer (1857)

Returning to Utah in 1857, Parley P. Pratt was arrested by authorities in Arkansas on charges brought against him by Hector McLean, former husband of one of Parley's converts and plural wives. When brought before the court in Arkansas, Judge Ogden, fully convinced of Parley's innocence, not only later visited him at the jail to bring him his horse and see to his release, but even offered him a gun and knife for his defense against the vengeful McLean. Unfortunately, Parley turned down the latter offer. Discovering that Parley had fled westward, McLean caught up with the unarmed Parley west of Van Buren, and with a gun and knife, assassinated the apostle.[280]

And Wyoming Gains (1857)

In assessing the results of the so-called "Mormon War" of 1857, often overlooked is the land the Saints lost. As the American army approached Utah, the Saints burned and abandoned Ft. Bridger in territory that they had claimed as part of Utah. When the Territory of Wyoming was organized in 1868, friends of the gentiles in that area urged Congress to include that portion of Utah containing Ft. Bridger as part of Wyoming. Pleased to do anything to lessen the Mormon influence and power, this was done and Utah and the Saints lost another eight thousand square miles, almost ten percent of the future state of Utah.[281]

A Friend in Need (1857)

In the spring of 1857, as the federal government was preparing plans for the invasion of Utah, the Mormons were

---

280 Pratt, Parley P., Jr., pp. xxvii-xxviii.
281 Long, E.B., p. 6.

starting their own defensive preparations, including the erection of a gun factory on Temple Square. Their manufacture of colt-type revolvers at the rate of twenty per week may be evidence of Samuel Colt's agents giving the Saints permission to duplicate his patented revolvers. Colt who regarded Brigham as "the one really great leader living" and a "true statesman who knows how to rule and does so," had presented Brigham with a pair of his finest gift revolvers. Brigham shortly after purchased several hundred Colt revolvers, paying cash.[282]

Fancher Train Stories (1857)

History generates numerous apocryphal stories, whose value, other than being merely interesting, tell us much of Mormon folklore. Such is the case with the surviving children of the Mountain Meadows Massacre. One of these stories concerns Charlie Fancher, son of the Fancher train captain. We do know that he was taken into the home of John D. Lee who was later executed for his part in the massacre. We know that Lee claimed he paid the Indians $150 for the life of the boy who is later returned to relatives in the East. After that the boy disappears to emerge in folktales. In one he returns to the West as an outlaw called Idaho Bill and is killed in a gunfight. In another he returns to avenge his father's death, is converted to Mormonism, marries a Mormon girl, and dies in the faith.[283] Although the stories may not be facts, Mormon folklore is a fact and that will persist.

Another Mountain Meadows? (1857)

Shortly after the Mountain Meadows massacre, while the war hysteria was still at a peak in Utah, another gentile

---

282 Arrington, *Great Basin Kingdom*, p. 465fn.
283 Birney, p. 199.

emigrant train was following the route of the ill-fated Fancher train. A brief encounter between some Pahvantes Indians near Beaver and that train, headed by Captain Duke, might well have resulted in another massacre by the now aroused Indians who were determined to exterminate this group. They were saved only by a detachment of Mormon militia sent from Parowan who worked out a compromise and then guarded the company safely for the next 300 miles. Knowing what had occurred at Mountain Meadows, the guides detoured the Duke train safely around the site of the previous tragedy where the bodies, dug up by wolves, were still visible.[284]

One Dress for All (1857)

When Johnston's Army set up Camp Floyd in 1857, the major victim was the nearby town of Fairfield. It was immediately inundated with gamblers, teamsters, prostitutes, and all the flotsam that follows any army. Still, some of the Saints stayed and tried to follow normal activities—including periodic dances. A well-dressed and attractive camp follower named Annie Lee frequented many of these Mormon dances. Because of her nicer clothing, acquired by morally questionable means, jealousy overcame some of the Mormon women and one night they forced her out back where they disrobed her and then took turns wearing her dress for a dance. Finally, ostracized by both societies, she took her leave of Frogtown, as it was called by the soldiers, and disappeared in history.[285]

The Invasion Changed Brigham (1857)

While Sir Richard Burton visited Utah in 1860, he observed a handcart train enter the valley but Brigham did not greet

---

284 Brooks, *The Mountain Meadows Massacre*, pp. 121-125.
285 Godfrey, Audrey M., "Housewives, Hussies, and Heroines, or the Women of Johnston's Army," *Utah Historical Quarterly*. Spring 1986, pp. 173-174.

them. He was informed that since the invasion of the army in 1857, bringing with them all kinds of disreputable followers, Brigham appeared far less in public and only when attended by friends who were armed. Unlike the fearlessness of Joseph in mingling with the masses, Brigham had learned more caution and for good reason. Burton said he was informed by some gentiles that "many a ruffian, if he found an opportunity, would, from pure love of notoriety . . . try his revolver or his bowie-knife upon the 'Big Mormon'."[286]

Redeemable in Livestock (1858)

The early years in Utah were marked by a severe shortage of real money—currency, gold, specie, etc. The problem was exacerbated when it became necessary to finance the "Mormon War" of 1857-58. To solve the problem a church bank was established, called the Deseret Currency Association, avoiding the term "bank" which had a bad connotation since Kirtland. Since there was no gold to back up the notes that were to be issued, the capital stock became livestock, the only moveable assets the Church leaders thought the people would accept. To guarantee acceptance of the notes, amounting to nearly $80,000, the Saints were asked to sign their names to "sustain" this currency. It worked until gentiles starting buying up the notes at reduced rates and cashing them in for Church livestock.[287]

---

286 Burton, pp. 249-250.
287 Arrington, *Great Basin Kingdom*, pp. 189-192.

The Salt Offer Revisited (1858)

The incident of Brigham's offer of salt to Johnston's deprived Army in winter camp at Fort Bridger being rudely turned down is well known in Church history. Less known is Sam Houston's remarks in the U. S. Senate when word of the refusal reached Washington. He chastised Johnston and said if it was a fight Johnston wanted, the army would be beaten. He said Johnston missed a chance to make peace— "there is something potent in salt." Referring to near Eastern religions, he said, "it is a sacrament of perpetual friendship." The facts however, suggest otherwise—Brigham was merely rubbing "salt" into the wounds of an American army brought to a standstill by the outnumbered Saints.[288]

Herded by Ten Mormons! (1858)

The press, both at home and abroad, had a field day with the thought of an American army stopped by a few religious "fanatics" in the Utah Territory. Actually it was only a few who had burned the grass in advance of the army and destroyed hundreds of supply wagons that forced the army to set up winter encampment in the mountains well short of Salt Lake City. During the winter the Saints kept a relay of only ten mounted men above the head of Echo canyon to watch and report on any movements of Johnston's army. It was this information that prompted the London Punch to graphically picture a cartoon showing the "flower of the American army," as they termed it, half buried in the snow while being herded by ten "Mormons."[289]

---

288 Anderson, Nels, p. 190.
289 CHC, 4:302 fn.

A Confirmed Bachelor (1858)

It was not until April 1858 that President Buchanan finally decided he had acted in haste in sending an army against the Mormons before sending an investigating commission. Although Johnston's army was already in camp east of the Salt Lake Valley, two commissioners were chosen and sent west to confer with all parties. One of these was Ben McCullock, a hero of the Texas revolution and the war with Mexico. He was at the time a U. S. Marshal in Texas. According to a talk given by George A. Smith in the Bowery at the October Conference in 1865, the job given to the new Territorial Governor Cumming had originally been offered to McCullock. He had declined however, on the ground that a confirmed old bachelor ought not to interfere with polygamy.[290]

A Bloody Conflict Averted (1858)

Apparently unhappy with the inactivity of Johnston's Army outside of Salt Lake City in the spring of 1858, Congress passed an act on April 7, authorizing the president to call into service two regiments of volunteers for use in the Utah Territory. Although Buchanan did not call up any volunteers, he did make reference later to the "number of our brave and patriotic citizens anxious to serve their country" in Utah. The reason for concern by the Saints was given by Senator Albert G. Brown from Mississippi when he objected to such an act, referring to the Saints' old persecutors in Missouri and Illinois, who would "go with a view of shedding blood; they go for vengeance, and they will have it." A war would be inevitable, he concluded.[291]

---

290 JD, 11:181.
291 Roberts, CHC, 4:374.

Mosquito Coast Refuge? (1858)

As the Saints began another tragic exodus from their homes in the spring of 1858 with the advance of the U. S. Army toward Salt Lake City, a refuge had to be found. A very brief consideration was given to an offer made by some representatives of a Colonel Kinney of California for 30 million acres of land on the Mosquito Coast of present day Honduras. Although some anti-Mormons in Washington believed this offer, at ten cents per acre, to be an answer to the "Mormon Question," Brigham became adamant against it, the more it was suggested. "I would not go to that country," he said, "if it was covered 15 inches deep with gold and we owned it all." Fortunately, a compromise was reached, making another refuge unnecessary at that time.[292]

The Sebastopol Speech (1858)

The decision by Brigham to burn Salt Lake City if the U. S. Army attempted to ransack or occupy the city, may have been prompted by the siege of Sebastopol by British forces in the Russian Crimea only two years previously. As the Russians retreated after a long siege, they left nothing but smoking ruins. On March 21, 1858, Brigham described his willingness to destroy all the Saints had accomplished in the valley if necessary—mentioning Sebastopol several times. "They may have 'Sebastopol' after it is vacated, but they cannot have it before." Although men stood ready to torch the city if necessary, the army marched through it with perfect discipline and encamped forty miles south.[293]

---

292   Stott, pp. 105-106.
293   Stott, pp. 58-59.

A Change of Plans (1858)

The exodus of the Salt Lake City residents southward as the U. S. Army under Colonel Johnston moved into the valley in 1858 is a well-known story. Not as well known is the fact that original plans were to go north—not south! Fort Limhi on the Salmon River in Oregon Territory would have been a critical, halfway base of supply and refitting as the Saints moved north to the Beaverhead region of western Montana, then on to the Bitter Root Valley and if necessary, into Canada. Unfortunately, in February, before the exodus began, Fort Limhi was attacked and laid siege by a large force of Bannock and Shoshoni Indians. With that critical base and supply station eliminated, an alternative route south, already considered, was selected.[294]

"Poorest and Most Helpless" (1858)

Much of the month of March in 1858 was spent by church leaders in organizing the move south as Johnston's army prepared for their "invasion" of Salt Lake City. The organization seemed perfectly coordinated, with only one part a little difficult to understand. According to Hosea Stout, "It was decided to send 500 families from this city immediately to be selected from among those who had never been driven from their homes and from that class to take the poorest and most helpless. This 500 was to be selected by the bishops from the several wards." He further wrote that the plan "was to be an ensample to other citis [sic] wards and settlements throughout the territory." Why selecting the least experienced and "poorest and helpless" would be an ensample, he doesn't say.[295]

---

294 Bigler, David, L, "The Crisis at Fort Limhi 1858," *Utah Historical Quarterly*, Spring 1967, p. 125.

295 Brooks, *On The Mormon Frontier*, 2:655.

"A Force in the World" (1858)

As the Saints in the Salt Lake Valley began their mass exodus southward before the advance of the U. S. Army into Salt Lake City, one would expect derision in the American press for their failure to stand and fight. Such was not the case in most respectable presses. The New York Times stated it well in June, 1858, when it noted, "When people abandon their homes to plunge with women and children into a wilderness, to seek new settlements, they know not where, they give a higher proof of courage than if they fought for them . . . a faith to which so many men and women prove their loyalty, by such sacrifices, is a force in the world."[296]

When Mormons Attacked Mormons (1858)

An important northern settlement for the Utah Saints was Fort Limhi, on the Salmon River [now Lemhi River] in the Oregon Territory. It was erected in 1855 by missionaries to the Bannock and Shoshoni Indians and in the spring of 1858 was intended to be a major link in the escape route of the Saints as they abandoned the Salt Lake Valley. However, that was not to be for on February 25th the outpost was attacked by about 250 hostile Bannock and Shoshoni Indians. The Saints lost two killed and five wounded before taking refuge in the stockade. It was several weeks before help from the Salt Lake Valley was able to lift the siege. The attackers were baptized Indians who had been talked into the raid by gentile mountain men.[297]

---

296 CHC, 4:418 fn.
297 Bigler, David L., "The Crisis at Fort Limhi 1858," *Utah Historical Quarterly*. Spring 1967, pp. 121-136.

Can It Be True? (1858)

As Johnston's Army marched through Salt Lake City in June 1858, they saw for the first time what they believed they had been sent to eradicate—and some of them began to doubt what they had been told. One soldier in that army wrote: "But oh how beautiful is this city... A whitened sepulcher, 'A den of thieves & murders,' the emigrants say, but to our eyes alone it would seem to be an abode of purity and happiness, a going back to the Golden Age. I say to myself, 'Can it be true?' this story of their crime & in spite of the evidence I am dissatisfied. I know it is true but feel that it cannot be. Grey hairs & venerable forms walk the streets—are they too chief of sinners?"[298] The "evidence" he speaks of is the anti-Mormon propaganda he had encountered before his journey west.

Honoring the Battalion (1858)

When Colonel (now General) Johnston's army finally entered Salt Lake City in 1858 after a cold winter delay, they were met with a nearly deserted city. Except for a few men, many of them former Mormon Battalion members, who stood ready to burn the city if the army attempted to take it over, the inhabitants had fled south. Commanding the dragoons making up the rear guard of the army was Colonel (later Major-general) Philip St. George Cooke who had commanded the Mormon Battalion on its famous march during the War with Mexico. Recognizing some of his former Battalion comrades, Colonel Cooke removed his hat in respect as he rode past them.[299]

---

298 Arrington, *Great Basin Kingdom*, p. 193.
299 Anderson, Nels, p. 81fn.

Free to Leave (1858)

As the federal army started its expedition to the Utah Territory to put down the Mormon "rebellion," Easterners were delighted at the prospect of finally freeing the Mormon women from their forced bondage. With this in mind, one of the first acts of the new Territorial Governor, Alfred Cumming, was to issue an order promising all territorial residents who wished to "escape," safe passage out of Utah. After his April 24 announcement, 50 men, 33 women, and 71 children appeared and were certified for safe conduct out of the Territory. Unfortunately, records do not indicate how many of these may not have been Latter-day Saints, but simply gentiles seeking cheap, safe passage back East.[300]

"The Height of Absurdity" (1858)

In typical Mormon fashion, the Saints made the best of a bad situation —the military occupation of Utah. They owned a toll road through Provo Canyon that the contracted firm of Russell, Majors and Waddell had to use to supply the army at Camp Floyd. One of the gentile teamsters described the situation: "Here a saintly keeper, slate in hand, kept tally of our wagons as they lumbered past, the toll being one dollar per ton, $1,250 for our train. The road belonged to the Mormon Church—otherwise Brigham Young. Paying an enemy toll to enter his conquered territory was the height of absurdity." Absurd perhaps, but it helped fill the depleted coffers of the Mormon Church.[301]

---

300 Anderson, Nels, p. 182.
301 Arrington, *Great Basin Kingdom*, p. 198.

Strange Compliment to Brigham (1858)

Thomas L. Kane, the Mormon friend who was primarily responsible for a peaceful ending of the Utah War, paid Brigham Young a mysterious compliment in his unpublished Utah journals when he stated: "Next to myself—this is modest—our country owes more to Brigham Young than to any other human being in our generation. The efforts he had made to save us, (?) have perhaps before this, cost him his life." Then Kane, who resisted his wife's efforts to bring him to a religious life, stated, "since a certain day last fall, at least since the 1st of March 1858, (when Kane was meeting with Brigham to enact a truce with the U.S. Army) he has been laboring for his salvation upon his knees, without the honor of a noble Christian."[302]

An Unsound Prophet (1859)

The leader of the notorious apostate Morrisites, Joseph Morris, was a Welchman who converted to the gospel in 1849. Becoming of unsound mind, if he wasn't already, he wrote to Brigham Young in September 1859, informing him that he was prepared to take his place as the greatest prophet who ever lived. He believed he was Moses reincarnated, the seventh angel mentioned in the book of Revelation and that the Prophet Joseph had only been his forerunner. Such claims would not be that unusual in religious history except he was able to gather together between five and six hundred followers from the ranks of "faithful" Saints before he was shot down by a sheriff's posse in 1862 along with sixteen followers. He had been holding prisoner and threatened with death, some dissidents from his community.[303]

---

302 Poll, Richard D., "Thomas L. Kane and the Utah War," *Utah Historical Quarterly*. Spring 1993, p. 135.
303 Roberts, CHC, 5:48.

A Curse to the Masters (1859)

Newspaper editor Horace Greeley visited Salt Lake City in the summer of 1859 and interviewed Brigham Young. It seemed very appropriate to ask about Brigham's views on slavery since the Compromise of 1850 had not forbid it as it did in California. In 1851 the Territorial Legislature had made it legal for owners to bring slaves into Utah but urged them to voluntarily free them if the slaves desired. It is difficult to imagine them not wishing freedom. There were only 29 in the entire territory in 1860. Brigham told Greeley that Utah, when admitted to the Union would enter as a free state. He said, "I regard it generally as a curse to the masters."[304]

Never On a Sunday (1859)

With the arrival of Colonel A. S. Johnston's army in Utah, came the installation of several federal officers to replace the Mormon officials. Among the federal judges was Charles E. Sinclair—not too atypical as to competence, tolerance or morality. His honor, whose court included Salt Lake City, was often seen staggering through the streets of the city, drunk and helpless. His primary claim to fame was in the case of Thomas Ferguson, sentenced for shooting and mortally wounding Alexander Carpenter, both being non-Mormons. He isn't remembered just for ordering the first execution in the Utah Territory but for ordering it done on a Sunday. Later—when he was either sober or reminded of the inappropriateness of the execution, it was changed to a Friday.[305]

---

304 Long, E. B., p. 12.
305 Bancroft, p. 540.

"Civilizing" the Saints (1859)

The anti-Mormons had great expectations for the presence of the U. S. Army and federal officers in the Utah Territory after the Saints reluctantly permitted their entry in 1858. *The New York Tribune* in January of that year announced that if the Saints "should not be brought to reason as to these matters by the precept and example" of the army and civil officers, then the country must "resort to the remedy of dispersing them by fire and sword." A year later, as a result of the increased lawlessness brought on by the army and its attending influx of camp followers and gentile traders, the police force of Salt Lake City had to be increased from 50 to about 250. This prompted Brigham to later tell a departing federal officer, "I wish you would tell them that I am here, watching the progress of civilization."[306]

Drop-outs (1859)

Although seldom mentioned in Mormon history, "drop-outs" in the trek westward were not uncommon. The official journal of the first handcart company mentions thirty-three persons dropping out en route. Two of the most interesting desertions were in the eighth handcart company of 1859. At the Big Sandy mail station two mountaineers said they were looking for wives and two young women, one of them having a lover in the company, offered themselves as wives. A company member, William Atkin, believed the starving condition of the company may have been a factor and reported that one of the girls later brought her mountaineer husband to Salt Lake City and the other one returned to her first lover who forgave and married her.[307]

---

306 CHC, 4:456, 462 & 468.
307 Hafen and Hafen, pp. 174 & 199.

Don't Go Near the Walker! (1859)

The Walker Brothers were Mormon immigrants from Great Britain who started a very successful business in Salt Lake City in 1859, but later left the Church. Because of their apostasy and the belief of Church leaders that the economic welfare of the Saints depended on them patronizing Mormon owned businesses, businesses owned by gentiles and anti-Mormons were boycotted. In fact, members who purchased from such companies as Walker Brothers were often forced to ask forgiveness in Ward meetings. A stanza that was widely quoted at this time was "Brigham Young, may I go buy? Yes, my son and daughter. You can buy from the good Co-op, but don't go near the Walker."[308]

A Very Profitable War (1859)

Contractors get rich in any war and Horace Greeley, editor of *The New York Tribune*, who visited Utah in 1859, gave examples of government contracts which he believed might have been a factor in keeping Colonel Johnston's army in Utah after the 1857 Expedition. Allowed twenty-two cents per pound for transportation of all goods west to the army, contractors, "by a little dexterous management at Washington" were allowed to sublet their contracts for flour in Utah at seven cents per pound and still get their twenty-two cents per pound for "transportation from the East." That one item alone for just one year meant a profit to the unscrupulous suppliers of $170,000.[309] Anti-Mormonism was expensive.

---

308 Fife, pp. 96-97.
309 CHC, 4: 526.

An Unusual Mission Call (1859)

Camp Floyd, established by Johnston's army in 1857, boasted a theater that was even able to attract Latter-day Saints to its stage. One of the most popular and talented was Mercy Tuckett. In 1859, she refused to appear in any more productions there when she was asked to take part in a parody that ridiculed the Prophet Joseph. Although she was inactive in the Church and would later divorce her Mormon husband, she was not anti-Mormon and her descendants in the church today are proof of this. The most interesting aspect of her life however was not the Camp Floyd incident but that she began her stage career in Utah by being called on a "mission" by President Young to perform in the Bowery and later the Social Hall.[310]

Uncommon Astuteness (1860)

World traveler Sir Richard Burton had heard all the propaganda about Brigham Young but was determined to make up his own mind when he visited Salt Lake City in 1860. President Young was certainly not what he heard. "The Prophet is no common man" he wrote, and noted his absence of bigotry, dogmatism, and fanaticism and especially his sense of power. He said "There is a total absence of pretension in his manner, and he has been so long used to power that he cares nothing for its display. The arts by which he rules the heterogeneous mass of conflicting elements are indomitable will, profound secrecy, and uncommon astuteness." After three weeks the Englishman left, with profound respect for his host.[311]

---

310 Godfrey, Audrey M., "Housewives, Hussies, and Heroines, or the Women of Johnston's Army," *Utah Historical Quarterly.* Spring 1986, pp. 170-171.

311 Burton, p. xxix.

Advice to Young Men (1860)

In April 1860, Brigham Young announced the opening of one of the first academies in Utah—the Union Academy with Orson Pratt as principal. Located in the old Union hotel (afterwards Deseret Hospital), this school for young men was often visited by general authorities. One of the most unusual visits was by Heber C. Kimball. One day he entered, removed his high-crowned straw hat, made a profound bow to the young men, looked at his audience without saying a word for a minute, and then very impressively, said, "Boys, never call your father the old man." With another bow, and without saying another word, he turned and left.[312]

Mormon Women (1860)

World traveler and author Richard Burton visited Utah in 1860 and his resulting book *City of the Saints* is probably the most insightful look at nineteenth century Mormons—especially Mormon women. Contrary to what had been written about dull and drab-looking sister Saints, he found them "exceedingly pretty and attractive." Noting that many were from the British Isles, he noted that the beauty of the English women, "a sex which is early taught and soon learns to consider itself creation's cream" improved in Utah. While many of the English immigrants were "of that solid and sometimes clumsy form and dimensions that characterize the English . . . others had much of the delicacy of figure and complexion which distinguishes the American women."[313]

---

312 Whitney, Orson, p. 439.
313 Burton, pp. xxiv & 251.

That Worthless Copper! (1860)

President Young was known for his opposition to any kind of mining except iron and *The Deseret News* seemed to reflect that feeling. An article appeared in that paper in 1860 announcing the discovery of "a specimen of virgin copper found in Cedar Valley." The article went on to say that "in these days, gold is the principal thing sought after and a man who would engage in copper mining in an inland country like this, might by some, be considered in a state of insanity." If only those editors and Brigham could see in that same vicinity today the largest open pit copper mine in the world.[314]

Purse & Scrip—Yes! (1860)

After the restoration of the Church in 1830, Mormon missionaries were advised to travel with neither purse nor scrip but to rely on the Lord providing through the generosity of friends and fellow Saints. In 1860, Brigham announced at a Sabbath meeting in the bowery, that from this time forward he wanted the Latter-day Saints "in this territory to fit out our own missionaries, to clothe them and give them money to take them to their destined fields of labor." He had announced in a meeting of bishops in Salt Lake City just previously, that the elders abroad "had to beg so much of the people" that it "must be stopped." The poor Saints in Europe and England could ill afford to spare from their small incomes.[315]

314 Spencer and Harmer, p. 253.
315 CHC, 5:84-85.

Ox-teamology (1860)

Joseph Young, a nephew of Brigham, who had captained a wagon train that left Utah in the spring of 1860 and returned that fall, was invited to deliver a sermon at the October general conference on "the science of Ox-teamology," describing the possibilities of future "down and back" trains. Such wagon trains could take produce and food for migrating Saints eastward and bring back the immigrants and needed freight. These "down and back" trains were started in 1861 and during a six-year period, utilizing nearly 2,000 wagons, 2,500 men, and 17,500 oxen, were able to transport thousands of tons of goods and machinery and helped bring in over 20,000 immigrants. The entire operation, costing an estimated $2,400,000 was borne by voluntary labor, teams, supplies and provisions.[316]

---

316   Arrington, *Great Basin Kingdom*, pp. 207-209.

8

Striving For Integration
(1861–1870)

Enriching the Saints (1861)

With the outbreak of the Civil War, the Union Army that
had entered the Salt Lake Valley in 1858 under Colonel
Johnston, was withdrawn from the territory. Unable to transport all of the supplies that had accumulated since their
"invasion," the government was prompted to sell the surplus
after destroying the munitions. Ironically, the very government
that had planned to hurt and humiliate the Saints with the
presence of the army, ended up only enriching them. The
Saints purchased some $4 million worth of property at 4 _
cents on the dollar. Sadly, the whole Utah Expedition fiasco,
according to some estimates, cost the government at least $40
million.[317]

The Rag Mission (1861)

It's not the kind of mission that one dreams of being called
to and it was a blow to the pride of George Goddard, a well-
known Salt Lake businessman. But a new paper mill had been
erected to supply badly needed newsprint in the Utah Territory
and a paper mill required rags for the manufacture of such

---

317   Brown, Cannon, & Jackson, p. 98.

paper in the nineteenth century. Thus, Brother Goddard was given the task by Brigham Young of preaching the cause of rags around the territory. This he effectively did for three years, carrying a basket on one arm and an empty sack on the other. Traveling door-to-door and pulpit-to-pulpit, he was able to acquire over 100,000 pounds of rags during his successful mission.[318]

An Impressive Chandelier (1861)

One of the earliest and most impressive public buildings in Utah was the Salt Lake Theater built in 1860-61 with three balconies and seating 3,000 persons. One impressed visitor, author F. H. Ludlow, was given a tour by Brigham Young at the completion. Asked to estimate the value of a large gilded central chandelier, Ludlow replied probably a thousand dollars in New York. Extremely pleased, the Prophet revealed that he had made it himself from an ox-cart wheel and chains that he had gilded and covered with gilt vines, leaves and tendrils made from tin he had also patterned himself. Ludlow described it as a piece of work that would have been creditable to any New York firm.[319]

Do Nothing! (1861)

When Utah Territorial Governor Alfred Cumming returned to his home in Georgia at the beginning of the Civil War, he was temporarily replaced by acting governor Wootton. When Mormon editor Thomas B. H. Stenhouse asked the departing governor how he expected Wootton would get along in his new role, Cumming replied, "Well enough, if he will do nothing.

---

318 Humphreys, A. Glenn, "Missionaries to the Saints," *BYU Studies*, Autumn 1976, p. 77.

319 Arrington, *Great Basin Kingdom*, pp. 212-213.

There is nothing to do. Alfred Cumming is Governor of the Territory, but Brigham Young is Governor of the people. By____, I am not fool enough to think otherwise. Let Wootton learn that, and he will get along." Not a man of towering intellect, Cumming had learned something that future Territorial Governors were never willing to accept.[320]

The End of Isolation (1861)

The most important single event ending the isolation of the Saints in the Salt Lake Valley occurred on October 17, 1861. If it had occurred five years sooner, the Federal military operations against the Mormons might never have occurred. On October 18, Brigham Young was able to instantly communicate to the East, via the telegraph completed the day before, that "Utah has not seceded, but is firm for the constitution and laws of our once happy country." It did, however, do much to allay Eastern suspicions of where the loyalty of the Mormons lay in regard to the War Between the States. With almost instant communication, delayed information such as that which prompted "Buchanan's Blunder" would be a thing of the past.[321]

Nothing to Tax (1861)

One of the least known early federal taxes was authorized by Congress in 1798 and was levied directly upon the states according to the value of the dwellings, land, and slaves within those states (and later territories). When the Civil War began, the Union badly needed the revenue from such taxes to carry on the war. The amount decided by the federal government, owed by the Territory of Utah in 1861 was $26,982, with two

---

320 Long, E. B., p. 32.
321 Long, E. B., pp. 42-44.

thirds to be paid in gold and silver coin, of which the Saints had very little. There was one hitch, however. Federally owned land was exempt and since the Indian title to Utah lands had not been settled, all land in Utah was technically exempted and there was nothing to tax. To demonstrate loyalty, the Saints paid the tax nevertheless.[322]

Brigham the Squelcher (1861)

In his book *Roughing It*, Mark Twain recalled a visit he had made with his brother Orion to Salt Lake City ten years earlier. Known by this time for his biting satire about Mormonism, he was nevertheless able to make himself the "fall guy" in his party's early interview with Brigham Young. Despite his attempts to "draw him out," the prophet, according to the twenty-six-year-old Clemens, merely glanced at him as a "benignant old cat (would) look around to see which kitten was meddling with her tail." Twain settled into an "indignant silence." As they were taking their leave, he later said, the Mormon Prophet "put his hand on my head, beamed down on me in an admiring way and said to my brother: 'Ah—your child, I presume? Boy, or girl?'"[323]

Clean Tithing Money (1861)

The construction of about 500 miles of the Western Union Telegraph System in the intermountain west was contracted by the Saints through Brigham Young. Upon its completion in 1861, Brigham for his part in setting up or delivering telegraph poles, was handed $11,000 in gold. He later said at a small meeting in the historian's office, "I did not touch that gold with

---

322 Long, E. B., p. 44.
323 Mulder & Mortensen, p. 346.

my fingers or flesh until it was all paid in. I then put it in a vessel of water, cleaned it, and said what words I wished over it (doubtless words of consecration). I then delivered every dime of it over for tithing."[324]

Peculiar Habits (1861)

Because of the measures taken by missionary leaders to preserve order, decency and cleanliness onboard emigrant ships, Mormon companies were normally desired by the captains of ships who had experience with such groups. In 1861 however, when a large group of Welch and German Mormons attempted to book passage on the Great Eastern, the management of the huge, jinx-haunted, iron ship refused them passage. Although the steamship sailed with only one-fortieth of her passenger capacity, the managers preferred not to add 300 Mormons on the ground that they had "peculiar habits." Three years later, after years of deficit operation, the ship had to be sold. Could it have been the management?[325]

Baptiste the Grave Robber (1862)

John de Baptiste had been a grave digger for many years, but he carried a terrible secret. His secret would never have been discovered if friends had not obtained permission to remove Moroni Clawson's remains from the city cemetery in Salt Lake City to Big Cottonwood. The body had no clothes. The grave digger, Baptiste, was suspected, arrested and confessed. His home was found to be filled with boxes of clothing from an estimated 300 burials. He had been stealing clothing from the dead since his grave-digging career began in Australia. In fact,

---

324 CHC, 4:554 fn.
325 Arrington, *Great Basin Kingdom*, pp. 103 & 448fn.

his criminal practice there had been so profitable that he had been able to build a house of worship and donate it to the Methodist Church. It was felt that execution was too kind for "Salt Lake City's greatest villain" as *The Deseret News* called him. Instead he was branded, his ears cut off, and he was exiled to an island in the Great Salt Lake from which he eventually disappeared.[326]

Pure and Holy Entertainment (1862)

The Salt Lake Theater was dedicated on March 6th, 1862, with Daniel Wells giving the dedicatory prayer, in which its intended wholesome use was made manifest. He asked that the Lord "suffer no evil or wicked influences to predominate or prevail within these walls." Brigham Young, in some following remarks, continued the theme of wholesome entertainment by saying that "those on the stage should ever be as humble and just as if they were on missions preaching the gospel. No impure thoughts should be inspired there, nor no impure words expressed. Truth and virtue must abound and characterize every person engaged on that stage, or they should be immediately ejected from the building."[327]

Hands That Hold Chickens (1862)

Prices for seats at the opening of the Salt Lake Theater varied from fifty to seventy-five cents, but money was scarce, so barter was not uncommon. Artemus Ward mentioned one evening's receipts included two hams, a live pig, a churn, sixteen strings of sausages, a wolfskin, several bushels of grain, a set of children's undergarments, and a silver coffin plate. One

---

326 Devitry- Smith, John, "The Saint and the Grave Robber," *BYU Studies.* Vol. 33, No. 1, pp. 6-43.
327 CHC, 5:133-134.

of the more interesting barter stories, apocryphal perhaps, relates a theater attendee with a date, paying with a turkey and receiving two live spring chickens as change. Rather than holding hands that evening, he sat through the entire performance holding a chicken under each arm.[328]

No Finished Temple! (1862)

The story of the removal of the original foundation of the Salt Lake Temple because the stones "were not laid solid, but were laid on chinky, small stones," according to Brigham Young, is well known. Less known is what else he said when he made the announcement of the intended foundation replacement in 1862. Although, as he said, he expected the temple to stand through the millennium, he also said, "I do not want to quite finish this temple, for there will not be any temple finished until the one is finished in Jackson County, Missouri, pointed out by Joseph Smith." This little known prophecy was recorded in *History of Brigham Young*, Ms., 1862, as well as Woodruff's journal on August 23rd, 1862.

A Legal Church Army? (1862)

During the Civil War, when the federal government decided to raise a volunteer regiment to guard the mails between Forts Bridger and Laramie, Brigham Young reminded Lincoln that there was a militia already—the Nauvoo Legion. Lincoln responded by wiring Brigham, instead of the territorial governor who officially controlled the Utah militia, asking for the use of the legion. This quasi-recognition that the Mormon Church had its own militia army, controlled by the priesthood

---

328 Pyper, p. 110.

and not official government authorities, may have been an error on the part of the President of the United States, but it was nevertheless tantamount to recognizing a Mormon Church army. Needless to say, the gentiles were offended and the legion was soon replaced by Colonel Connor and his California volunteers.[329]

An Aspiring Actor (1862)

A dancer in the first performance at the Salt Lake Theater in 1862 was the talented Sara Alexander, who would later go on to perform successfully in New York and San Francisco. Living in the Lion House to teach dance to some of Brigham's daughters, she was considered one of the Prophet's wards. Thus, when an actor from the east visited Salt Lake to perform at the theater and fell in love with Sara, he felt obligated to seek Brigham's approval. He called on the Mormon Prophet and made his request. "Young man," the president replied, "I have seen you attempt Richard III and Julius Caesar with fair success, but I advise you not to aspire to Alexander." The marriage did not come off.[330]

A Reversal of Roles (1862)

Although Brigham was no longer Utah's territorial governor, President Lincoln asked him for a Mormon troop to protect the Overland Mail route from the east into Utah in 1862. Within an hour of receiving the telegram to raise, equip and arm such a troop for a three-month period, Brigham had issued such an order. The commander of this armed force was none other than the mountain fox of the Utah War of 1857, Lot

---

329 Anderson, Nels, p. 216.
330 Spencer and Harmer, p. 157.

Smith. Only five years previously he was stalking and burning government supply trains in the same area he was now defending for Uncle Sam, with the federal government paying the bill. History doesn't record the satisfaction he must have felt for this strange reversal of roles.[331]

A Laid-back President (1862)

John Bernhisel, the Utah Territorial delegate to Congress, met with President Lincoln in January 1862 with complaints about Governor Dawson who had recently left Utah after only three weeks on the job. He was an incompetent and heartily disliked Federal official and Bernhisel had a number of affidavits to present to Lincoln. The president's response was "I have no recollection how I came to make the appointment. I have been trying to recollect, but have less recollection about it than any important appointment that I have made." Bernhisel added in his letter to Brigham Young, "The President appears to take matters and things very easy; neither the war nor anything else seems to trouble him."[332]

Plow Around Them (1863)

Brigham Young's opinion of Abraham Lincoln seemed to vary with the most recent news from Washington, but in June of 1863, he wrote to George Q. Cannon reminding him that Lincoln had promised to leave the Saints alone. This seemed to match the story that Stenhouse related about the president's view of the Saints. He compared the Mormons to a knotty green hemlock log on his frontier farm back in Illinois. It was too hard to split, too wet to burn and too heavy to move, so he

---

331 Schindler, p. 318.
332 Long, E. B., p. 60.

plowed around it. And that was what he intended to do with the Saints. If they left him alone, he would "plow around them."[333]

An Apostate's Testimony (1863)

John W. Rigdon visited the Utah Territory in 1863 and left, convinced that the Book of Mormon was a fraud and he would be able to persuade his father, Sidney, to verify his opinion. Arriving home in 1865, he urged his father, with so few years left, to "give me all you know about it, that I may know the truth." Sidney's response: "My son, I can swear before high heaven that what I have told you about the origin of that book is true." After Sidney's death and shortly before his mother's death, he asked his mother and she confirmed what John's father had told him. "This she said to me in her old age and when the shadows of the grave were gathering around her; and I believed her."[334]

Cannon Balls and Revelations (1863)

Joseph Morris, an ignorant and mentally unstable Mormon, apostatized and formed a small dissident group in 1863. Imprisoning some members who tried to escape his group, he was besieged in a make-shift fort by a sheriff and his posse trying to serve writs. During the siege he received a "revelation" that if they did not surrender, "not one of his faithful people should be destroyed." Before his group had a chance to discuss his "revelation" a cannon ball from the posse crashed into the fort, killing two women. Morris himself was later killed and the "Morrisites" arrested or dispersed. One of the leaders, John Parsons, who had read the misguided "reve-

---

333   Long, E. B., pp. 191-192.
334   CHC, 1:234-235.

lation" to the group, later traveled the territory, reading an epistle of Brigham Young's, telling the deluded followers to go back to work.[335]

Order No. 11 (1863)

On one occasion while the Prophet Joseph was imprisoned in Liberty Jail during the winter of 1838-39, General Doniphan had him brought to his law office for consultation. Overhearing the general discuss taking some land in Jackson County as a legal fee, Joseph advised him against it, predicting that land would be visited by fire and sword. Twenty-five years later the notorious Order No. 11 was issued by Union General Thomas Ewing to devastate that part of Missouri in order to put an end to Confederate bushwhacking against Union forces. The order was carried out with a vengeance, and for years the devastation was a visible reminder of Joseph's prophesy. History does not record whether Doniphan was an owner of any of the property destroyed by Union troops.[336]

As Bad As Sand Creek (1863)

The Sand Creek Massacre of Cheyenne Indians in Colorado Territory by white militia in 1864, in which at least 400 men, women and children were massacred, has been recorded as one of the worst atrocities in American history. Equally bad in some ways was the massacre of almost an equal number of Bannock and Snake Indians in what was called the "Battle" of Bear River in Utah the year previously. The leader of the volunteer troops from Fort Douglas, Colonel Connor, a bitter anti-Mormon, was later rewarded by being made a general, for the attack in which

---

335 CHC, 5:46-47.
336 Roberts, CHC, 1:537-538.

about ninety of the slain were children and women. An eyewitness reported that many of the women were killed because they refused to quietly submit to being raped.[337]

"A Remarkable Result" (1863)

The ship *Amazon* departed from London for America on June 4th, 1863, with over eight hundred Latter-day Saints. Shortly before it sailed, Charles Dickens visited the ship and described his impressions later in his book *The Uncommercial Traveler.* He stated that he "went on board their ship to bear testimony against them if they deserved it," as he believed they would. But he said "these people are so strikingly different from all other people in like circumstances whom I have ever seen . . . they were in their degree the pick and flower of England." Impressed by their organization, mild language, temperance, and education, he finally "went over the *Amazon's* side, feeling it impossible to deny that, so far, some remarkable influence had produced a remarkable result."[338]

Brigham and the Midget (1863)

One of P. T. Barnum's star circus attractions was the three-foot four-inch midget Charles Stratton, better known as Tom Thumb. Shortly after Tom's marriage to another of Barnum's midgets in 1863, the couple toured the United States, stopping in Salt Lake City where they visited the Mormon Prophet and other church leaders in the Beehive House. The story is told, possibly apocryphal, that perched on a chair in the parlor, the diminutive performer turned to Brigham. "There is one thing I cannot understand about you Mormons, and that is, to put it

---

337 CHC, 5:33-34.
338 CHC, 5:92-93.

bluntly, this here polygamy." After a slight pause, Brigham calmly replied, "Don't worry, when I was your size I didn't understand it either."[339]

Gold! So What? (1863)

Silver ore was discovered twenty-five miles southwest of Salt Lake City in 1863. This prompted the Church leaders to continue speaking out against prospecting or gold seeking as they had been doing since the California gold rush. They seemed to be successful in keeping the Saints in agriculture, but was it because of their sermons and editorials? It seems the Saints had already figured out that if they made any rich finds, gentiles would jump their claims, knowing that the anti-Mormon Territorial judges would give preferential treatment to the claim-jumpers. Prospecting, with federal judges on the Utah benches, would be an exercise in futility.[340]

Every Vote Cast (1863)

The parade of federal officials appointed to govern the territorial affairs of Utah between 1857 and 1896 were for the most part uniform in their incompetence, corruption, and bigotry. An exception was Chief Justice John F. Kinney, appointed originally by President Pierce, and removed by Lincoln in 1863 because of his opposing party affiliation. He had been so fair in his administration of justice and equality to the Saints, a virtue detested by the anti-Mormons, that after his removal, he was elected by the Mormons as delegate to Congress. Not only was this a unique honor bestowed on a gentile by the Saints, but he received every vote cast in the election. Judge Kinney made his final home in Utah where he died in 1902.[341]

---

339 Anderson, Nels, p. 390.
340 Arrington, *Great Basin Kingdom*, pp. 202 & 473fn.
341 CHC, 4:195.

First—Rate Methodists (1863)

Like the Prophet Joseph, Brigham was constantly preaching the importance of secular learning as part of the doctrine of eternal progression. He stressed this concept in the Bowery in Salt Lake City in October 1863. He referred to "those who have been with us for years, and many of them have, apparently, little or no capacity for improvement or advancement." He likened such Saints to Protestant fundamentalists who believe they have achieved the epitome of progression "at the time of their religious birth." If such "first-rate Methodists" as he called them, "were truly born of God, their path would shine brighter and brighter unto the perfect day."[342]

Bleed Her to Death (1863)

John M. Bernhisel, Utah's first delegate to Congress when the Utah Territory was organized in 1850, served his people well until 1863 when he returned to Utah to take up his original practice of medicine. He was one of the few Latter-day Saints to have graduated from a medical school—which may not have been a good thing. He seemed to have retained the earlier school of medical thought regarding bleeding, which the Prophet Joseph had discouraged years before. Brigham Young was also opposed but said little to Bernhisel who had served the Saints so well. On one occasion, when an associate protested Bernhisel's bleeding of a patient, the doctor replied, "bleed her to death," meaning, bleed her until she faints. Unfortunately, we don't know the results of that particular visit.[343]

---

342   JD, 10:268.
343   Barrett, Glen, "Delegate John M. Bernhisel, Salt Lake Physician Following the Civil War," *Utah Historical Quarterly*. Fall 1982, p. 355.

Tabernacle or Tonic Sol-Fa Choir? (1863)

Tonic Sol-fa was a method of singing using non-musical notations used in a singing school inaugurated in Brigham Young's schoolhouse in 1860 by David Calder, a clerk in Young's employ. Within a short time the school had produced a choir that dwarfed the Tabernacle Choir that in 1861 had only "about a dozen persons." In 1863 the Tonic Sol-Fa singers performed with 260 young men and women all dressed in white. By 1884 however, the Tonic Sol-Fa singers were a thing of the past and the Tabernacle Choir was improving, even, according to *The Logan Utah Journal*, to the point of becoming "as good as that of our Logan choir."[344]

Control Your Applause, Please! (1864)

There seemed to be few subject limitations to President Young's sermons. On October 8, 1864, he preached against whistling and undue applause at the theater, especially "those who scream, whistle, stamp, and indulge in many other unwise [and] reprehensible demonstrations." A visiting English Bishop who attended the Salt Lake Theater with Brigham reported that the president "did not like much noise and if the applause became loud and vigorous, his well-known face would be seen protruding from the curtain of his box and looking round, and lo! At once all was hushed." The bishop left Salt Lake City wishing that "we could have recreation of the same sort in England."[345]

---

344 Hicks, pp. 49 &102.
345 Walker, Ronald W. & Starr, Alexander M., "Shattering the Vase: The Razing of the Old Salt Lake Theater," *Utah Historical Quarterly*. Winter 1989, p. 71.

Fortunes of War (1864)

On March 24th, 1864, arrangements were made for an exchange of prisoners of war at Richmond, Virginia. By one of the strangest ironies of that war, two old friends of the Latter-day Saints obtained their release from prison on that day. Both had been closely involved in the same cause back in 1857; bringing a peaceful end to the "Mormon War" in Utah. Now they were on opposite sides. Thomas Kane, captured by Jackson's troops, was released at the same time and place as Governor Alfred Cumming, whom Kane had helped install as the new Territorial Governor of Utah to replace Brigham Young. Cumming, a Georgian, had spent two years in a Union prison along with his wife. History doesn't record whether these one-time allies recognized or greeted each other on that occasion.[346]

The Big Ten (1864)

One of the hits of the 1864 theater season in Salt Lake City was Utah's first fairy-play, "The Mountain Sylph," with ten of Salt Lake City's prettiest and most popular girls playing the part of the charming sprites. These girls, all sisters, were called the "Big Ten," not because of their size but because they were the oldest girls in their family, which separated them from their younger siblings. The play was a success, not only in the talent displayed but in the girls' blue tarlatan skirts which fell midway between the knees and some very shapely ankles. These rather risqué costumes brought no rebuke from the very proud father that evening. Brigham Young could be an indulgent father when it was practical.[347]

---

346 CHC, 4:545-546.
347 Pyper, pp. 120-123.

Luxuries or Vices? (1864)

Brigham Young estimated that in 1864 the territory spent, in hard-to-acquire gold and silver, nearly $100,000 on tobacco, and thousands more on tea, coffee, and liquor. Although the leaders had been preaching against the use of these Word of Wisdom prohibitions for several years, it was more a saving of money than violating a commandment. "We can produce them or do without them," Brigham said. In fact, in 1861, the Prophet told Orson Hyde that southern Utah could "cheerfully contribute their efforts to supply the Territory with," among other products, "tobacco." He wanted Utah's Dixie to produce the territorial supply of tobacco so as to eliminate "paying to outsiders from sixty to eighty thousand dollars annually for that one article."[348]

Short-lived Gratitude (1864)

Like his humorist contemporary Mark Twain, Artemus Ward enjoyed making fun of the Latter-day Saints in his popular writings and lectures. In an 1860 issue of *Vanity Fair,* Artemus wrote of an imaginary trip to Salt Lake City and his departure. "I packt up my duds & left Salt Lake, which is a 2nd Soddum & Germorrer, inhabited by as theavin & on-principled a set of retchis as ever drew Breth in any spot on the Globe." In 1864 he actually did visit the Saints and Brigham Young, but before leaving fell seriously ill with mountain fever. He was nursed back to health by Relief Society sisters and was sent daily gifts of wine and fruit by President Young. He described his good care in a letter to Twain before he left Utah but

---

348 Arrington, *Great Basin Kingdom*, p. 216-223l

returned to New York to continue his vicious anti-Mormon humor.[349]

Not His Field of Expertise (1865)

Ulysses S. Grant would visit Utah when he became President, but the first record we have of his opinion of the Saints was in a message he sent to Patrick Connor, commander of Fort Douglas, shortly after the conclusion of the Civil War in 1865. It was a message influenced, perhaps, by information that Connor had sent him. Grant wrote: "It is not believed that an institution like Mormonism can exist permanently in force and close communication with the civilized world."[350] It was perhaps Connor he was referring to when he visited Salt Lake City in 1875, and was reported to have said, "I have been deceived."

Appomattox and Plural Marriage (1865)

When the Civil War ended at that little courthouse in Virginia, the Latter-day Saints who were toying with the idea of independence, knew only that their chance for a sovereign state was now gone with the Union intact. What they didn't realize was that the victory for federal sovereignty at Appomattox gave new and unchallenged impetus for the federal authorities to crush any attempts by states, but especially federal territories, to claim sovereignty in its internal affairs. The war had destroyed one of the twin relics of barbarism—slavery—and now the victorious political forces felt renewed strength to destroy its twin—polygamy.

---

349 *BYU Studies*, Vol. 14, No. 2, p. 280.
350 Long, p. 264.

The Handicapped Artist (1865)

Going on a mission in the early days of the Church was seldom easy, but for Carl it was especially difficult because of his handicaps. Not only was his hearing deficient but he was very nearsighted. Crossing the plains as he started his mission in 1865 he was assigned night guard duty. Keeping his eye on what he thought was his large white mule, he discovered in the morning that he had been watching a large white rock and the herd and other guards were nowhere in sight. Fortunately Carl did not let his handicaps deter him from his primary love and talent. He was an artist and although some critics might debate his talents, his reputation for recording early church history is firmly established. He was C. C. A. Christensen whose original paintings today, when available, are worth tens of thousands.[351]

Defense Is No Excuse (1865)

When the Black Hawk Indian War erupted in Utah in 1865, the Saints appealed to the federal government for the military aid that was always given to other territories. The answer they received from General Sherman, commanding the department of the plains, was to depend "on the militia to compel the Indians to behave." This they were forced to do over a three year period at a cost of over a million dollars and dozens of Saints killed and with no help from the federal authorities in either troops, supplies or money. After the war ended, the Saints were then harshly condemned by eastern newspapers and officials for their "new means taken to organize and drill the militia" (i.e. fighting the Indians) as evidence of their preparation for "an open conflict with the representatives of the government."[352]

---

351 Nibley, Preston, *Missionary Experiences*, pp. 200-208.
352 CHC, 5:158.

Brigham Was the Judge (1866)

The first Catholic Church in Utah was built on Second East Street, between South Temple and First South Streets, on a lot purchased by the Reverend Edward Kelly, at the request of Bishop O'Connel of California. After the purchase it was discovered there was an error in the title to the property. Rather than going to court, the seller and Reverend Kelly appealed to the Mormon Prophet, Brigham Young, to act as arbitrator and they agreed to submit to his decision. After studying the evidence and examining the deed, Brigham found in favor of the Catholics and the deed was handed over to Father Kelly. The Reverend later reported that his first mass in Salt Lake City was in the old Assembly Hall, placed at his disposal by the Mormons.[353]

A "Generous" Offer Refused (1866)

As gentile merchants in Utah became increasingly hostile to Church rule in the Territory, Church leaders encouraged the Saints to purchase only from faithful members. As a result, the gentile merchants devised a scheme that was not only profitable but might easily have brought about greater federal condemnation and control. In 1866, twenty-three gentile merchants submitted to the Church a proposal to abandon the Territory if the Church would: (1) make payment on all outstanding accounts owed them by any Saints and (2) pay the merchants for all property, homes, merchandise, etc at cash value minus 25 percent. Brigham refused this "generous" offer, saying the Mormon merchants would like to find purchasers on the same basis.[354]

---

353   CHC, 5:493.
354   CHC, 5:212.

Who's a Mormon? (1866)

Much of the legislation introduced in Congress in the late nineteenth century to abolish polygamy in Utah, is now viewed as unbelievable by constitutional standards. None, however, appear so distorted and biased as the Wade bill introduced by Senator Wade of Ohio in 1866. Fortunately, a majority of senators must have recognized the absurdity of the bill. Among a number of provisions that would at that time have destroyed all self-government in Utah (which did occur within the next two decades), it would also have destroyed the Mormon Church. Church authority to make rules and regulations in relation to fellowship in the church would have been denied, making membership in the Church totally meaningless, thus abolishing a religion by an act of Congress.[355]

An Unbelievable Apostasy (1867)

The loss of a testimony of the Restored Gospel has not been that unique in early Church history—even by a general authority. But when Joseph F. Smith was called to the Quorum of the Twelve in 1867, it was to fill a vacancy resulting from a most unbelievable apostasy—a disbelief in the atonement of Jesus Christ. Amasa Lyman who had been a member of that Quorum since 1842, was brought before the Council of Twelve in 1867 on charges of heresy. It was discovered that since 1862 he had believed and taught that men were not saved through any atonement made by the Savior. After briefly asking for forgiveness and publishing his error, he again reaffirmed his heretical belief and was excommunicated on May 6th, 1867.[356]

---

355 CHC, 5:226.
356 CHC, 5:271.

Short Talks Please! (1867)

The new large tabernacle west of the Salt Lake Temple was not yet complete or dedicated when the first general conference was held in it in 1867. Following tradition, men and women were seated separately and the conference began on a Monday. The prophet selected the subjects for talks, including the need to educate women for business in order to free men for construction and agriculture. Brigham said he had no idea when the conference would end because of the number of subjects to be covered so he would ask for short sermons. The conference lasted for three days.[357] Brigham should see the exacting organization and disciplined management of such conferences today.

Known for His Prophecies (1867)

Heber C. Kimball was famous for his accurate prophecies. When his beloved wife Vilate died in 1867, he said he would follow her shortly. Eight months later he died from a serious fall from a wagon. He had once promised a hard working but poor Saint that within a year he would have a team and wagon of his own. A year later the brother mentioned to Heber that he had only been able to acquire one horse. Brother Kimball told him he had watched him and he had been faithful and hard working. Therefore he was to pick out a matching horse from Heber's own stable along with a harness, saying, "If the Lord will not fulfill my prophecies, I will myself."[358]

---

357   Grow, pp. 67-68.
358   Anderson, Nels, p. 110fn.

Keeping Them Out (1868)

As the Union Pacific Railroad neared Utah in its transcontinental construction, the Latter-day Saints contracted to furnish the labor once it reached Utah territory. They did the same thing with the Central Pacific, with Brigham himself taking the contract to build the grades for the most difficult gorges. This was not merely a means of earning some railroad dollars as is commonly believed. An article in *The Millennial Star* in 1868, mentions a less known reason. It was done, the Church newspaper pointed out, to prevent "5,000 or 6,000 Irish, German, and other laborers crowding through our peaceful vales."[359]

Laziest Boy in the Ward (1868)

Bishop Edwin Woolley once offered to help a widowed mother with some home repairs but was turned down. The good sister said her young son would build her a new home someday. The bishop told some friends that it could never happen since her son was "the laziest boy in the whole thirteenth ward." The bishop even learned that instead of painting a fence as his mother asked, the boy had hired two other boys to do the job, paying them with money he earned playing marbles. He got the job done in half the time and had money left over. Such a young man with that business sense could make a good leader, and Heber J. Grant did, successfully leading the Church through the Great Depression.[360]

---

359 Hansen, p. 144.
360 Arrington, *From Quaker to Latter-day Saint: Bishop Edwin D. Woolley,* p. 464.

Separate But Not Equal (1868)

The first Relief Society Hall was dedicated in the fifteenth ward in Salt Lake City in 1868. This was the time when the Relief Society was the most independent of all church organizations—even to having separate facilities, furnished with all the furniture needed for learning better methods of homemaking. Even the operating expenses were not connected to the Church but were raised by member dues. In fact, in 1892 the society was incorporated as a separate legal entity called the "National Woman's Relief Society" and transacted its own business with its own board of trustees. This semi-independent status existed until the 1920s when the Relief Society was brought back into the chapels to share facilities and administration.[361]

Brigham Comes First (1868)

In June 1868 Heber C. Kimball lay dying after being paralyzed as a result of a fall from his wagon in Provo the previous month. On that hot June day, his old friend of over three decades, Brigham Young, sat fanning the dying man. Their love and companionship for all those years was coming to an end and many were concerned over the effect this would have on the President of the Church. In fact, it was at the invocation of Heber's funeral that such thoughts apparently prompted George Q. Cannon to ask the Lord to comfort Brigham in his loss. This was before he thought of asking for comfort for Heber's family.[362]

---

361 Bushman, Claudia L., pp. 231-232.
362 BYU Studies, Vol. 18, No. 3, p. 408.

The End of An Era (1868)

The year 1868 saw the passing of an important era in Latter-day Saint history—in two ways. That year witnessed the end of the ox train method of Mormon immigration into Utah with the completion of the transcontinental railroad in 1869. The era of the long hard journey by wagons had lasted for twenty-two years. The year 1868 also marked the last of the Atlantic crossings by sail with the arrival of 457 British, Swiss, and German Saints on the sailing ship Constitution. It had been six weeks in the crossing. The next shipload of Mormon immigrants, numbering 600, arrived in the steamship Colorado. That ship made the crossing in two weeks.[363]

"We're In Favor!" (1869)

The Washington Chronicle in February 1869 reported that polygamy only existed where women were degraded. They could be elevated, the report continued, "by giving them additional power and by this means polygamy would be destroyed." Thus, believing that Mormon women would vote against plural marriage, a "Bill to Discourage Polygamy in Utah" was introduced in the House of Representatives in March 1869 and a similar bill in the Senate the next day. When the Utah delegate, William Hooper, heartily showed his support and *The Deseret News* seemed elated, Congress became suspicious and lost interest in this method of suppressing polygamy. Neither of the sponsors brought the bill to a vote in Congress.[364]

---

363 CHC, 5:114.
364 CHC, 5:324-325.

The Quincy Excursion Party (1869)

The hospitality of the citizens of Quincy, Illinois when the Saints were driven from Missouri in 1838-39 is well remembered. The Saints also remember the generosity of such Quincy citizens as mayor John Wood who not only personally supplied goods to the impoverished refugees but after the Nauvoo exodus in 1846 made two trips, taking supplies to the suffering Saints on the plains of Iowa. Less remembered, however, is the visit to Utah thirty years later by a group known as the Quincy Excursion Party. Several Quincy citizens, including the former 1839 mayor, wanted to renew their friendship with their former friends and beneficiaries in Utah.[365]

There Was a Reason (1869)

Statehood was withheld from Utah for half a century, allegedly because of the Mormon practice of plural marriage. Another major reason however, was the control that anti-Mormons believed the Church had over the temporal affairs of its members. To a large extent this was true but there were reasons for which the federal government itself was responsible. One of the first things the government did in newly settled territories was to establish a land office to allow the citizens to file claims for ownership of property. They refused to do this in the Utah Territory until 1869, twenty-two years after the Saints arrived. Such refusal necessitated the Church establishing control over the rights and claims of land ownership—a major temporal necessity of life anywhere.

---

365 CHC, 5:277.

Divide and Conquer—Maybe! (1869)

The late nineteenth century saw many plans in Congress for punishing the Mormon Church for their practice of plural marriage. One of the most interesting was a scheme introduced by James Ashley, a representative from Ohio. The bill proposed giving a large strip of the Utah Territory on the west to Nevada and a similar strip on the east to Wyoming and Colorado, leaving Utah with a narrow central strip which would have been only 59 miles wide at some points. It took a *New York Times* correspondent to point out that with the large LDS population attached to Nevada (10,000) and Wyoming (25,000), there would then be three Mormon Territories instead of one. The idea was quickly dropped.[366]

Does the Lord See the Humor? (1868)

When Heber C. Kimball died in 1868, he left a son, J. Golden Kimball, noted in church history for his sense of humor. Heber's was just as keen as J. Golden's however, although not as well known. On one occasion, while kneeling in a prayer circle, he was offering up an ardent petition for some of his fellow men. Everyone in the circle was startled when Heber suddenly burst into laughter. Regaining his composure, he apologized, still conversing with his Heavenly Father, by remarking, "Lord, it makes me laugh to pray about some people."[367]

---

366 CHC, 5:230.
367 Whitney, Orson, p. 427.

The "Presidentess" (1869)

Eliza R. Snow earned this title by the early Utah Saints because of the influence she had on her husband, Brigham Young. She was married to Brigham in name only after the death of her first husband, the Prophet Joseph. She was valued so highly by President Young, however, that she always sat on his right at the dinner table and in the prayer room. Although Brigham is credited with the formation in 1869 of the Retrenchment Society, the forerunner of the Young Women's Mutual Improvement Association, his daughter Clarissa Spencer later claimed that Eliza Snow was the "power behind the throne in organizing" it. Formed originally to encourage more simple dress among young women, Clarissa claimed that Eliza was most extravagant in her own dress.[368]

Lost in History (1869)

The completion of the transcontinental railroad in 1869 is usually considered the end of the pioneer journeys west. Although a few wagon trains still went west, most Saints arrived in Utah via the railroad. During the previous twenty-two years, it has been estimated that more than 68,000 Mormon pioneers, 9,600 wagons, and 650 handcarts made the 1,000-mile journey. The majority of those who died along the way were buried in unmarked graves and as often as not, their names have been lost in history. The actual number who died along the way will never be known, but the best estimate by scholars is that some 6,000 did not reach their destination.[369]

---

368 Spencer and Harmer, pp. 76-78.
369 *Church News*, July 28, 1990.

Ned Buntline In Utah (1869)

Known primarily as the first of the dime novelists, the originator of the name "Buffalo Bill" for William Cody, the creator of the "Know-nothing" party, a wild adventurer with a long criminal record, and a popular writer and lecturer, Edward Judson used the pen name Ned Buntline. Traveling to Salt Lake City in 1869, he remained for some time, even writing poetry for *The Deseret News*. His main activity while in the city of the Saints, however, was lecturing on a subject that had little to do with the wild adventure stories for which he was noted. His topic was "The Industrial and Social Importance of Total Abstinence from the use of Intoxicating Drinks, as Exemplified by the People Here."[370]

How to Kill a Town (1869)

The town of Corinne was established when the transcontinental railroad was being completed in northern Utah in 1869. Settled primarily by gentile railway workers, it quickly mushroomed into a tough border town as well as a hotbed of anti-Mormonism. Faced with the prospect of this anti-Mormon town becoming a major railroad and metropolitan center in Mormon Utah, Brigham Young acted promptly. Purchasing property in the nearby Mormon community of Ogden, he offered the land to the Union Pacific and Central Pacific officials free of charge if they would locate their depot and shops there. The officials quickly accepted the offer and Ogden became a major railroad junction. And Corinne, the last of the "Hell on Wheels" railroad camps, died away to virtually a ghost town.[371]

---

370 CHC, 5:276.
371 Campbell, p. 315.

Horses and Asses (1869)

Although the Mormon leaders in Utah wanted a railroad, they did so with mixed emotions, knowing the type of humanity that would accompany it. Charles R. Savage, the well-known Mormon photographer who was present at the "wedding of the rails" in 1869, verified this in his journal as he prepared for the joining of the rails. "I was creditably informed that 24 men had been killed in the several camps in the last 25 days. Certainly a harder set of men were never before congregated together . . . their presence would be a scourge upon any community . . . At Blue River the returning demons . . . were being piled upon the cars in every stage of drunkenness . . . Verily the men earn their money like horses and spend it like asses."[372]

---

372 Richards, Bradley W., "Charles R. Savage, the Other Promontory Photographer," *Utah Historical Quarterly*. Spring 1992, pp. 146-147.

9

Striving For Respect
(1870-1877)

Prisons Large Enough (1870)

Tired of being judged as subservient partners to husbands, a mass meeting of Church women was held in the tabernacle in 1870 to protest anti-Mormon legislation pending in Congress. Speaking for the five thousand women present, Phoebe Woodruff said, "If the rulers of our nation will so far depart from the spirit and the letter of our glorious Constitution as to deprive our (husbands) of citizenship, and imprison them for obeying this law, (Cragin and Cullom bills) let them grant us this our last request, to make their prisons large enough to hold their wives, for where they go we will go also." What affect this meeting had on Congress is difficult to judge but neither bill was enacted into law.[373]

The First Woman to Vote (1870)

The first law granting women political suffrage was in the Wyoming Territory in December 1869 but there was no election pending at that time. Within two months, on February 12, 1870, the women of Utah were granted the same privilege and only nine days later there was a municipal election in Salt Lake

---

373 CHC, 5:232-233.

City. The first woman in line on that day and the first woman in the United States to formally vote in a political contest, according to contemporaries, was Seraph Young, a grandniece of Brigham Young. How ironic that a woman from a religious group accused of degrading women was the first to exercise her equal right to vote and that the United States Congress, allegedly vowing to help Mormon women gain greater rights, would deprive them of that right by the Edmunds-Tucker Act of 1887.[374]

The "Wooden-Gun Rebellion" (1870)

When the Utah militia received some new musical instruments in 1870, they issued an invitation to members to hear the music and accompany it by drill. Because a previous federal official had issued an order forbidding such drills except under his orders, several officers were arrested by federal officials and imprisoned at Fort Douglas on charges of treason. With more logic a grand jury failed to indict any of the participants. The rebellion's name came from the wooden guns carried by some boys who were mimicking their elders. With tongue in cheek, the LDS periodical, *Keep-A-Pitchinin*, called the event "the most daring and desperate attempt on the peace and safety of a nation ever recorded in the annals of crime."[375]

Not Like His Father (1870)

As anti-Mormon legislation was being considered in Congress in 1870, Alexander Majors of the freighting company Russell, Majors and Waddell, was asked to testify. Familiar with the Mormons as a result of supplying the army stationed

---

374 Jenson, *Encyclopedic History*, p. 959.
375 Walker, Ronald W., "The Keep-A-Pitchinin or the Mormon Pioneer was Human," *BYU Studies*. Spring 1974, p. 340.

in Utah, he was asked his opinion of polygamy and Mormon women. He testified they were intelligent with high religious impulses and that Congress should admit Utah as a state. "They are paying their taxes, they are behaving themselves, except as regards polygamy, as well an any other community." His defense of the Saints was in vivid contrast to that of his father, Benjamin Majors, a member of the mob-committee that forced the Saints from Jackson County, Missouri in 1833.[376]

Brigham's Belief in Women (1870)

It was difficult for gentiles to believe that the Saints and especially Brigham, really believed in granting equal rights to women. After Mormon women gained the right to vote in 1870, Brigham was asked by a skeptic if he really would want to see women in such offices as sheriff. Brigham answered by refer-ring to one of his wives, Harriet Cook Young who had given a major speech in a mass meeting of women in January in defense of plural marriage. He said if Sister Harriet, who happened to be six feet tall, "went out after a man she would get him every time." We have no record of Sister Harriet's reaction to such a comment, if she heard of it.[377]

Transformation of an Anti-Mormon (1870)

General P. E. Connor, commanding the troops at Camp Douglas during and after the Civil War, was notorious for his anti-Mormonism, once referring to the Mormon Church as "disloyal and traitorous to the core." His association with the people and Church leaders over a period of time seems to have lessened his bitterness toward the Saints to the point that when

---

376 CHC, 5:235.
377 Alexander, Thomas G., "An Experiment in Progressive Legislation: The Granting of Woman Suffrage in Utah in 1870," *Utah Historical Quarterly,* Winter, 1970, p. 27.

Brigham was arrested on murder charges advanced by the apostate Bill Hickman and ordered into court, General Connor objected. He even offered to sign bonds to the extent of $100,000 in favor of Brigham if he could be admitted to bail. Bail was not admitted however, and the prophet was put under house arrest until the case was disposed of in his favor.[378]

False Preaching Yes—Dancing No! (1870)

Although he dearly loved Bishop Woolley, Brigham didn't hesitate to chastise him when he felt it necessary, which he did in February 1870. The bishop had rented the Thirteenth Ward hall for a dance to raise funds to refurbish the building. The meetinghouse, Brigham said, should be used only for "sacred purposes." Brigham himself, however, had previously given permission, very reluctantly, for the use of the same meeting-house by the Godbeites, one of the most notorious apostate groups in nineteenth century Utah. In that instance, however, William Godbe, who owned three to four thousand dollars worth of shares in the meetinghouse, threatened to close the chapel if not granted permission. Brigham could be very prac-tical when the situation demanded it.[379]

A Challenge Ignored (1870)

When J. P. Newman, Chaplin of the U. S. Senate and pastor of the Metropolitan Church in Washington traveled to Salt Lake City in 1870 to challenge President Young to a public debate on polygamy, Orson Pratt picked up the gauntlet and expertly humbled the pompous divine. At the time of this debate, the editors of the Mormon humorous periodical, *Keep-*

---

378 CHC, 5:69.
379 Arrington & Bitton, p. 59.

A-Pitchinin, issued their own challenge to Newman. If he would try polygamy for six months, the Saints would try monogamy, after which there would be a public discussion of the matter. Furthermore, there would be an exchange of pulpits, while the Mormon preachers would draw Newman's salary and he would draw theirs. Needless to say, the challenge was ignored.[380]

Martin Didn't Know (1870)

Before Martin Harris arrived in Salt Lake City in 1870 to rejoin his fellow Saints, he was told of the church doctrine of rebaptism, based on Revelation 2:5 which requires those who have fallen to "repent, and do the first works." Martin said he had not been excommunicated but if rebaptism meant to renew his covenants before the Lord, he would obey. It was apparent at that time that no one else believed he had been cut off from the Church, since he himself applied for rebaptism once he arrived in Utah. It was not until the middle of the twentieth century that evidence found in the Historian's Office in Salt Lake City indicates Martin had been excommunicated by a High Council Court in Kirtland but was apparently never informed.[381]

Nothing to Fear (1871)

Unlike many of the sectarian visitors to Utah, the Latter-day Saints were extremely tolerant of opposing religious doctrines. In a discourse in Ogden in 1871, Brigham told his people, "If you have visits here from those professing to be "Christians," and they intimate a desire to preach to you, by all

---

380 Walker, Ronald W., "The Keep-A-Pitchinin or the Mormon Pioneer was Human," *BYU Studies.* Spring 1974, p. 339.
381 Nibley, Preston, *The Witnesses of the Book of Mormon,* p. 132.

means invite them to do so." Accord to all "who may wish to occupy the stands of your meeting houses to preach to you, the privilege of doing so." He added, "Place your children . . . in a position or situation to learn everything in the world that is worth learning." Visiting speakers were often astonished at the large number of attentive Saints in their congregations. They just made little headway in converting them.[382]

Excessive Bail Perhaps? (1871)

In October 1871, Brigham Young was arrested by a federal marshal on a spurious charge of adultery. Later another false charge was added—murder. This last charge was for the killing of two brothers on the Sevier River in 1857, a murder that the notorious apostate Bill Hickman claimed was ordered by Young. The U.S. Attorney asked that bail be set at $500,000, an amount five times that of Jeff Davis only five years previous. Put into a comparable dollar amount today (2002), the bail would be between seven and ten million dollars. Even this exorbitant bail was denied by Judge James McKean.

One-Man Power (1871)

At the age of sixty-eight, Ralph Waldo Emerson visited Salt Lake City and Brigham Young with a group of friends en route to California. Apparently unimpressed, Brigham made nothing of the visit and *The Deseret News* didn't even report it. Known somewhat for his anti-Mormonism, Emerson and his party started the meeting off on the wrong foot and Brigham let them know it. Making reference to Utah's accomplishments under the directing power of a single man, the Mormon Prophet

---

382 CHC, 5:496.

replied, "It's easy to talk about that! We have no more of it than they have elsewhere!" As the group later learned, Brigham had given a sermon that very day on the subject of "one-man power" in which he soundly condemned those who could not see the Lord rather than himself behind all the accomplishments.[383]

The Hayloft Court (1871)

One of the most hated federal judges, J. B. McKean, was appointed to the Utah Territory in 1871. He was eventually removed in disgrace, but one of his first decisions was to remove the territorial marshal because he was a Mormon. In retaliation, he found himself ousted from his courtroom by the Mormon landlords of the building. For the next year and a half, the Federal Court in Salt Lake City was a hayloft over a livery stable. Actually, acquiring court space appeared to be a consistent problem for federal judges as they prosecuted the Saints. In 1884 Attorney General Brewster ordered the Federal marshal to rent the rooms over the courtroom in order to remove the "objectionable parties." Those rooms were a brothel.[384]

Never In Public (1871)

When Brother Briant Stringham died in 1871, Erastus Snow who was scheduled to be one of the speakers was unable to take the stand—he was crying so. Brother Stringham was obviously much loved for his nature and dedication to the Church. He had been one of the original 1847 Pioneers and held several important positions in the Restored Church. He aided in the

---

383 Mulder & Mortensen, pp. 382-383.
384 Cresswell, p. 119.

administration of President Young's property, was supervisor of the Church lands and livestock, and had served as a counselor to the well-known Edwin Woolley, bishop of the Thirteenth Ward. But Brother Briant is today an inspiration to members who find public speaking a challenge. He was so bashful that even as a member of the bishopric, he "was never known to respond to a call either to pray or speak in public."[385]

Curiosity at West Point (1871)

The first Latter-day Saint to attend West Point was Willard W. Young, son of the Mormon Prophet and Clarissa Ogden Chase Young. Part of his preparation for West Point was driving a supply wagon between Salt Lake City and the Missouri River when he was only fourteen. He was recommended to West Point by Congressional delegate William Hooper, whose daughter he later married. When he entered as a cadet in 1871, Mormon persecution was at a peak and he was a curiosity but not the only one. Before graduating near the top of his class four years later, New York papers were carrying stories of two curiosities at West Point, encouraging visitors to see two "firsts"—a black cadet and a Mormon.[386]

Just Take Aim (1871)

It is difficult today to understand the hostility of federal officials appointed to rule the Saints in Utah in the late nineteenth century. When Daniel Wells, as lieutenant general of the Utah militia, ordered the militia with its bands to march in the upcoming July 4th parade in 1871, acting Territorial Governor George Black forbid them. He called upon General De

---

385 Arrington, *From Quaker to Latter-day Saint*, p. 321.
386 Spencer and Harmer, p. 138.

Trobriand, commander of U. S. troops at Camp Douglas, to fire upon the militia if they attempted to march. De Trobriand agreed to call upon his troops to "take aim," but the order to fire would have to be given by the acting governor. The governor was unwilling to give the order himself and the episode passed without the blood bath wanted by Black.[387]

"Embrace It In Your Heart" (1871)

The suppression of plural marriage did not suddenly begin with Wilford Woodruff in 1890 or even with his predecessor, John Taylor. It began with President Young in 1871 when he announced that as long as a man embraces "the law of celestial marriage in his heart and not take the second wife (he) is justified before the Lord." A year before he died he had closed the Endowment House, an act which fostered a decline in new plural marriages in the Salt Lake Valley. Following the Woodruff Manifesto in 1890, members were quick to recall the early signs of the eventual suppression. Anthon Lund recalled in his journal in 1900: "President Young once proposed that we marry but one wife."[388]

Mountain Law in the Daytime (1871)

Mountain Common Law was a law centuries old and practiced by not only the Latter-day Saints in Utah but other Americans in the early West. It was "death to a seducer" by relatives without penalty. But there were generally observed rules of conduct. In 1871, Henry Davis was accused of killing Richard Brown, a Provo resident. At the trial, John J. Baum rose and admitted the murder, saying Brown had seduced his

---

387 CHC, 5:360.
388 Anderson, J. Max, p.104.

niece. Davis was of course freed and Baum was charged with the murder, but his defense was "mountain law." He also was acquitted but as *The Salt Lake Daily Herald* explained, "What we object to . . . is the hour at which it was done. We are most strenuously opposed to deeds done in the dark."[389]

An Overlooked Invitation (1872)

As opposed to any compromise on the plural marriage question as the Mormon authorities seemed to be, they offered Congress a covert invitation to propose a compromise in 1872. Included in the proposed constitution that the Utah legislature (with Church government approval) submitted to Congress was a clause providing that any change suggested by Congress would become a part of the constitution if ratified by the people of Utah. It is unlikely that this clause was added without Church authorities recognizing the possibility of a recommended change in the Church doctrine of plural marriage. This certainly left open the door for a compromise and a chance for all parties to save face. The anti-Mormons, favoring an unconditional surrender by the Saints, ignored the invitation.[390]

The Long Conference (1872)

By tradition, the spring session of the semi-annual General Conference of the Church is held the first weekend of April. And that was the case in 1872, but it didn't end when it was supposed to. On January 2nd Territorial Judge McKean had placed Brigham Young under house arrest on murder charges brought about by excommunicated Bill Hickman. Although the charges were later dismissed, Brigham was still confined to his

389 Cannon II, Kenneth L., "'Mountain Common Law': The Extralegal Punishment of Seducers in Early Utah," *Utah Historical Quarterly.* Fall 1983, p. 320.
390 Anderson, Nels, p. 287.

home in April and could not attend the conference. George A. Smith, acting in Brigham's place, held the conference over week after week until Brigham was released on a writ of habeas corpus on April 28. The president was then able to personally attend and give his people his blessing.[391]

To Save Time, Perhaps? (1872)

Elizabeth Kane, with her husband Thomas, visited Utah in 1872 and left a most sympathetic and vivid account of visits to homes and church services. She described a sacrament service in Nephi that was typical throughout the church at that time. The concluding speaker stopped long enough for the blessing of the bread and then continued his talk while the bread was being passed. He then halted again for the blessing of the water. "While the water was being handed round, another hymn was sung; one of a set of beautiful fugues of which the Mormons are particularly fond. Then the services were concluded with a blessing, and the congregation dispersed."[392]

An Embarrassed Nation (1872)

In an effort to gain useful facts from the western world, over one hundred members of the new Meigi government of Japan started a world tour in 1872, beginning with the United States. Heading east toward Washington, the government party was held up by snow-blocked train tracks east of Utah, forcing them to spend nineteen days in the Mormon capital. The nation felt humiliated to think of the impression this important delegation would have of their country while residing so long in polygamous Utah as well as finding the

391 Pusey, p. 117.
392 Kane, Elizabeth, *Twelve Mormon Homes*, pp. 45-46.

Mormon leader under house arrest by federal authorities. There is little question that the delegation formed opinions of Americans and made lasting memories during their unplanned stay.[393]

"A Mind Free From Care" (1872)

Mrs. Thomas Kane and her husband, while visiting Utah in 1872, accompanied Brigham Young on his annual journey to St. George, stopping at a number of homes on the way. A keen observer, she was frank in her characterization of the Mormon prophet. She noticed his people loved him and wrote they "talked away to (him) about every conceivable matter, from the fluxing of an ore to the advantages of a Navajo bit, and expected him to remember every child in every cotter's family. And he really seemed to do so, and to be at home . . . I noticed that he never seemed uninterested, but gave an unforced attention to the person addressing him, which suggested a mind free from care."[394]

Not Just Two Counselors! (1873)

With the increasing burdens of office, in 1873 Brigham chose an additional five brethren to serve as his counselors—Lorenzo Snow, Brigham Young, Jun., Albert Carrington, John W. Young, and George Q. Cannon. In the 1873 April Conference he stated that he now had "seven brethren to assist him in this capacity." This was not unique however. Joseph had done the same thing when after Sidney Rigdon and Frederick Williams were sustained as counselors, he selected Oliver Cowdery, Joseph Smith, Sen., Hyrum Smith, and John Smith,

---

393 Butler, Wendy, "The Iwakura Mission and Its Stay in Salt Lake City," *Utah Historical Quarterly*. Winter 1998, pp. 26-47.

394 Kane, Elizabeth, *Twelve Mormon Homes*, p. 101.

his uncle, as additional counselors. The minutes of that meeting said all seven leaders were "to be considered the heads of the church."[395]

Petticoat Domination! (1873)

Like many others of their gender, nineteenth century Mormon women felt it was improper for male doctors to attend women in childbirth or treat female disorders. Convincing Brigham Young of this, he announced in 1873 that "the time has come for women to come forth as doctors in these valleys of the mountains." When some sisters responded to his announcement, he set apart Ellis Shipp, Margaret Shipp and Romania Pratt to go east to medical schools, each of whom obtained a medical degree and returned to Utah to encourage other sisters to enter the field. The last quarter of the nineteenth century found a higher percentage of women from Utah studying medicine than any other state or territory. By the end of the century, male doctors were complaining of "petticoat domination."[396]

Like Mother, Like Son (1874)

When Arthur became deputy U. S. marshal in Utah in 1874, he seemed to enjoy his job and as a former Mormon, he became good at it. He served papers on polygamous husbands, including Brigham Young and even served as guard while Brigham was under house arrest in 1875. Although raised as a Latter-day Saint, his mother had experienced polygamy-related problems with Joseph Smith in Nauvoo and became bitterly anti-polygamous and apparently had great influence

---

395 CHC, 5:506.
396 Bushman, Claudia L., pp. 58-59.

on her son Arthur. It must have been especially galling to Arthur's mother when her husband and Arthur's father, Orson Pratt, was chosen to publicly announce the doctrine of plural marriage for the first time in 1852.[397]

Not For Lack of Trying (1874)

That such co-operative societies as Orderville were started by the Saints in the second half of the nineteenth century is well known. Less known is the actual number. The big push came in 1874 by Brigham Young, largely to promote moral reform as well as to emphasize the principle of consecration. Brigham told the Bishops responsible, however, not to push their members further than they were willing to go in co-operative living. The result was over 220 United Order organizations taking a number of organization forms, but nevertheless co-operative. Most of these were set up in 1874 throughout the Utah Territory, Nevada, Idaho, and Arizona, with the last one established at Cave Valley, Chihuahua, Mexico in 1893.[398]

General Doniphan in Utah (1874)

During the last week of May 1874, Brigham Young had a most notable visitor to his office on South Temple Street. General Alexander Doniphan of Missouri, whom the Saints held in such high esteem because of his refusal to carry out General Clark's order to execute Joseph and six of his associates on the public square at Far West in 1838, came to visit the people whom he had described as a "peaceful, sober, industrious, and law-abiding people." Although he does not mention

---

397   Van Wagoner, Richard S. & Mary, "Arthur Pratt, Utah Lawman," *Utah Historical Quarterly*. Winter, 1987, pp. 22-35.
398   Arrington, Fox, and May, pp. 414-419.

the Saints in his brief autobiography, he is reported to have once said about the Mormon leaders he met in Missouri in the 1830s: "I have never met a group of men who had native intelligence and understanding and force of character that have even quite equaled the group of men-leaders gathered about Joseph Smith."[399]

Brigham Incarcerated (1875)

In February 1875 Ann Eliza Webb Young sued Brigham for divorce plus a substantial divorce settlement and alimony. The trial was held before Judge McKean, bitterly anti-Mormon. He granted the divorce and ordered the payments. Brigham refused on the grounds that Ann Eliza knew at the time of marriage that Brigham already had a legal wife. He refused to comply with the court order and McKean charged him with contempt and fined him $25 and sentenced him to one day in prison. On March 1, 1875 the seventy-three-year-old Prophet entered the penitentiary for twenty-four hours—the only time he would ever spend behind bars.[400]

Planned As It Went (1875)

The construction of the very unique tabernacle on Temple Square was started in 1863, but not dedicated until 1875. Part of the reason for the delayed dedication (it was being used as early as 1867) was that its plans were still being made as it was constructed. The design for the interior was not even started until 1867, the year it was first used for conference. Four months before the conference, Truman O. Angell recorded in his diary, "I got along with the penciling on the drawing of

---

399 Maynard, Gregory, "Alexander William Doniphan: Man of Justice," *BYU Studies*, Vol. 13, No. 4, p. 472.
400 Roberts, *Life of John Taylor*, p. 322.

Tabernacle seating and flooring arrangement." The location of the stand and organ and slope of the floor had not yet been decided. The balcony was an afterthought and was found to improve the acoustics in a remarkable manner.[401]

Sent By A Nephite (1875)

Three of the Twelve whom the Lord chose as his apostles in the New World after his resurrection were given permission to tarry on earth as translated beings until he came again. They would administer as holy messengers in the latter days. Stories of the "three Nephites" abound in Mormon folklore, but Orson Pratt, speaking as an apostle himself, spoke of such administrations in a discourse given in the Twentieth Ward Meeting House in February 1875. He referred to more than fourteen hundred Indians who had so far been converted to the Restored Gospel and said that in almost every case the conversion had been made because a messenger, speaking their language, came to them, instructed them and told them to go to the Mormons to request baptism.[402]

A Man Without Vanity (1875)

When George A. Smith died in 1875, the Church lost one of its greatest leaders and also perhaps, one of its least vain. Perhaps with his size, over three hundred pounds, he believed there was nothing to be vain about. Like many men who prematurely lose their hair, he resorted to a wig, but unlike many, he didn't care who knew. He was reported to have had at least five in different colors—to match his moods, he said. In front of some Indians in southern Utah he once removed not

---

401 Grow, pp. 98-99.
402 JD, 17:299-300.

only his wig but his false teeth, causing them to flee in fright. It is difficult to imagine a general authority, preaching to the Saints, removing his hairpiece and mopping his brow, as Brother Smith often did to the amusement of the Saints.[403]

Apostle Yes, President No! (1875)

Two years before his death, Brigham Young placed apostles Orson Pratt and Orson Hyde after John Taylor in the Quorum of the Twelve. The reason given was a need to readjust the seniority in the Quorum because of the one-time excommunications of Pratt and Hyde. Although Brigham had at one time refused to let Orson Pratt resign from the Quorum, he apparently didn't want him as Church President. Pratt's philosophical writings irritated the president so much that the First Presidency and the Quorum published point-by-point condemnations of Pratt's views in 1865. Woodruff once made reference to Pratt's "unyielding stubbornness, and of upbraiding the Twelve for not being manly, for not declaring their views the way he looked at it."[404]

A Lesson Learned (1875)

Like many young missionaries who find themselves unprepared when they begin their missions, such was the case with Junius Wells, son of the well-known Daniel Wells. At the age of eighteen, he was introduced to his first audience in Liverpool by the branch president. He recalled, "being a son of President Wells, there was much expected of me. It took the president of the branch several minutes to introduce me, but it took me just one and one-quarter minutes to say all that I knew." He must

---

403 Pusey, p. 113.
404 VanWagoner & Walker, p. 215.

have learned fast—just two years later in 1875, by call of Brigham Young, Julius organized the Young Men's Mutual Improvement Association, designed to give young men speaking experience for missionary work.[405]

If You Don't Shoot Him, I Will (1875)

As the gentiles started flooding Utah in the late 1800s, fathers and Church leaders found it difficult to keep some of their daughters from the clutches of fly-by-night charmers. In 1875 a young gentile miner was asked to appear before a Bishop's Court to determine his intentions toward a young lady in Washington, Utah. He scoffed when he appeared before the bishop and said, "If you have a real charge, I demand a trial by a real court." An attending elder said, "Bishop, I favor giving this man one hour to think it over. If he stays and you don't shoot him, I will." Ten minutes after being sent outdoors to make a decision on responding respectfully to the court, the elders found him riding toward Silver Reef, never to return.[406]

Eliza Recants—Slowly (1876)

Eliza Snow wrote several articles for the *Woman's Exponent* and perhaps one she should not have written. In September 1875, the *Exponent* reprinted by popular request a previous article by Eliza justifying the literal resurrection of the body. Brigham had not objected the first time, but this time, without referring to Eliza as his wife, he had printed in the next issue a refuting quote: "As the prophet Joseph Smith once [said], 'It has just one fault and that fault is, it is not true.'" History is silent as to Eliza's reaction during subsequent

---

405 Humpherys, A. Glen, "Missionaries to the Saints," *BYU Studies*, Autumn 1976, p. 82.
406 Anderson, Nels, pp. 339-340.

encounters with her husband, but six months later, in a tiny notice in the same magazine, Eliza recanted: "Permit me to say that I fully concur in the views expressed by Pres. Young."[407]

Karl Maeser's Mission (1876)

Karl Maeser was given the responsibility in 1876 of establishing the Brigham Young Academy in Provo (later called BYU). As its first president and only teacher, he was responsible for instructing the entire first year's enrollment—twenty-nine students. As an inspiring teacher, Karl had some worthwhile experience. He had served a mission in Virginia shortly after arriving in the United States as a convert. While in Richmond and financially impoverished, he visited a music store and there impressed a customer with his ability to play the piano. As a result he was able financially to complete his mission by giving piano lessons to the daughters of the gentleman he met in the store—former President of the United States, John Tyler.

Reporting the Custer Massacre (1876)

Within five years of the completion of the first transcontinental telegraph line in Utah, the Saints had their own Deseret Telegraph, tying together the numerous Mormon settlements in the Territory. It was by way of this telegraph that the world first learned of the massacre of the Seventh Cavalry at Little Big Horn in 1876. A rider from the army command post at Fort Hall rode all the way to Franklin, Idaho, and from there the Mormon operator relayed the news to federal authorities and the news media in the east. Ironically it was the outbreak of Indian hostilities in Utah that prompted the Church leaders to push the completion of the Deseret Telegraph in 1865.[408]

---

407 Ursenbach, Maureen, "Three Women and the Life of the Mind," *Utah Historical Quarterly*. Winter 1975, p. 39.

408 Campbell, p. 278 fn.

David's Discovery (1877)

In January 1877, David Smith, born after the death of his father Joseph in 1844, was committed to the Illinois Hospital for the Insane where he resided until his death in 1904. The causes of mental illness were little known at that time, but his brother Joseph III was convinced of the reason. Young David had been sent as a missionary from the Reorganized Church to the Utah Saints in 1869 and again in 1872, contrary to his mother's wishes. Joseph III later wrote that "there was inculcated into my brother's mind the idea that his father was either a polygamist in practice or that he was the spiritual author of the Utah plural marriage philosophy."[409] This was probably true, for while in Utah he had discovered evidence of several of his father's plural wives.

After Thirty Years (1877)

Eight months before his death and nearly thirty years since he had last been in a temple, Brigham Young dedicated the St. George Temple on January 1, 1877. Wilford Woodruff read the dedicatory prayer in place of the ailing president, after which Brigham was carried upstairs for the dedication of the second floor and the sealing rooms. A week later President Young's daughter, Susa Young Gates was privileged to be the first to be baptized for the dead in the new temple—for a deceased friend. She had also been the first to be rebaptized and confirmed on the day of dedication, along with 223 others. As a resident of St. George, she then became a worker and recorder in the temple.

---

409 Edwards, Paul, "The Sweet Singer of Israel: David Hyrum Smith." *BYU Studies*, Winter 1972, p.

Was It Amelia's Palace? (1877)

When President Young died in 1877, the official Church President's residence then under construction was not yet finished. After his death, the story emerged that it was built for his favorite wife, Amelia Folsom. The driver of a tourist hack is credited with given it the name of "Amelia's Palace" and when a later owner, Mrs. Emery Holmes insisted upon calling it by that name, it stuck. Actually Amelia did live there briefly after Brigham's death but so did Mary Ann Angell, his wife when plural marriage was first introduced. Within three years of President Young's death, the Gardo House, as it was officially called, was sold to the Church and became the residence of both Presidents Taylor and Woodruff. The name "Gardo" came from a Spanish book that President Young had especially enjoyed.[410]

All Except Three! (1877)

Shortly after the dedication of the St. George Temple, Wilford Woodruff was visited by the spirits of the founding fathers appealing for their temple endowments. The story of Brother Woodruff being baptized by Brother McCallister for the signers of the Declaration of Independence and other early eminent men is well known. Less known is what followed those baptisms. At a talk given in the tabernacle in Salt Lake City later that year, he reported, "I then baptized him (brother McCallister) for every President of the United States, except three; and when their cause is just, somebody will do the work for them." He did not mention the names of the "unworthy" three presidents.[411]

---

410   Spencer and Harmer, p. 210.
411   JD, 19:229.

A Wealthy Midwife (1877)

Patty Sessions, the well-known Mormon midwife, drove a four-ox team the entire distance across the plains in 1847. She later claimed she entered the Salt Lake Valley with only five cents that she had found on the trail. Thirty years later, through hard work and frugality, she had been able to donate hundreds of dollars to the Perpetual Emigration Fund and the tithing fund as well as doing numerous deeds of private charity. Even more remarkable, she had become a stockholder in the Z.C.M.I. to the amount of twelve to thirteen thousand dollars. By today's adjusted inflation value, that stock would have been worth at least half a million dollars.[412]

Why the Church Didn't Cooperate (1877)

Numerous attempts were made by the federal government to bring to justice those responsible for the Mountain Meadows massacre of 1857. Critics of the Mormon Church have laid the blame for the lengthy delay at the feet of the Church for their unwillingness to cooperate. There was actually a most logical reason for the lack of cooperation. Each attempt degenerated into an attempt to charge and convict Brigham Young for the crime, although the evidence in the very beginning indicated Brigham was not involved. Shortly before the prophet's death, after the government abandoned such attempts to implicate him, the Church authorities cooperated and John D. Lee, although not the only guilty one, was finally brought to trial and executed.[413]

---

412 Tullidge, p. 428.
413 Pusey, p. 108.

At the Crime Scene (1877)

Little thought is given to the fact that John D. Lee was executed at Mountain Meadows, the site of the massacre for which he was found to be so responsible—other than that it was appropriate. That was not the primary reason for selecting that site. It was the idea of William Nelson, a United States Marshal, a bitter anti-Mormon. It was his hope that forcing Lee to face death on those very grounds where so many emigrants had been killed would be such an emotional trauma for Lee that he would break down and make a confession that would link Brigham Young with the crime. In his final statement at the scene, he accused Brigham of moving away from the teachings of Joseph Smith and although he would have seemed justified, he refused to implicate the Church President in the massacre.[414]

"Fiend of Hell" (1877)

That John D. Lee was deeply involved in the Mountain Meadows massacre, there is no doubt. The extent of his participation may be, however. The most damning account is the story of his involvement in the slaying of two teenage girls, repeated by Jacob Hamblin at Lee's trial. Although Hamblin said Lee told him of his part in the killing of the girls shortly after the massacre, it is a fact that Lee and Hamblin were not on friendly terms at this time and after this story surfaced, Lee would refer to his fellow Saint as "dirty fingered Jake," or the "old fiend of hell." The facts may never be known but because of Hamblin's reputation for integrity, his testimony as a prose-

---

414   Birney, pp. 214-215.

cution witness in 1876 was key evidence in Lee's guilty verdict.[415]

Brigham and God (1877)

Brigham Young was not known to be especially humble when discussing his role in building the Lord's Kingdom in the Great Basin—nor did he necessarily have need to be. After his death in 1877, there arose a classic story, and although possibly apocryphal, it is nevertheless an appropriate characterization of the church president's secular accomplishments. Brigham was conducting a visiting clergyman around the prosperous Salt Lake Valley, when the impressed visitor commented on what an amazing job Brigham and God had accomplished. Brigham responded, "Yes, and you should have seen it when the Lord had it alone!"[416]

415   Brooks, *The Mountain Meadows Massacre*, p. 107.
416   England, Eugene, "Brigham's Gospel Kingdom," *BYU Studies*, Vol. 18, No. 3, p. 373.

10

The Church Survives
(1877–1890)

When Heber Was a Red (1878)

Utah may have been a frontier in the 1870s, but it was also baseball country—especially Salt Lake City. In 1878, it boasted two first-rate teams that played and consistently beat other Intermountain West teams. One of these, the Red Stockings was a newcomer to baseball and received its support primarily from the local Latter-day Saints. Although the older established team, the Deserets, was favored, the two played for the championship in 1878. Surprisingly, the Reds won three out of five games, helped to a major degree by their new second baseman—Heber J. Grant. Heber was more certain of his worthiness as a team member than he was four years later when he was called as an apostle at the age of twenty-five.[417]

An Apostate's Testimony (1878)

The story of David Whitmer's repeated testimonies, as the last survivor of the three witnesses, is well known in Mormon history. Less known is the testimony of John Whitmer, David's brother, as the last of the eight witnesses. Shortly before he died in 1878, he bore a moving testimony of the Book of

---

417 Cannon II, Kenneth L., "Deserets, Red Stockings, and Out-of-Towners: Baseball Comes of Age in Salt Lake City, 1877-79," *Utah Historical Quarterly*. Spring 1984, pp. 146-149

Mormon and his witness of the original plates. After he was excommunicated in 1838, Theodore Turley bluntly asked him, in the presence of anti-Mormon friends, why he once bore witness and now doubted. This would have been his opportunity to admit he never saw the plates. Instead, however, he merely said, he saw the plates and the characters thereon, but since he couldn't personally translate them, he didn't "know whether it is true or not."[418]

A Lightning Strike By Brigham? (1878)

Brigham Young was not happy with the tower of the St. George Temple. It had a squat-domed cupola and Brigham wanted it changed to a taller more majestic dome. Unfortunately, the prophet died before he could bring about the change he wanted. The year following his death, either Brigham or the Lord brought about the change with a lightning strike. The low awkward tower was damaged enough that it was thought profitable to rebuild the dome the way Brigham had desired. Under Truman Angell's direction, William Folsom designed a higher domed structure and Brigham finally got what he wanted.[419]

Evarts' Folly (1879)

Secretary of State Evart, a member of President Hayes' cabinet, was apparently writing without thinking when he sent an official circular letter to American diplomatic officers in various European countries, including England, Germany, Norway, Sweden, and Denmark, urging them to warn those governments that "No friendly power" would deliberately

---

418 Anderson, Richard Lloyd, p. 131.
419 Cannon & Whittaker, p. 165.

encourage "criminal enterprises" in the United States. They should therefore attempt "to prevent the departure of those proposing to come to the United States as violators of the law by engaging in such criminal enterprises." In other words prevent the emigration of Mormons because they might end up engaging in plural marriage. Needless to say there was a storm of protest over such an absurd violation of international law, both at home and abroad, and the idea was allowed to quietly die.[420]

The Greatest Hardships (1879)

The eighty families who were assigned to the San Juan Mission in the fall of 1879, suffered greater hardships in reaching their destination than any other pioneers in the American West. What began as an expected six-week journey to their destination in Southeastern Utah turned out to be six months. Their incredible feats of cutting by hand and blasting chutes down rock cliffs and lowering their wagons by ropes down such "impassable" crevasses as the "Hole-in-the-Rock" above the Colorado River ranks as unequaled feats in American pioneering. With their goal the remote settlement of Montezuma, they gave up eighteen miles short, too exhausted to continue, and founded the little settlement of Bluff, Utah.[421]

Sufficient Brains (1880)

Years after plural marriage had been abolished by the Church, Heber J. Grant attempted to correct some false impressions about the practice. He pointed out that the practice was less widespread than believed (less than two percent of

---

420 CHC, 5:550-551.
421 Miller, *Hole-IN-The-Rock*. Chaps. VIII – X.

the population were liable under the Edmunds-Tucker act) and leaders were cautious in granting permission. For the two years he presided as President over the Tooele Stake (1880-1882) he received only two applications for plural marriages—both of which he rejected. One he refused because of the man's drinking problem and to the other he said, "What is needed in your family is sufficient brains to take care of one wife and one family."[422]

Who Owned The Temple? (1880)

The RLDS Church gained ownership of the Kirtland Temple despite their failure to hold legal title because of their use and possession over a period of several years. This is called being awarded title by "adverse possession." It should be noted that the court was asked to determine ownership not between the RLDS and LDS Churches but between the RLDS Church and two of its leaders—Joseph Smith III and Mark Forscutt— in order to quiet title to Kirtland real estate that had been in question for over three decades. The court decision, however, was used by the RLDS Church as evidence of the legitimacy of the RLDS Church over the Utah Church although the Utah Church was not even represented at the court.[423]

Ignorant Foreigners?

In the fight for political control of Utah in the nineteenth century, numerous slanderous charges were made. One of the most common was that Utah was made up largely of ignorant foreigners unfit to be citizens of the United States. Census statistics of 1880 tell a different story. Wisconsin, California,

---

422 Berrett & Burton, 3:122.
423 Walker, Ronald W. (ed.), "The Historians' Corner," *BYU Studies*, Vol. 25, No. 3, p. 110.

Minnesota, Dakota, Arizona, and Nevada all had higher percentages of foreign-born citizens, with Nevada showing over 70% to Utah's 44%. As to literacy, statistics at the same time pointed out that of all the states and territories in the Union there were but "thirteen showing a lower percentage [than Utah] of total population who could not read." In fact the highly literate state of Connecticut had the same as Utah, 3.37 percent.[424]

In A Hurry! (1880)

A plural marriage anecdote from frontier Utah reveals more about the primitive state of travel at that time than anything else. When John D. Rees died in 1880, he left three wives who would live into the twentieth century. One of these, Mary Morgan Rees, who had been his first wife, received word while living in Bingham City, that John had received a call to take another wife. Distressed over this information, she set out to walk to Salt Lake City, over fifty miles distant, to confer with Brigham Young on the matter. Along the way she was offered a ride in a neighbor's wagon, but refused with a blunt, "No, thanks. I'm in a hurry!"[425]

A Letter to God, Please! (1881)

The little town of Bluff in Southeastern Utah experienced Indian problems long after they had disappeared in the rest of territory. In 1881, an Indian named Navajo Frank was caught stealing horses but escaped. After several more such incidents, he was located and warned by the Saints that if he persisted he would "take sick and die." He laughed at the threat but turned

---

424 Berrett and Burton, 3:162-163.
425 Beecher, Maureen Ursenbach, "Under the Sunbonnets: Mormon Women with Faces," *BYU Studies*. Summer 1976, p. 484.

over the horses. Several months later, thin and haggard, he was seen by Thales Haskel who had given him the warning. Navajo Frank pleaded with Haskel to write a letter to the Lord telling him he would never again steal from the Mormons if his life was spared. Haskel made no promises but Navajo Frank recovered to live another twenty years—without stealing.[426]

Fumigating the Territory (1881)

It seems that every church in the country had a "solution" to the "Mormon Problem" in the nineteenth century. One of the most radical, even criticized by other denominations, was found in 1881 in the *Chicago Interior*, a publication of the Presbyterian Church. It called for throwing open all Mormon property in Utah for a "takeover" by any men who wanted free land. "The army will keep out of the way" to allow the invaders "to finish up the pest, fumigate the territory, and to establish themselves in ninety days after the word 'go' is given." The *Congregationalist* of Boston, to its credit, referred to its sister Protestants' plan "as amazing as it is wrong."[427]

Not Brigham's Church (1881)

Bishop Edwin Woolley's testimony was not unique for the pioneer Saints, but perhaps the way he expressed it was. When he died in 1881, he was remembered for a sight altercation with Brigham Young, who could at times be quite sarcastic. As their minor confrontation ended, Brigham said, "Now, Bishop Woolley, I guess you will go off and apostatize," to which the bishop replied, "If this were your church, President Young, I would be tempted to do so. But this is just as much my church

---

426 Austin, Thomas E., & McPherson, Robert S., "Murder, Mayhem, and Mormons: The Evolution of Law Enforcement on the San Juan Frontier, 1880-1900," *Utah Historical Quarterly*. Winter 1987, pp. 40-42.

427 CHC, 6:41.

as it is yours, and why should I apostatize from my own church?"[428]

That Mormon Look (1881)

James Garfield, the second American president to be assassinated, was shot by Charles J. Guiteau, with motives not entirely clear. But it was 1881 and the height of anti-Mormonism, so it was not unexpected to immediately hear reckless charges that the assassin must have been a Mormon—charges especially from ministers of the gospel. The Rev. T. DeWitt Talmage, preaching at the Brooklyn New York tabernacle, suggested the time would come when it will "be found that he was a paid agent of that old hag of hell [i. e. the 'Mormon church]." Talmage described Guiteau as having not only the look of "Mormon ugliness" but "the spirit of Mormon licentiousness; of Mormon cruelty; of Mormon murder."[429]

Childhood Deaths in St. George (1881)

The death rate in Mormon Nauvoo, especially among children, is well known in Latter-day Saint history. According to the Sexton's death list published in the *Nauvoo Neighbor*, forty-four percent of all deaths in that river town were of children five and younger. A study was made years later of the age of persons interred in the municipal cemetery in St. George, Utah. During St. George's first twenty years, ending in 1881, sixty-four percent of all deaths were of children four and under. The author of the study concluded that although the death rate declined over the next forty years, it remained high until the residents discontinued drinking water from open irrigation ditches.[430]

---

428 Arrington & Bitton, p. 61.
429 CHC, 6:26-27.
430 Anderson, Nels, p. 360.

Just A Question Of Semantics (1882)

The Saints have a tendency to forget that during the persecutions that raged in the late nineteenth century over plural marriage, there were many allies outside the church. One of the best was Senator Joseph E. Brown of Georgia. In February 1882 he made an eloquent but futile speech in the Senate opposing the Edmunds bill. He sarcastically told his fellow colleagues that the problem could be solved by the Mormons merely changing the name of their marriage relationship—suggesting that prostitution itself would never be legislated against. He seemed to strike at the heart of the persecution when he stated: "The clamor is not against the Mormon for having more than one woman, but for calling more than one his wife."[431]

Threat to Public Morality? (1882)

Primarily because of the church doctrine of plural marriage, non-Mormons throughout the last half of the nineteenth century were accusing the Saints of being a "threat to public morality." A comparison of criminal activities by Mormon and non-Mormons in Utah and Idaho at the height of such charges should be a definitive response. Statistics derived from the 1880 census brought down to 1882 when it was compiled, police and penitentiary figures, and federal commission reports show a dramatic contrast. Saints made up over 80 percent of the population of Utah and Idaho, but they accounted for only 12 percent of the criminal acts. If a non-Mormon was almost seven times as likely to commit a criminal act, who was the threat?[432]

---

431 Mulder and Mortensen, p. 411.
432 Berrett and Burton, 3:91.

Dragging In The Tabernacle (1883)

Wilford Woodruff, the senior member of the Quorum of the Twelve, called it "the most interesting Exhibition I ever witnessed in my life." The "exhibition" was a concert performed in the Tabernacle in 1883 conducted by Evan Stephens with a 450 voice childrens' Sunday School choir. It must be assumed that the adulation was for the vocal quality of the huge choir which Stephens had put together from Sunday School classes throughout the city and not for the performance of Brother Stephens himself. Stephens, a twenty-eight-year-old Welch bachelor, appeared at the concert in a mock prima donna performance in drag.[433]

Was It Worth It? (1883)

A single line in church chronology tells us little about a man's faith. Such was in the case of Joseph Toronto, an early Church pioneer. For July 6, 1883, the one-line obituary read, "Joseph Toronto, once a missionary to Italy, died at Salt Lake City." In 1845, as the temple was nearing completion in Nauvoo and the Saints were preparing for their exodus west, Brigham Young recorded that on July 8 Joseph Toronto handed him $2,500 in gold and said that he wanted to give himself and all he had to the building up of the Church and the kingdom of God and would thereafter look to Brigham for counsel and protection. To put such an offering into perspective, in today's dollar value that would be nearly $200,000.[434]

---

433 Hicks, pp. 101-102.
434 HC, 7:433.

His Last Thoughts (1883)

The last words of General Thomas L. Kane demonstrated the character of one of the most influential and knowledgeable gentile friends the Saints had during their persecutions in the nineteenth century. His wife wrote George Q. Cannon, after her husband's death, that in his final lucid moments he said: "My mind is too heavy, but do send the sweetest message you can make up to my Mormon friends—to all, my dear Mormon friends." She then added in the letter, "Nothing I could 'make up,' I am persuaded, could be sweeter to you than this evidence that you were in his latest thoughts."[435] The appreciation of the Saints for Kane's friendship was demonstrated in 1970 by the purchase and establishment of the Kane Memorial Chapel as a Church historical site in Kane, Pennsylvania.

One of Two Women (1884)

Several sister Saints had driven ox teams across the plains, but Vienna had done it at the age of sixty. She was unique in a number of ways. As a wealthy, educated woman from Boston she had learned of Joseph Smith and traveled alone to Kirtland where she was baptized and donated all she owned to the Church. She had attended the sick in Zion's Camp near Fishing River, gone through the Ohio, Missouri and Illinois persecutions and after half a century of faithful service, died in 1884 at the age of ninety-six in Utah. But the most unique thing about this sister was that of all the revelations directed by the Lord at 130 individuals in the Doctrine and Covenants, only two were directed at women—Emma Smith and Vienna Jacques.

---

435 CHC, 6:104.

A Charge Laid To Rest (1884)

The most persistent anti-Mormon charge in the nineteenth century was that the Book of Mormon was based on an early manuscript by Solomon Spaulding. The charge was difficult to refute since the 'Spaulding Manuscript' came up missing. In 1884, however, the President of Oberlin College, Jas. H. Fairchild, was visiting Honolulu to go over some acquisitions offered by an L. L. Rice, a former Ohio editor. In the collection he discovered the long-lost manuscript by Spaulding. Recognizing it as the alleged origin of the Book of Mormon, Fairchild and Rice immediately set about comparing the two writings. Their conclusion, verified by later scholars: "(We) could detect no resemblance between the two, in general or detail." The Spaulding manuscript now resides at Oberlin College.[436]

The Red Hot Address (1884)

On August 10, 1884, a mob attacked the home of the Condor family at Cane Creek, Tennessee, killing two Mormon missionaries, Elder Gibbs and Elder Berry, as well as two young men of the family who tried to defend the Mormons, and seriously wounding the mother of the young men. The mob had become incensed over a news report reprinted from the anti-Mormon *Salt Lake Tribune* that reported an address given at Moab, Utah by a Bishop West, advocating the assassination of the Utah's Territorial Governor Murray. As it turned out, no such address had ever been made—there was not even such a person as Bishop West. Needless to say, the *Tribune* showed little remorse for its false and inflammatory report.[437]

---

436 *Contributor*, Vol. 10, Nov. 1888 – Oct. 1889, p. 20.

437 CHC, 6:83-102.

Not Nice But Understandable (1884)

After the murders of the two Mormon missionaries in Tennessee (described in "The Red Hot Address"), the federally appointed governor of Utah, Eli H. Murray, felt compelled to contact the Tennessee governor, W. B. Bate, about the killing of two of "his" citizens. He did so with tongue-in-cheek, saying "the charges of preaching polygamy do not excuse murder. I trust that you may bring the guilty to punishment.... But the murdered Mormon agents in Tennessee were sent from here, as they have been for years, by the representatives of organized crime." He then suggested that Tennessee representatives in Congress be less indifferent to Mormon lawlessness so that such killings would not continue.[438]

One-time Foes Join Forces (1885)

When President John Taylor went on the underground in 1885, he had to take with him, in addition to his close friend and counselor, and nephew, George Q. Cannon, a few trusted individuals to serve as guards and coachmen. One of these was Charles H. Wilcken, a veteran of the German army and holder of the distinguished Iron Cross for bravery, who had come to Utah with Colonel Johnston's army in 1858 and had attached himself to the Church and as protector to Brigham Young. Upon Brigham's death he became a protector to Brother Cannon and thus President Taylor. Joining the group of "protectors" and becoming one of Wilcken's closest friends, was Samuel Bateman, who had led the a platoon under Captain Lot Smith in the guerrilla action against Wilcken and his military companions years earlier.[439]

---

438   CHC, 6:99.
439   Larson, *The "Americanization" of Utah for Statehood*, pp. 155-156.

And Women Also! (1885)

It is a general impression that Mormon sisters were merely bystanders while their husbands went off to prison for unlawful cohabitation in the 1880s. Today we take for granted the constitutional guarantee that women cannot be forced to testify against their husbands, but such was not the case in Territorial Utah. Wives were hunted down, arrested and if they refused to testify, were sentenced to prison. On September 15, 1885 we find Miss Elizabeth Starkey and Miss Eliza Shafer sent to prison by Judge Zane. In October 1884, Lydia Spencer, who refused to testify, was sent to prison.[440] Others were Belle Harris, Annie Gallifant who was pregnant at the time, and Nellie White who served a month and a half in the penitentiary.[441]

Demise of Orderville (1885)

The longest lasting of all the United Orders started by the Church in the late nineteenth century was Orderville in southern Utah. Its demise, like all the other United Orders, is usually ascribed to its antipathy to human nature and individualism. These were certainly major contributing factors, but the *coup de grace*, as with plural marriage, was brought about by the federal government. The enforcement of the 1882 Edmunds Act, beginning in 1885, forcing more and more Church leaders either into prison or the underground, effectively deprived Orderville of its functioning leadership. The Church was able to function with its leaders underground, but a small, close-knit, laboring community with so few surplus resources could not.[442]

---

440 Jenson, Andrew, *Church Chronology*, pp. 116 & 123.
441 Hoopes and Hoopes, p. 86.
442 Arrington, Fox & May, p. 291.

Stealing Postage Stamps? (1885)

When the infamous and hated federal judge, W. W. Drummond sat on the bench in Utah, the Saints had more to detest than his open hostility to their faith. Their opinion of him as an immoral and corrupt individual was amply proven by his life after helping to bring about the "Mormon War of 1857." It was apparently all downhill after that. In 1880, Abraham O. Smoot, former mayor of Salt Lake City, met Drummond as a seedy-looking sewing machine salesman in St. Louis. The Saints next heard of him being sentenced to a House of Corrections for stealing postage stamps in 1885 and finally they learned of his death as a pauper in a Chicago grog shop in 1888.[443]

An American Pogrom (1885)

Many non-Mormons find humor in the polygamy the Saints once practiced, but they should find little humor in the official measures their government once took against polygamists. Raids on churches themselves were common, with congregations arrested or subpoenaed en masse. In 1885, a deputy marshal actually took over the podium at a regional conference to announce the arrest of members in the congregation and to serve subpoenas. *The Deseret News* in 1886 reported a raid led by U.S. Marshal Elwin Ireland on the Seventeenth Ward meeting house in which eighty-year-old Bishop McRae was arrested along with others.[444] The humor the anti-Mormon *Tribune* found in such raids seems lacking today.

---

443 CHC, 4:206.
444 Panek, Tracey E., "Search and Seizure in Utah: Recounting the Antipolygamy Raids," *Utah Historical Quarterly.* Fall 1994, pp. 324-325.

A Dangerous Priesthood? (1885)

Just as many have interpreted the Civil War as a contest over slavery when the real issue was the sovereign power of states versus the federal government, many have misinterpreted the conflict between the federal government and the Saints in the nineteenth century as a contest over plural marriage. In reality it was the power of priesthood authority that was the issue. "Not polygamy but the power of the priesthood is the real danger," reported the *Springfield* [Mass.] *Union* in 1885. This sentiment was honestly voiced by Territorial Governor West in 1888 who said "This priesthood not only rules the Church, it governs the state . . . [it is] a power more absolute and despotic than any other known to civilization."[445] Most Saints would merely debate the word "despotic," not "absolute."

Sweatbox For The Faithful (1885)

In August 1885 Rudger Clawson, serving a four-year prison term for unlawful cohabitation and polygamy, had a confrontation with warden G. N. Dow. Brother Clawson, who is remembered for his presence at the murder of Joseph Standing while they were missionaries in Georgia and for his later membership in the Quorum of the Twelve, refused to participate in a Protestant religious service at the prison. He was willing to attend but not participate in required rites. For this he was sentenced to being locked in an iron sweatbox in the prison yard under the hot August sun. Carrying his cot like a cross, the twenty-eight-year-old Mormon was marched to his confinement. There he spent three days and nights.[446]

---

445 Larson, *The "Americanization" of Utah for Statehood*, pp. 207 & 245.
446 Hoopes & Hoopes, pp. 107-109.

Getting Hit Where It Hurts (1885)

The obvious hotbed of anti-Mormon sentiment and activity in the 1880s was Salt Lake City and seemed to be promoted by gentile merchants. One weapon the church had, however, was patronage by the Mormon community. Asking members not to deal with the more notorious anti-Mormon establishments was effective, but the church authorities found another weapon—the general conferences. Such conferences brought thousands of Saints into Salt Lake City twice a year, where they spent thousands of dollars with the merchants. During the years 1885, 1886 and 1887, annual and semi-annual conferences were moved to Logan, Provo and Coalville. The outcry from the gentile merchants indicated these moves were most effective.[447]

The Half-Mast Incident (1885)

On July 4, 1885, the national flag was flown at half-staff over several buildings in Salt Lake City as an expression of sorrow over the loss of civil liberties in the Utah Territory. Although not intended, this act was considered an insult to the flag by anti-Mormons and Civil War veterans—ironically even Confederate veterans. Public anticipation became intense that the Mormons would again dishonor the flag on Pioneer Day, July 24th. Even military camps in the west were put on alert for violence in Utah and veteran groups organized to punish the Saints for the anticipated "insult." On July 23rd ex-President Ulysses S. Grant died and the next day, Utah's Pioneer Day, flags were flown at half-staff nationwide.[448]

---

447 CHC, 6:168-169.
448 Roberts, *Life of John Taylor*, pp. 401-405.

Political Terrorism—Idaho Style! (1885)

Idaho had its share of anti-Mormonism—sometimes more dramatic than Utah. When the anti-Mormons gained the majority in the territorial legislature in 1885 they were able to pass the infamous Election Test Oath bill. This bill effectively barred Latter-day Saints from voting, serving as jurors, or holding public office. It was later reported in a Boise newspaper that the territorial governor Bunn was opposed to the legislation and refused to sign it. He was then visited by an anti-Mormon delegation who became "exceedingly wrathful and after a short heated controversy, Smith (a mob leader) arose, and pulling a gun from his pocket said: 'Governor, you will not leave this room alive unless you sign that bill and sign it at once.'" The governor then had to bear the condemnation of the Saints for signing it.[449]

And Just a Misdemeanor! (1886)

During the height of the anti-polygamy persecutions, President Taylor went into hiding and George Q. Cannon had to act in his place. On February 13th, with a reward of $500 placed for his capture on charges of polygamy, Cannon was arrested at Humbolt, Nevada. On his way back to Salt Lake City, President Cannon fell from the rear of the train and was injured. Rumors of his attempted escape spread and a force of twenty-seven soldiers from Fort Douglas was sent to escort the injured prisoner back. Taken to the U. S. Marshall's office, he was released on a bail of $45,000. And all of this cost and effort was for a charge considered merely a misdemeanor.[450]

---

449 Berrett and Burton, 3:81.
450 Jenson, *Church Chronology*, pp. 128-129.

Convicting Jesus (1886)

When Saints were barred from serving on juries in polygamy cases in Utah and Idaho, it became most profitable for anti-Mormons to serve. George Taylor, arrested for unlawful cohabitation in Provo in 1888, noted that his trial lasted only six minutes, thus making it possible and very profitable for jurors to be paid for several such trials each day.[451] Thus, to guarantee selection for jury duty, they were more than willing to return the verdicts the anti-Mormon officials wanted and findings of not guilty would be rare indeed. The classic example of such perverted justice is that of United States marshal Fred DuBois who boasted in open court in 1886 that "he had a jury impaneled to try unlawful cohabitation cases that would convict Jesus Christ if he were on trial."[452]

Just A Job! (1886)

One of the most detested U. S. Attorneys in Utah was W. H. Dickson, who was not only zealous in his prosecution of the Saints, but in calling for more federal restrictions. Speaking to some Civil War veterans in 1886, he referred to the Mormon Church as "steeped in disloyalty," and asked for support in the disfranchisement of all members of that Church. The following year Dickson left his job and in 1890 was defending the Saints in federal court in the case of *The Late Corporation of the Church of Jesus Christ of Latter-day Saints v. United States.* Such 'side-switching' was not uncommon; several former prosecuting federal attorneys in Utah were later hired and worked tirelessly to defend the Mormons against laws they had once zealously endorsed and whose passage they had encouraged.[453]

---

451   Bushman, Claudia L., pp. 151-152.
452   CHC, 6P:213-214.
453   Cresswell, pp. 116 & 127.

And $2.25 In Coins! (1887)

Convinced that the Saints were using the "wealthy" Perpetual Emigrating Fund to strengthen polygamy in Utah, the federal authorities moved to destroy the organization. In 1887, Congress added an amendment to the Edmunds-Tucker Bill disincorporating the P.E.F. and federal officials assumed charge of the assets. On November 18, United States Marshall Frank Dyer proceeded to take over the property that consisted of a safe, a desk, records, account books, promissory notes, paper of various kinds, and $2.25 in defaced silver coins. When the safe was opened Marshall Dyer discovered the company's assets, consisting of $417,968.50 in promissory notes, uncollectable and of no value.[454]

A Profitable And Pleasurable Job (1887)

Candidates were eager for the job of U. S. Marshals in the Utah Territory. Appointed to serve papers and arrest polygamous Saints, they found such jobs both profitable and pleasurable. Fred Bennett, who published a story of his job in 1887, wrote "I found the greatest pleasure in attending strictly to that business." In addition to an annual salary of $200.00 they received $2.00 for each warrant, attachment, summons, or other writ served. For an arrest they claimed $20.00. With such rewards at stake, it is little wonder that the federal officers were so diligent in issuing subpoenas to children, as well as adults or invading homes without proper authorization. They had little to fear of reprimands from anti-Mormon federal courts.[455]

---

454 Larson, *Prelude to the Kingdom,* p. 278.
455 Panek, Tracey E., "Search and Seizure in Utah: Recounting the Antipolygamy Raids," *Utah Historical Quarterly.* Fall 1994, pp. 319-323.

Hailstones From Hell? (1887)

In 1887, while Rudger Clawson was in the territorial prison for unlawful cohabitation, he met a murderer by the name of Fred Hopt who was executed while Clawson was there. Being a Catholic, Hopt was visited by a priest shortly before his execution. Probably asked by the priest to consider his eternal destination, he told the warden that if there was an afterlife, he would send a hailstorm within forty-eight hours. The storm came—with two-inch hailstones. The effect of this "miraculous" event on the other prisoners, Clawson did not say.[456]

547 Years For A Misdemeanor (1887)

In one of their rare Supreme Court victories in the nineteenth century, the Saints rejoiced when Lorenzo Snow was released after serving only a portion of his eighteen-month sentence for polygamy. He and many other Saints had been sentenced by federal judges on a "segregated" sentence basis. By this judicial theory the offense was segregated into time periods and thus they could be given a sentence for each time period. Since the sentence for this misdemeanor was normally six months in prison and a $300 fine, this could be multiplied by the years spent in living a plural marriage as was Snow—or months, or weeks or even days or minutes. If by days, Snow would have received a sentence of 547 years and a $328,500 fine.[457]

---

456 Hoopes and Hoopes, p. 130.

457 Driggs, Ken, "Lorenzo Snow's Appellate Court Victory," Utah Historical Quarterly. Winter 1990, pp. 81-93.

If They Build It, Will They Come? (1887)

Under pressure from American women outside of Utah, Congress appropriated money for the building of a home in Salt Lake City for "escaped" polygamous wives. Awarded a federal grant of $40,000, the Industrial Home Association issued its first annual report in 1887. It showed a total of eleven "saved" women. Awarded more federal money in 1888, the number of women given "sanctuary" dropped to five and the following year six women entered for their room and board. Actual records from the association do not indicate if any of those women were "escaped" or repentant wives or merely homeless gentiles seeking free housing. Finally Congress refused more money and the building became federal offices.[458]

A Study In Scarlet (1887)

One of the most prominent nineteenth century anti-Mormon authors was Sir Arthur Conan Doyle, penman of a lurid anti-Mormon novel, *A Study in Scarlet*. Thirty-six years later, the elderly Doyle decided to visit Utah in his spiritualist crusade, but was apprehensive because of his early anti-Mormon writings. Although he still held the same views on Mormonism, he was given a warm reception and five thousand packed the Tabernacle to hear his message on spiritualism. Interestingly enough, the only one to bring up the subject of his anti-Mormon writing was a non-Mormon, Dr. G. Hodgson Higgins, who suggested that Doyle apologize for his previous falsehoods about the Saints. He refused, believing that the good people he now met could not alter their past. The Saints didn't seem to care about an apology.[459]

---

458 Larson, *The "Americanization" of Utah for Statehood*, pp. 226-228.
459 Homer, Michael W., "'Recent Psychic Evidence': The Visit of Sir Arthur Conan Doyle to Utah in 1923," *Utah Historical Quarterly*. Summer 1984, pp. 264-274.

Holiness To The Lord (1888)

It took forty years to build, but the Washington Monument was finally opened to the public in 1888. Stones for the interior walls had been solicited years earlier from hundreds of organizations, countries and local governments, including the Territory of Deseret. After years of sitting in storage in Washington, the Utah stone was put in place and can now be seen midway up the monument on the inside. Carved from limestone from Manti, Utah, the stone shows a symbolic beehive with the word Deseret and a phrase that is now reserved strictly for Latter-day Saint temples—Holiness to the Lord.[460]

Worthy For Prison (1888)

It was exasperating for federal officials. A prison sentence is normally a punishment and causes shame, remorse and intimidation but that was not the case with Latter-day Saints imprisoned for polygamy. This is best illustrated by the words of two convicted cohabs, typical of the many who were imprisoned in the late nineteenth century. John Lee Jones wrote, "I thank the Lord that I was considered worthy to be one of the number that was imprisoned for maintaining one of the pure principles of the Everlasting Gospel" and Levi Savage wrote in his prison journal in 1888, "If I were here for a crime I would consider this part of my life literally wasted, but as it is I rejoice."[461]

---

460 Thayn, Florian H., "A Little Leavening." *BYU Studies*, Spring 1981, p. 221.
461 Larson, *The "Americanization" of Utah for Statehood*, p. 206.

Where's The Seer Stone? (1888)

One of the most significant events of President Woodruff's administration was the dedication of the Manti Temple. He later wrote: "Before leaving I consecrated upon the altar the Seer Stone that Joseph Smith found by revelation...and carried by him through life." There have been two principal questions surrounding this stone. Was it used in translating the Book of Mormon? In spite of evidence in favor of that view, Joseph Fielding Smith believed it was not.[462] The second question is where is the stone today? B. H. Roberts, from conversations with President Joseph F. Smith and from his own knowledge, reported in 1930 that it was in possession of the President of the Church. It is reasonable to assume that is where it is today.[463]

They Could Be Bought (1889)

Charles Henry Wilcken, a friend and bodyguard to such church leaders as George Q. Cannon and Wilford Woodruff during the polygamy raids in the later 1880s, once confirmed to Abraham Cannon who had just escaped arrest, that he, Wilcken, had "bought Doyle (U. S. Marshal) off, and got his promise that ... [Cannon] should not be molested nor should any other person without sufficient notice being given for them to escape." Wilcken also got from the Marshal the names of fifty-one others about to be arrested in Utah and Emery counties. Historical evidence now suggests there were several other marshals on the Mormon payroll, which is believed to be the reason why so many polygamists escaped arrest.[464]

---

462 McConkie, 3:224-226

463 CHC, 6:230-231.

464 Seifrit, William C., "Charles Henry Wilcken, an Undervalued Saint," *Utah Historical Quarterly.* Fall 1987, pp. 317-318.

Blossom Like A Rose! (1889)

Many of the pioneer Saints of 1847 had reason to question the seemingly hopeless prophesy of Brigham Young's that the Salt Lake Basin would one day "blossom like a rose." And yet four decades later it seemed dramatically fulfilled. The Department of Agriculture under President Benjamin Harrison awarded a five-hundred-dollar prize for the best five acres of wheat grown in the United States to William Gibby in Salt Lake County while a farmer in Spanish Fork, Utah County, won a cash prize for the best yield of potatoes per acre.[465]

---

465 Hinckley, Bryant S., *The Faith of Our Pioneer Fathers*, p. 14.

11

A New Era Begins
(1890-1921)

Temple Take-Over (1890)

The federal confiscation of church property provided by the terms of the Edmunds-Tucker Act of 1887, except for houses of worship, resulting in the impoverishment of the church before the Manifesto was issued in 1890, is well known. Less known is a threat by the government that prompted the Lord to reveal to President Woodruff the need to suspend the practice of plural marriage. A month before the revelation, which came in September 1890, it was learned that the government planned to take over the Logan, Manti, and St. George Temples reneging on a promise by the U. S. Solicitor General who had promised that the federal authorities would not go that far. The Lord knew the Manifesto was essential in saving the Church.[466]

Not What We Expected! (1890)

Aided by federal authorities and fraud, a non-Mormon government was installed in Salt Lake City in March, 1890. Only nine months later a mass meeting of gentiles met in the Methodist Church to denounce the changes that had occurred since "their" people had assumed power. Houses of prostitu-

---

466 Hoopes and Hoopes, p. 147.

tion and gambling were opening with no limitations, saloons were now open on the Sabbath and crime was rampant. On the night before the meeting there had been six highway robberies. A set of resolutions was adopted saying that the new city government "by its failure to enforce the laws against gambling, brothels, the sale of liquor to minors, and the opening of saloons on Sundays... is thereby imperiling the cause of morality in this city."[467] Was that an admission of greater morality under Mormon rule?

My Revelation Tops Yours! (1890)

When plural marriage was officially abolished in 1890, many polygamists had problems of caring for wives that the federal government wanted them to abandon. One who didn't have that problem lived in Paragoonah and had his wife to thank. Earlier, he had desired a plural wife, but afraid to ask his wife for permission, he told her he had a revelation to take another wife and thus she must give her consent. The next morning she announced her own revelation, which was to shoot any woman who became her husband's plural wife. Since hers seemed to top his, the matter was permanently dropped.[468]

Volunteer to be Republican (1891)

The major problem with bloc voting, practiced by the Saints in their early history, was that if their party lost, they would have no friends in public office. Recognizing the disadvantage of a single political party, the Saints decided in the late 1800s to divide their votes. This would obviously have to be done by Church mandate, so at a meeting held at Beaver, Utah,

---

467 *Latter-day Saints Millennial Star*. Liverpool, England: January 19 & 26, 1891.
468 Young, Kimball, p. 123.

on June 22, 1891, where Church leaders from several stakes were present, Apostles F. M. Lyman and A. H. Cannon presided and explained the need to divide votes between the two major parties. They then asked to see the hands of those who would volunteer to become Republicans. In some parts of Utah it was necessary to designate voters who would be Republicans.[469]

Ella Jensen Brought Back to Life (1891)

The miracle of healing is not unique in the Restored Church, but bringing a person back to life is certainly uncommon. One such case occurred in 1891 at Brigham City, Utah and involved Lorenzo Snow's niece, Ella Jensen. Lorenzo was speaking in the Brigham City Tabernacle when he was informed of the death of his niece two hours earlier. He quickly left the meeting with the stake president, Rudger Clawson and went to the Jensen home where he found the nineteen-year-old Ella washed and laid out for viewing. Brother Snow was inspired to bless young Ella that she might return to life, which he did with Brother Clawson's aid. An hour after the two brethren left the home, Ella opened her eyes and asked for her uncle who she said had called her back. She lived for another sixty-five years.[470]

First American Factory (1891)

It was not the first factory in America, but the first to be erected with American-made machinery by American workmen. The date was October 8, 1891 when the factory wheels in Lehi, Utah, began to slowly turn. A week later, the product, twenty tons of pure white sugar made from sugar

---

469 Anderson, Nels, pp. 327-328
470 Packer, pp. 251-252.

beets, was ready. For years beet sugar manufacturing had been considered a risky venture and the Saints had seen their previous attempts come to naught. Shortly after this success, President Woodruff visited the Lehi sugar factory and watched as the sacks of sugar were loaded aboard rail cars. He wept tears of joy seeing the culmination of a four-decade pioneer dream come true.[471]

Blasphemous To Bostonians (1892)

In the late nineteenth century Salt Lake City was visited by many interesting national figures. One was Dr. Charles W. Eliot, president of Harvard, who visited the city in 1892 and was warmly received. He responded warmly, comparing the pioneer Mormons to the Pilgrim Fathers. When word of this flattering discourse reached New England, the 'proper' descendants of the Pilgrims and Puritans considered such an analogy blasphemous and responded furiously. President Eliot, who would hold his position for forty years, was unmoved by the protest. In fact, a few conservative papers in New England, with tongue in cheek, thought the analogy might be appropriate, even in the matter of morals.[472]

A Flattering Request Indeed! (1893)

In September 1890, President Woodruff announced the end of plural marriage and eight months later Benjamin Harrison, the President of the United States, visited Utah. Perhaps it was that trip that influenced the country's president to do something in 1893 that made many Saints feel they had finally "arrived" in national respect. Actually they still had far

---

471 Berrett and Burton, 3:228-232.
472 Cowley, p. 579.

to go, but in that year President Harrison's wife lay at the point of death and he asked for the prayers of the Presidency of the Church in behalf of himself and wife. President Woodruff thought it remarkable that the Church had reached the point where the President of the United States would request the prayers of the First Presidency. It was indeed![473]

Hiring The Handicapped (1893)

At a time when handicapped workers nationwide were refused work and forced to live on charity, the Saints were finding meaningful work for them. When the Salt Lake Temple was completed in 1893, it had been under construction for forty years and during that time even the handicapped were hired to work on it. John F. Bennett, who later became prominent in banking in Utah, recalled that as a thirteen-year-old he was assigned the task of carrying tools between the Church blacksmith shop and the temple site. He also led two blind boys with strings, assigned to the same task. This job, for which he was paid twenty-five cents a day, was turned over to the two boys when they were able to do the job without being led by strings.[474]

Opening The Temples (1893)

When the Salt Lake Temple was dedicated in April 1893, the *Chicago Tribune* reported that "the building was worth a trip across the continent" to see. This was an appropriate observation since it was the first Mormon temple to open its doors to the general public before its dedication. Coming shortly after the discontinuance of plural marriages, the public

---

473 Cowley, p. 580.
474 Spencer and Harmer, p. 277.

showing marked the beginning of an aggressive public relations campaign to dispel the numerous perverted rumors the
public believed about the inner workings of Mormon temples.
Its success was evident when the *Los Angeles Times* noted the
hundreds of gentiles visiting the temple and observing "the
splendor and gorgeousness of which was great surprise to all
beholders."[475]

Moslems Yes, Mormons No! (1893)

One of the major events of 1893, in connection with the
World's Columbian Exposition in Chicago, was the World's
Parliament of Religions. The stated purpose was "to promote
brotherhood among religious men of diverse faiths." And yet
when the Church of Jesus Christ of Latter-day Saints requested
admission, they were denied because they would be a
disturbing element "on account of its plural marriage system"
which it had renounced three years earlier. At the conference a
Muslim representative was permitted two addresses in defense
of their doctrines, including polygamy. The Saints were finally
given permission to meet in a small side room but could not
speak to the main body. They refused the invitation.[476]

The Overlooked Connection (1894)

Wilford Woodruff's revelation on the law of adoption at the
April Conference in 1894, that henceforth Saints should be
sealed to their own parents rather than to apostles and Church
leaders, had an immediate response. During the rest of 1894
and in 1895, there was a significant increase in the number of
dead and living sealings. It appeared that many who had hesi-

475 Bishop, M. Guy and Holzapfel, Richard Neitzel, "The 'St. Peter's of the
New World': The Salt Lake Temple, Tourism, and a New Image for Utah,"
Utah Historical Quarterly. Spring 1993, pp. 147-148.

476 CHC, 6:236-240.

tated in being sealed to non-family members, now came forward without hesitation for family sealings. It was not mere coincidence that the vital new need to seek out information on families resulted in the Church-sponsored Genealogical Society of Utah being organized only seven months after the prophet's revelation which clarified the law of adoption.[477]

His Wife Came Back (1894)

The name of Mary Jackson Ross who died in October 1894 will normally cause little recognition among students of Mormon history—unless we add the name Woodruff. She was the first plural wife of Wilford Woodruff, sealed to him in the Nauvoo Temple after the exodus from that city began in 1846. Unfortunately, she was not happy in the marriage, left Wilford and married another man. In her declining years she regretted the separation and asked Wilford to accept her back into his eternal family. He was not only magnanimous to her but to the children of her second husband, and when she died had her interred in his own burial lot.[478]

Other Nauvoos (1895)

The city of Nauvoo, coined by the Prophet Joseph from Hebrew roots meaning place of rest and beauty, sounds like it should be a unique name for an American town. Actually there are or have been six other towns in the United States with the same name, the last named being in of all places the state of Missouri. Records show a post office established on its southern border in 1895, probably by the first postmaster who had visited Nauvoo, Illinois. There is also a small village in

---

477 Irving, Gordon, "The Law of Adoption: One Phase of the Development of the Mormon Concept of Salvation, 1830-1900," *BYU Studies.* Spring 1974, pp. 312-313.
478 Cowley, p. 588.

north central Pennsylvania; one in Walker County, Alabama; Dyers County, Tennessee; a little fishing village swallowed up by Sea Bright, New Jersey; and another swallowed up by West Portsmouth, Ohio. Most of these were probably named by missionaries or former residents of Nauvoo, Illinois.[479]

Politics And Bedfellows (1896)

There has always been a streak of independence among Latter-day Saint women, which has occasionally led to less than tranquil marriages. The first woman state senator in the United States won her election in 1896, which was Utah's first election as a state. Normally a husband should be proud, but Angus Cannon found it difficult to conceal his disappointment. It so happened that he was running on the Republican slate for that office and his wife, Martha Hughes Cannon was on the Democratic slate. She won—he lost. He later wrote that he was "not going to separate" from his wife "but will try and keep as near as I can and be happy." Eventually it was Martha who decided to separate—living the last years of her life in California.[480]

You Can't Serve Two Masters (1896)

Even though he was a member of the Quorum of the Twelve, being unable to serve two masters was a truism that Moses Thatcher refused to accept. When the general authorities issued a manifesto urging leading men of the Church to seek counsel before accepting political offices that would interfere with Church duties, Apostle Thatcher refused to sign. Not being in harmony with his brethren of the Twelve Apostles, he

---

479 Kimball, Stanley B., "Discovery: 'Nauvoo' Found in Seven States," *Ensign*. April, 1973, p. 21.
480 Cannon & Whittaker, pp. 390-391.

was not sustained at the General Conference in 1896, and thus dropped from the Quorum—an extraordinary occurrence. Brother Thatcher, a faithful pioneer of the Church remained active in the Church and in politics the rest of his life, determined to serve both masters.[481]

No Hard Feelings (1896)

When the Brigham City tabernacle was destroyed by fire in 1896, Stake President Rudger Clawson set out to rebuild it. One way to raise funds, he decided, was to appeal for donations among the more prosperous citizens of Salt Lake City. One man he approached was the judge who had earlier given Clawson one of the longest prison terms for unlawful cohabitation for LDS polygamists. When asked for the donation for a Mormon House of worship, Judge Charles Zane gave Clawson $10—comparable to no less than $150 to $200 in today's rate of exchange. Obviously both Zane and Clawson had forgotten the past.[482]

Office For Polygamous Son (1896)

The Industrial Christian Home for polygamous wives erected in Salt Lake City in 1888-89, failed completely to attract wives "escaping" from polygamous unions. Despite numerous attempts to keep it afloat, the gentile supporters finally were forced to close its doors in 1893. It then served briefly as offices for the Utah Commission before it was finally turned over to the new state officials in 1896, including the first elected governor of the state of Utah, Heber M. Wells. It is unlikely that the promoters of the home for polygamous wives

---

481 Jenson, Andrew, *Church Chronology*, p. 211.
482 Hoopes and Hoopes, p. 168.

could have ever conceived that their "solution" to end plural marriages would shortly be the official office for the son of one of the best-known polygamous fathers in Utah—Daniel H. Wells.[483]

The "High Hat Law" (1897)

After the admission of Utah as a state in 1896, three women were elected to the state legislature, despite objections that women would be more likely to pursue trivial interests. Although that was not the case, one legislator, Eurithe K. LaBarthe, came close to fulfilling that warning Her most memorable contribution in Utah legislative history was the introduction and passage of the so-called "High Hat Law." That bill provided that "any person attending a theater, opera-house or an indoor place of amusement as a spectator shall remove headwear tending to obstruct the view of any other person." Although considered "freak" legislation by some men, it became the men who benefited the most and approved it most heartily.[484]

Most With The Least (1898)

Described in the *LDS Biographical Encyclopedia* as "one of the most remarkable men that ever figured in the history of the Mormon Church," Christopher Layton is seldom mentioned in Church histories. With one exception, he may be remembered for little other than his lengthy and dedicated work for the Church as well as his temporal success in businesses in Utah. The one exception that gives him distinction is having the largest number of offspring with the fewest wives. Whereas

---

483 Larson, Gustive O., "An Industrial Home for Polygamous Wives," *Utah Historical Quarterly*. Summer 1970, pp. 262-275.

484 White, Jean Bickmore, "Gentle Persuaders: Utah's First Women Legislators," *Utah Historical Quarterly*. Winter, 1970, pp. 38-39.

Heber C. Kimball fathered the most with forty-two wives and John D. Lee fathered sixty with nineteen wives, Christopher Layton was the sire of sixty children with only ten wives. Perhaps some credit should go to his wives also.[485]

The Monster Petition (1898)

The Church issued its manifesto forbidding plural marriage in 1890 and in 1896 Utah was admitted into the Union. Then in 1898, the first election for Utah's representatives to Congress was held. By an easy margin, B. H. Roberts was elected to the House of Representatives—but the House refused to seat him. Although he met the Constitutional requirements, his seat was denied because of his previous involvement in the plural marriage system. In the hearings that resulted in the denial, a petition bearing 7,000,000 signatures reached Congress. It was revealed the petition resulted from a letter sent to Sunday Schools and other groups across the nation by the "National Anti-Polygamy League," urging even children to sign and in "the interest of this great moral work" one could sign more than once.[486]

Attending Own Funeral? (1898)

Sixteen years before his death in September 1898, Wilford Woodruff wrote the directions he wished his loved ones to follow for his funeral. The directions were common to what was expected in many late nineteenth century funeral customs such as the kind of coffin, the care of his body, etc. There was however, one paragraph in his sheet of instructions that must have caused, if not comment, at least some wonder. He had

---

485 Jenson, *LDS Biographical Encyclopedia*, 1:363.
486 Berrett & Burton, 3:168-169.

written, "If the laws and customs of the spirit world will permit, I should wish to attend my funeral myself, but I shall be governed by the counsel I receive in the spirit world."[487] This causes one to wonder whether we do attend our own funeral.

Go South, Lorenzo (1899)

One morning in the spring of 1899, President Lorenzo Snow awoke and told his associates of a revelation from God telling him to travel to St. George in southern Utah that at the time had been experiencing an eighteen- month drought. Not knowing the reason for his trip, he nevertheless left, accompanied by a few other church leaders. It was not until he was sitting on the stand in the St. George Tabernacle that the Lord revealed the reason for his visit. He was prompted to promise the people that they would be blessed and the drought broken if they would pay their honest tithing, a doctrine that was being largely neglected throughout the Church, in spite of numerous sermons on the subject. Now however, the tithings started flowing in, the drought was broken, the church became debt free, and tithing seemed to take on a new meaning.[488]

A Membership For Sale (1899)

The apostasy of Frank Cannon, whose hateful writings against the Church caused the Saints so much distress in the early twentieth century, could be explained by a number of reasons—failure to be reelected U.S. Senator, opposition to polygamy, moral weaknesses, etc. A major initiating factor, however, seemed to have been money. In 1899, the Church began issuing $500,000 worth of bonds to lessen church

---

487 Cowley, p. 622.
488 Hoopes and Hoopes, pp. 179-181.

indebtedness. Cannon asked for permission to sell those bonds in Washington—at a sizeable commission. President Snow at first agreed, but when Joseph F. Smith pointed out the bonds could easily be disposed of in Utah with no commission, the offer was withdrawn, bringing down on the Church the wrath of Frank Cannon. After his nemesis, Joseph F. Smith, became Church President, he joined the enemies of the Church in their campaign of defamatory venom.[489]

A Miracle Nevertheless (1900)

Heber J. Grant's mother, Rachel, became deaf in her later years but never accepted the finality of her disability. In 1900, congregations throughout the West were asked and did pray and fast that her hearing might be restored. Numerous blessings seemingly did little good, but she never gave up hoping for a miracle. Eight times she was baptized for the miracle that continually eluded her. Susa Young Gates witnessed one of those baptisms, in which Rachel would inevitably emerge from the water, still deaf but smiling nevertheless. It was at this time, Susa said, that she witnessed the miracle—a faithful Saint who so readily and joyfully accepted God's refusal to hear her prayer. The miracle was within Rachel herself.[490]

Deacon Or President? (1903)

Reed Smoot, elected as Senator from Utah in 1903, fought a lengthy congressional battle with anti-Mormons before being given his seat in 1907. He was to hold that seat for thirty years, gaining a notable reputation as a statesman even among non-Mormons, but still an object of bigotry because of his faith. He

---

489 Yorgason, Blaine M., *From Orphaned Boy to Prophet of God*, p. 328.
490 Cannon & Whittaker, p. 35.

later reported that he was twice offered the Republican nomination for President of the United States if he would denounce his membership in the Church. When later asked if that wouldn't have been worth it, he replied, "If I had to take my choice of being a deacon in the Church of Jesus Christ of Latter-day Saints, or being President of the United States, I would be a deacon."[491]

Teddy R. Tried (1905)

During the Congressional hearings designed to prevent Reed Smoot from being seated as a Senator from Utah, the chief counsel for the anti-Mormons was Judge R.W. Taylor, a bitter enemy of the Saints. President Teddy Roosevelt, who had earlier spoken in defense of Elder Smoot, saying it would be an outrage to turn him out because of his religious belief, took a clever route in support of Smoot. Unable to prevent the proceedings, he appointed Taylor to a federal judgeship in Ohio, hoping to deprive Smoot's opposition of their lead counsel. It threw them into confusion, but Taylor, in spite of the ethics of continuing as counsel, stayed until the committee gave an unfavorable recommendation. Smoot still won the Senate vote.[492]

Lot's Wife And Reed Smoot (1907)

After a battle by anti-Mormons, Apostle Reed Smoot took his seat in the United States Senate in 1907 and soon acquired the title of the "Sugar Senator" for his efforts to protect the sugar industry that the church was involved in with its own sugar factories. Some historians claim the famous Smoot-

---

491 Hinckley, Bryant S., *The Faith of Our Pioneer Fathers*, p. 202.
492 Berrett & Burton, 3:202.

Hawley Tariff Bill was designed specifically for that purpose. Senator Smoot became so well known for his protection of domestic sugar production that the comedian Will Rogers likened him to Lot's wife who was turned into a pillar of salt. "If Reed ever glances back," Will said, "we are going to have a human sugar bowl on our hands."[493]

Better Than Tandem Polygamy (1910)

Another friend of the Latter-day Saints was Frederick Vining Fisher, pastor of Ogden's First Methodist Church in 1910. After apostate Frank J. Cannon wrote some anti-Mormon articles in a national magazine, Fisher wrote an article titled "A Methodist Minister's View of Mormonism" for a New York magazine, *Outlook*. He emphasized three points. The Saints were a deeply religious people in the mainstream of Protestantism, they were born of the best blood of New England, and they were well educated. His greatest condemnation from religious leaders around the nation, however, resulted from his defense of polygamy. He said "it was practiced as religious duty, was not sensual and was infinitely better than tandem polygamy in the east." He continued throughout life as a defender of the Saints.[494]

Churchill And The Saints (1910)

Twenty years after the Manifesto halting plural marriage in 1890, polygamy was still a major charge being made against the church—especially in England. During the year 1910, eight debates took place in Parliament on the "Mormon Problem" in which the Home Secretary, Winston Churchill was asked what

---

493 Hoopes and Hoopes, p. 193.
494 Dawson, Janice P., "Frederick Vining Fisher: Methodist Apologist for Mormonism," *Utah Historical Quarterly*. Fall 1987, pp. 362-363.

he proposed to do. "Was he aware," a member asked, "of Mormon efforts to induce English women and girls to go to America and if so was he taking steps to stop them?" Replying to the implication that it was being done for immoral purpose, Churchill said he had determined it was not true and there was no ground for action. His reply prompted the *Liverpool Post and Mercury* to say, "The Home Secretary has an intelligent understanding of the situation and is friendly to the Church."[495]

The Last Kibbutz (1911)

As the Saints were fleeing persecution in Missouri in the 1830s, Jews were fleeing persecution in Europe, beginning their return to Palestine and 'back to the soil' after centuries of landlessness. Then in 1881, the Jewish 'back to the soil' movement spread to America with approximately forty agricultural communities being established by the Jews in New Jersey, the Dakotas, Kansas, Oregon, Colorado, Louisiana, and finally, in Utah. The first Jewish colonists arrived in Utah in 1911 and established the hamlet of Clarion, south of Gunnison on the Sevier River. Lack of water, funds, and experience doomed the experiment from the beginning. It ended in 1916, becoming the last Jewish attempt to colonize land in the United States.[496]

First Poet Laureate (1915)

Ninety-nine years after the final crop failure that forced Joseph Smith, Sr. to move from Vermont to Palmyra, his granddaughter was named the first poet laureate of California. Born Josephine, daughter of Don Carlos Smith, she was only three when her father died. Without Don Carlos, her mother

---

495 Hoopes and Hoopes, p. 254.
496 Goldberg, Robert Alan, "Building Zions: A Conceptual Framework." *Utah Historical Quarterly*, Spring 1989, pp. 165-179.

Agnes apostatized and little Josephine grew up, faithful to a promise made to her mother, not to discuss her Smith background. When her mother remarried and moved to California, Josephine changed her first name to Ina and took her mother's maiden name, Coolbrith. She became a beloved poet and today the place where her home stood when it was destroyed by the San Francisco earthquake and fire, is named Coolbrith Park.[497]

Seventy-Four Years To The Minute (1918)

The polished granite monument to Joseph Smith, dedicated at the homestead site in Sharon, Vermont, is well known to most Latter-day Saints. Less known is a similar shaft of Vermont granite erected to honor his brother Hyrum. Standing on the burial lot of Joseph F. Smith, Hyrum's son, in the Salt Lake City Cemetery, it is half the height of the monument in Sharon. It was unveiled precisely at the hour and minute of the martyrdoms, 5:20 p. m., June 27, 1918, seventy-four years after the Carthage assassinations. Representing two brothers who were separated neither in death or burial, the two monuments representing that union are separated by nearly two thousand miles.[498]

It Took A Long Time (1918)

It took much longer than most Latter-day Saints like to believe. Although the Word of Wisdom was received by the Prophet Joseph as early as 1833, the Lord apparently understood the difficulty of giving up such habits as tobacco and strong drinks and thus did not make it a commandment. Early Church leaders apparently believed the habits were more

---

497 BYU Studies, Vol. 23, No. 4, p. 448.
498 CHC, 6:429.

deeply entrenched than even the Lord suspected and made only periodic attempts to enforce the Word of Wisdom. Actually, it was not until the administration of a twentieth century Prophet, Heber J. Grant (1918—1945) that the revelation received by Joseph Smith became a requirement for advancement in the church and entrance to the temple.[499]

A Deadly Release (1921)

Emmeline Wells, aged ninety, had served as General President of the Relief Society when Heber J. Grant took office as Church President. When he suggested she be released, she responded that it would kill her. The President left her in office but three years later, when she became ill, he approached her again. Knowing that all previous leaders, except Emma Smith, had died in office, Emmeline felt humiliated but her attempts to prove her abilities were to no avail. President Grant was kind but firm. As he left her home, Emmeline started up the staircase. At the top she suffered a stroke and fell unconscious. For three weeks she lay in a coma before passing away on 25 April 1921.[500]

---

499 Kimball, Stanley, p. 204 fn.
500 Cannon & Whittaker, p. 336.

References

Allen, James B. and Leonard, Glen M.. *The Story of the Latter-day Saints*. Salt Lake City: Deseret Book Company, 1976.

American Almanac for the year 1838. Boston: Charles Bowen, 1837.

Anderson, J. Max. *The Polygamy Story: Fiction and Fact*. Salt Lake City: Publishers Press, 1979.

Anderson, Nels. *Desert Saints: The Mormon Frontier in Utah*. Chicago: Univ. of Chicago Press, 1966.

Anderson, Richard Lloyd. *Investigating the Book of Mormon Witnesses*. Salt Lake City: Deseret Book Company, 1981.

Arrington, Leonard. *From Quaker to Latter-day Saint: Bishop Edwin D. Woolley*. Salt Lake City: Deseret Book Company, 1976.

Arrington, Leonard. *Great Basin Kingdom*. Lincoln, Nebraska: University of Nebraska Press, 1966.

Arrington, Leonard J. & Davis Bitton. *Saints Without Halos*. Salt Lake City: Signature Books, 1981.

Arrington, Leonard J., Feramorz Y. Fox & Dean L. May. *Building the City of God*. Salt Lake City: Deseret Book Company, 1976.

Backman, Milton V., Jr.. *The Heavens Resound*. Salt Lake City: Deseret Book Company, 1983.

Backman, Milton V., Jr. & Keith W Perkins. *Writings of Early Latter-day Saints and Their Contemporaries—Database*. Provo, Utah: Religious Studies Center, 1996.

Bancroft, Hubert Howe. *History of Utah, 1540-1887*. San Francisco: The History Company, 1890.

Beecher, Maureen Ursenback. *Eliza and Her Sisters.* Salt Lake City: Aspen Books, 1991.

Bennett, Richard E.. *Mormons at the Missouri, 1846-1852.* Norman, Oklahoma: Univ. of Oklahoma Press, 1987.
We'll Find the Place, The Mormon Exodus 1846-1848. Salt Lake City: Deseret Book Co., 1997.

Berrett, William E. and Alma P. Burton. *Readings in L.D.S. Church History.* (3 vols.) Salt Lake City: Deseret Book Company, 1955.

Birney, Hoffman. *Zealots of Zion.* Philadelphia: The Penn Publishing Co., 1931.

Black, Susan Easton & William G. Hartley (eds.). *The Iowa Mormon Trail.* Orem, Utah: Helix Publishing, 1997.

Brooks, Juanita. *The Mountain Meadows Massacre.* Norman, Oklahoma: Univ. of Oklahoma Press, 1962.

Brooks, Juanita (ed). *On the Mormon Frontier: The Diary of Hosea Stout* (2 vols.) Salt Lake City: Univ. of Utah Press, 1964.

Brown, S. Kent, Donald Q. Cannon, & Richard H. Jackson. *Historical Atlas of Mormonism.* New York: Simon & Schuster, 1994.

Browning, John & Curt Gentry. *John M. Browning: American Gunmaker.* New York: Doubleday & Company, Inc., 1964.

Burton, Richard F.. *The City of the Saints* (ed. By Fawn Brodie). New York: Alfred A. Knoph, Inc., 1963.

Burton, Alma P. and Clea M. Burton. *Stories From Mormon History.* Salt Lake City: Deseret Book Company, 1960.

Bushman, Claudia L. (ed.). *Mormon Sisters: Women in Early Utah.* Logan, Utah: Utah State University Press, 1997.

Bushman, Richard L.. *Joseph Smith and the Beginnings of Mormonism.* Urbana and Chicago: University of Illinois Press, 1984.

Cairncross, John. *After Polygamy Was Made a Sin: The Social*

History of Christian Polygamy. London: Routledge & Kegan Paul, 1974.

Campbell, Eugene E.. *Establishing Zion: The Mormon Church in the American West, 1847-1869.* Salt Lake City: Signature Books, 1988.

Cannon, Donald Q. and David J. Whittaker, (eds.). *Supporting Saints: Life Stories of Nineteenth-Century Mormons.* Provo, Utah: BYU, 1985.

Cannon, George Q.. *Life of Joseph Smith the Prophet.* Salt Lake City: Deseret Book Company, 1972.

Cannon, George Q. & Wilford Woodruff (eds). *A String of Pearls.* Salt Lake City: Bookcraft, 1968.

Carter, Kate B.. *The Story of the Negro Pioneer.* Salt Lake City: Daughters of Utah Pioneers, 1965.

Cawalks, S. N.. *Incidents of Travel and Adventure in the Far West.* New York: Derby and Jackson, 1857.

Clayton, William. *William Clayton's Journal.* Salt Lake City: The Deseret News, 1921.

Cleland, Robert Glass & Juanita Brooks. *A Mormon Chronicle: The Diaries of John D. Lee, 1848-1876* (2 vols.) Salt Lake City: Univ. of Utah Press, 1983.

Coakley, Robert W.. *The Role of Federal Military Forces in Domestic Disorders 1789-1878.* Washington, D. C.: U. S. Government Printing Office, 1988.

Cook, Lyndon W. (ed). *David Whitmer Interviews: A Restoration Witness.* Orem, Utah: Grandin Book Company, 1993.

Cook, Lyndon W.. *Revelations of the Prophet Joseph Smith.* Salt Lake City: Deseret Book, 1985.

Cowley, Matthias F. *Wilford Woodruff: History of His Life and Labors.* Salt Lake City: Bookcraft, Inc., 1964.

Cresswell, Stephen. *Mormons and Cowboys, Moonshiners and Klansmen.* Tuscaloosa, Alabama: University of Alabama, 1991.

Devitry-Smith, John. "The Saint and the Grave Robber." *BYU Studies*, Vol. 33, No. 1.

Fife, Austin and Alta. *Saints of Sage & Saddle*. Bloomington, Indiana: Indiana University Press, 1956.

Ford, Gov. Thomas. *A History of Illinois*, 2 vols. Chicago: Lakeside Press, 1946.

Fox, Feramorz Y.. "The Consecration Movement of the Middle 'fifties," *Improvement Era*, February, 1944, No. 2.

Givens, George and Sylvia. *Nauvoo Fact Book*. Lynchburg, Virginia: Parley Street Publishers, 2000.

Grow, Stewart L.. *A Tabernacle in the Desert*. Salt Lake City: Deseret Book Company, 1958.

Gunn, Stanley R.. *Oliver Cowdery: Second Elder and Scribe*. Salt Lake City: Bookcraft, Inc., 1962.

Hafen, LeRoy R. & Ann W. Hafen. *Handcarts to Zion*. Glendale, California: Arthur H. Clark Company, 1960.

Hansen, Klaus J.. *Quest for Empire*. Michigan State Univ. Press, 1967.

Hicks, Michael. *Mormonism and Music: A History*. Urbana and Chicago: University of Illinois Press, 1989.

Hill, Marvin S.. *Quest for Refuge*. Salt Lake City: Signature Books, 1989.

Hilton, Hope. *"Wild Bill" Hickman and the Mormon Frontier*. Salt Lake City: Signature Books, 1988.

Hinckley, Bryant S.. *The Faith of Our Pioneer Fathers*. Salt Lake City: Deseret Book Company, 1965.

Holzapfel, Jeni Broberg & Richard Neitzel Holzapfel. *A Woman's View*. Provo, Utah: Brigham Young University, 1997.

Hoopes, David S. & Rooy Hoopes. *The Making of a Mormon Apostle: The Story of Rudger Clawson*. Lanham, Maryland: Madison Books, 1990.

Jenson, Andrew. *Church Chronology*. Salt Lake City: Deseret News, 1899.

Jenson, Andrew. *Encyclopedic History of the Church of Jesus Christ of Latter-day Saints*. Salt Lake City: Deseret News Pub. Co., 1941.

Jenson, Andrew. *Latter-day Saint Biographical Encyclopedia.* (5vols.) Salt Lake City: Western Epics, 1971.

Jessee, Dean C., ed. *John Taylor's Nauvoo Journal*. Provo, Utah: Grandin Book Company, 1996.

Journal of Discourses. Liverpool and London: Edited & Published by Amasa Lyman, 1860

Kane, Elizabeth Wood. *Twelve Mormon Homes*. Salt Lake City: University of Utah Tanner Trust Fund, 1974.

Kimball, Stanley B.. *Heber C. Kimball: Mormon Patriarch and Pioneer*. Urbana, Ill.: Univ. of Illinois Press, 1981.

Knight, Hal & Dr. Stanley B. Kimball. *111 Days to Zion*. Salt Lake City: Deseret News, 1978.

Larson, Gustive O.. *The "Americanization" of Utah for Statehood*. San Marino, California: The Huntington Library, 1971.

Larson, Gustive O.. *Prelude to the Kingdom: Mormon Desert Conquest*. Francestown, New Hampshire: Marshall Jones Co., 1947.

LeSueur, Stephen C.. *The 1838 Mormon War in Missouri*. Columbia, Missouri: University of Missouri Press, 1987.

Long, E. B.. *The Saints and the Union*. Urbana and Chicago: Univ. of Illinois Press, 1981

Ludlow, Daniel H.. *A Companion to Your Study of the Doctrine and Covenants* (2 vols.) Salt Lake City: Deseret Book Company, 1978.

Ludlow, Daniel H. (ed). *Encyclopedia of Mormonism* (4 vols). New York: Macmillan Publishing Co., 1992.

Maynard, Gregory. "Alexander William Doniphan: Man of Justice." *BYU Studies*, Vol. 13, No. 4.

McConkie, Bruce R.(ed.). *Doctrines of Salvation: Sermons and*

Writings of Joseph Fielding Smith (3 vols). Salt Lake City: Bookcraft, 1954-1956.

Merrill, Byron R. [et al.]. *The Heavens Are Open*. Salt Lake City: Deseret Book Company, 1993.

Miller, David E.. *Hole-In-The-Rock*. Salt Lake City: University of Utah Press, 1966.

Mormon Historical Studies, Vol. 1, No. 1, Spring 2000.

Mulder, William and A. Russell Mortensen (eds.). *Among the Mormons*. Lincoln, Nebraska: University of Nebraska Press, 1958.

Nibley, Preston. *Brigham Young: The Man and His Work*. Independence, Mo.: Zion's Printing and Publishing Co., 1936.

Nibley, Preston. *Missionary Experiences*. Salt Lake City: Deseret News Press, 1942.

Nibley, Preston. *The Witnesses of the Book of Mormon*. Salt Lake City: Deseret Book Company, 1968.

Otten, L. G. & C. M. Caldwell. *Sacred Truths of the Doctrine and Covenants* (2 vols). Springville, Utah: LEMB, Inc., 1983.

Packer, Boyd K.. *The Holy Temple*. Salt Lake City: Bookcraft, 1980.

Pratt, Parley P., Jr. (ed). *Autobiography of Parley P. Pratt*. Salt Lake City: Deseret Book Co., 1985.

Proctor, Scot Facer & Maurine Jensen Proctor (eds.). *The Revised and Enhanced History of Joseph Smith by His Mother*. Salt Lake City: Bookcraft, 1996.

Pusey, Merlo J.. *Builders of the Kingdom*. Provo, Utah: BYU Press, 1981.

Pyper, George D.. *The Romance of An Old Playhouse*. Salt Lake City: Deseret News Press, 1937.

Quincy, Josiah. *Figures of the Past*. Boston: 1883.(1856)

Reynolds, Philip C.. *Commentary on the Book of Mormon* (6 vols). Salt Lake City: Deseret Press, 1960

Roberts, B.H.. *A Comprehensive History of the Church of Jesus Christ of Latter-day Saints*. (6 vols.) Provo: BYU Press, 1965

Roberts, B. H.. *The Life of John Taylor*. Salt Lake City: Bookcraft Inc., 1963.

Roberts, Elder B. H.. *The Missouri Persecutions*. Salt Lake City: Bookcraft, 1965.

Schindler, Harold. *Orrin Porter Rockwell: Man of God, Son of Thunder*. Salt Lake City: University of Utah Press, 1966.

Seixas, J.. *Manual Hebrew Grammar for the use of Beginners*. Salt Lake City: Sunstone Foundation facsimile, 1981.

Sessions, Gene Allred. *Latter-day Patriots*. Salt Lake City: Deseret Book Company, 1975.

Smart, Donna Toland (ed.). *Mormon Midwife: The 1846-1888 Diaries of Patty Bartlett Sessions*. Logan, Utah: Utah State University Press, 1997.

Smith, Eliza R. Snow. *Biography and Family Record of Lorenzo Snow*. Salt Lake City: Deseret News Company, 1884.

Smith, George D. (ed.). *An Intimate Chronicle: The Journals of William Clayton*. Salt Lake City: Signature Books, 1995.

Smith, George D.. "Nauvoo Roots of Mormon Polygamy, 1841-46: A Preliminary Demographic Report," *Dialogue: A Journal of Mormon Thought*. Vol. 27, No. 1, pp. 1-72.

Smith, Joseph Fielding. *Answers to Gospel Questions* (5 vols). Salt Lake City: Deseret Book Co., 1972.

Smith, Joseph Fielding. *Church History and Modern Revelation*, 4 vols. Salt Lake City: Church of Jesus Christ of Latter-day Saints, 1946-1949.

Smith, Joseph Fielding. *Essentials in Church History*. Salt Lake City: Deseret Book Company, 1973.

Smith, Joseph, Jr.. *History of the Church of Jesus Christ of Latter-day Saints* (8 vols.) Salt Lake City: Deseret Book Company, 1980.

Spencer, Clarissa Young and Mable Harmer. *Brigham Young at Home.* Salt Lake City: Deseret News Press, 1947.

Stott, Clifford L.. *Search for Sanctuary: Brigham Young and the White Mountain Expedition.* Salt Lake City: University of Utah Press, 1984.

Tullidge, Edward W.. *The Women of Mormondom.* New York: Tullidge & Crandall, 1877.

Tyler, Sergeant Daniel. *A Concise History of the Mormon Battalion in the Mexican War.* Chicago: Rio Grande Press Inc., 1964.

Van Wagoner, Richard S. and Steven C. Walker. *A Book of Mormons.* Salt Lake City: Signature Books, 1982.

Whipple, Maurine. *This is the Place: Utah.* New York: Alfred A. Knopf, 1945.

Whitney, Orson F.. *Life of Heber C. Kimball.* Salt Lake City: Stevens & Wallis, Inc., 1945.

Yorgason, Blaine M.. *From Orphaned Boy to Prophet of God.* Odgen, Utah: The Living Scriptures, 2001.

Young, S. Dilworth. "Here Is Brigham . . ." *Brigham Young . . . the Years to 1844.* Salt Lake City: Bookcraft, 1964.

Young, Kimball. *Isn't One Wife Enough.* New York: Henry Holt & Co., 1954.

Index

accused murderer, 205
Delaware Indians, 11
Deseret Currency Association, 150
Deseret language, 123
Deseret Manufacturing Co., 117
Deseret name, 110
Deseret size, 105
Deseret University, 109, 112
Dickens, Charles, 178
Dilworth, Mary Jane, 91
Dixon, Illinois, 48
Doctrine & Covenants
    Section 136, 83
    Section 76, 49
    Section 81, 13
Doniphan, Alexander, 17, 20, 28,
    177, 210
    attorney for Saints, 28
    hired by Saints, 17
    supports the Saints, 18
    Utah, in, 210
Donner Party, 80
Douglas, Stephen A., 137
    named Little Giant, 47
Down and back trains, 164
Doyle, Arthur Conan, 241
Drummond, W. W., 234
Durfee, Edmund, 65
Duty, Mary
    most honored woman, 9

E

Edmunds-Tucker Act, 198, 224,
    245
Egan, Howard, 103
Election Test Oath, 237
Eliot, Charles W., 248
Emerson, Ralph Waldo, 132, 202
Emigration of Saints, 223
Emmett, James, 62, 82

Evart, Sec. of State, 222
Ewing, Gen. Thomas, 177
Expositor, 53, 54
Extermination order, 28

F

Fairchild, Jas. H., 231
Farmington, Iowa, 77
Fast offerings, 134
Fifteen-shooter, 103
Fillmore, 112
Fisher, Frederick Vining, 259
Flake, Green, 74, 110
Florence, Nebraska, 77
Floyd, John B., 42, 144
Foote, Irene Lane, 3
Ford, Thomas
    Expositor press, and, 53
    recommends division of
        Nauvoo, 60
Fory, Catharine, 45
Furniss, Norman, 141
Gallifant, Annie, 233
Garden Grove, 74, 78, 82, 93
Gardo House, 217
Garfield, James, 227
Gates, Susa Young, 216, 257
Gause, Jesse, 13
Genealogical Society of Utah, 251
General Epistles, 120
Gibby, William, 244
Godbe, William S., 200
Goddard, George, 167
Gold missions, 107
Golden plates, 5, 6
Goodyear, Miles, 102
Grand Island, Nebraska, 76
Grandin's Print Shop, 8
Granger, Oliver, 26
Granger, Sarah, 19

273

Grant, Heber J., 37, 189, 224
   baseball player, 221
   mission in Virginia, 37
   son of Rachel Ivins, 53
   Word of Wisdom, 261
Grant, Jedediah M.
   and Miss Floyd, 41
Grant, Rachel, 257
Grant, Ulysses S., 184, 236
Grave robbing, 171
Great Eastern, 171
Guiteau, Charles J., 227
Gunnison massacre, 123, 129
Gunpowder, 127

H

Hale, Emma
   Marriage to Joseph, 4
Half mast incident, 236
Hamblin, Jacob, 219
Hancock Country elections, 50
Handcart companies, 137
Handicapped workers, 249
Harding, Stephen, 8
Harlan, Edgar, 77
Harney, General William
   squaw killer, 145
Harris, Belle, 233
Harris, Martin
   116 pages, loss of, 5
   Book of Mormon printing, 8
   farm mortgage, 11
   rebaptism, 201
   rumored death, 45
Harrison, Benjamin, 244, 248
Harvard, 248
Haskel, Thales, 226
Haskell, Irene, 56
Haun's Mill massacre, 28
   desecration, 29

   peace agreement, 28
Henry VIII, 116
Hickman, Bill, 84, 139
   accuses Brigham, 200
Hinkle, George, 30
   guilt question, 33
Hodge, Irvine
   killed in Nauvoo, 64
Holbrook, Joseph, 39
Hole-in-the-Rock, 223
Holmes, Mrs. Emery, 217
Home teaching, 46
Hooper, William, 191, 204
Hopt, Fred, 240
Houston, Sam, 251
Howell, William—missionary, 114
Huntington, Dimick, 60
Huntington, William, 60
Hyde, Orson, 82
   Quorum suspension, 37

I

Icarians, 111
Illiteracy, 109
Industrial Christian Home, 253
Industrial Home Association, 240
Ireland, Marshal Ewin, 234
Ivie, James incident, 122
Ivins, Rachel, 52

J

Jackson County
   expulsion, 17
   marriage, first, 13
   slavery, 16
Jacob, Norton, 87
Jacques, Vienna, 230
Jedediah, 37
Jensen, Ella, 247
Jessup, Deacon, 3

Jackson County expulsion, 17
Lamanite mission, 11
Zion's fertility, 102
Presbyterian Church, 226
Priesthood
dangers of, 234
Pure Church of Christ, 12

Q

Quincy Excursion Party, 191
Quincy, Josiah, 132
Quorum of the Twelve
mission to England, 41

R

Red Stockings, 221
Rees, Amos
attorney for Joseph Smith, 32
Rees, Mary Morgan, 225
Reid, Amos
Governor of Utah, 11
Reid, John
defender of the Prophet, 11
Relief Society
beginning, 48
separate corporation, 189
suspension, 58
Religious toleration, 46
Remy, Jules, 131
Retrenchment Society, 193
Rich, Charles C., 94
Richards, Franklin D., 57
Rigdon, Sidney, 110
code name, 15
conversion, 11
July 4th speech, 32
law, study of, 28
Missouri explulsions, 27
overtures to Hinkle, 30
testimony, 176

Roberts, B. H., 71, 243
election, 255
Robinson, Captain
offer made to George A.
Smith, 29
Robinson, George, 111
Rockwell, Porter, 103, 139
daughter kidnapped, 106
Rocky Mountain Prophecy, 14
Rogers, Will, 258
Roosevelt, Teddy, 258
Run-away officials, 122
Russell, Majors and Waddell, 157,
198

S

Salt Lake Temple
construction, 119
marks location, 89
open house, 249
unfinished, 173
Salt Lake Theater
admissions, 172
controlling applause, 181
dedication, 172
Salt offer, 151
San Juan Mission, 223
Sand Creek Massacre, 177
Sandwich Islands, 59
Sanpete County, 131
Savage, Charles R., 196
Savage, Levi, 242
School of the Prophets, 19
School, first, 91
Sebastopol, 153
Seer Stone, 242
Seixas, 40
Seminole Indians, 25
Seneca Falls, 47
Sessions, Patty, 73, 218

Toronto, Joseph, 229
Transcontinental Railroad, 93, 190
Trobriand, Gen. De, 205
Trustee-in-trust, 44
Tucker, Pomeroy, 8, 11
Tuckett, Mercy—actress, 162
Turley, Theodore, 37
Tyler, President, 215

U

Umbrella as weapon, 97
Uncommercial Traveler, The, 178
Union Academy, 162
Union Pacific Railroad, 188
United Orders, 233
Upper California
    states included, 69
Urim and Thummin, 5
Utah Expedition
    costs, 145
    toll on, 143
Utah Lake, 60
Utah Territory
    division of, 192
Ute Indians, 122

V

Van Vliet, Stewart, 141
Victoria, Queen, 83
Violence in America, 18

W

Wade bill, 187
Walker Brothers, merchants, 160
Walker War, 123, 125
Walker, Cyrus, 48
Ward origin, 45
Ward, Artemus, 172
Warsaw Signal, 54

Washington County, 120
Washington Monument, 242
Watt, George E., 123
Wedding of the rails, 195
Wells, Daniel, 106
Wells, Emmeline, 78, 118, 262
Wells, Heber M., 253
Wells, Junius
    mission, 213
Western Union Telegraph, 170
White, Nellie, 233
Whitmer, David
    expulsion from Far West, 27
    Interview on stone box, 5
Whitmer, Elizabeth Ann, 14
Whitmer, John, 221
Whitmer, Mary, 7
Whitmer, Peter, Jr.
    Lamanite mission, 11
Whitney, Helen Mar, 23
Whitney, Newel
    code name, 15
Whittier, John Greenleaf, 61
Wight, Lyman
    Jackson County expulsion, 17
Wilcken, Charles H., 232, 243
Williams, Frederick G., 13
    conversion, 11
    Zion's Camp historian, 21
Willoughby Medical School, 23
Winter Quarters, 80
    deaths, 93
    population, 78
Winter Saints, 104
Wiswager, Brother, 38
Woodruff, Mary Jackson Ross, 251
Woodruff, Phoebe, 197
Woodruff, Wilford
    funeral, 255

281

law of adoption, 250
Presidential request, 248
Woolley, Bishop Edwin, 189, 200, 204, 226
Word of Wisdom, 115, 183, 261
World's Parliament of Religions, 250
Worrell, Frank, 103
Wyandot Indians, 11
Wyoming Territory, 147, 197

Y

Young, Ann Eliza Webb, 211
Young, Brigham
    assumes leadership in MO., 36
    bail, 200
    Bridger, meets, 86
    Catholics, and, 185
    conversion, 15
    crosses Atlantic, 40
    enters Valley, 89
    father as patriarch, 20
    father's membership, 39
    house arrest, 206
    Mark Twain, and, 170
    missionary travels, 42
    Mountain Meadows massacre, 218
    Nauvoo exodus delayed, 67
    Nauvoo wives, 72
    plural marriage, and, 209
    Presidency, assumes, 94
    prison, in, 211
    reactivates Relief Society, 58
    recruiting the Battalion, 75
    slavery views, 159
    temple burning, on, 77
    Tom Thumb, and, 178
    trial of assassins, 62
    views Joseph's body, 60
    views on women, 125
    views on women in office, 199
    warns army, 135
    western destination, 69
Young, Brigham, Jr., 131
Young, Harriet Cook, 199
Young, John, 39
Young, Joseph, 165
Young, Seraph, 198
Young, Willard W. at West Point, 204

Z

Z.C.M.I., 218
Zane, Judge Charles, 233, 253
Zion's Camp
    history of, 21
    training ground, 21

About the Author

George W. Givens spent twenty years teaching American History in schools in upstate New York, Arizona and Virginia before opening what became the largest family-owned bookstore in Virginia. George joined the LDS Church while living in Tucson, Arizona, in 1964. He and his wife Sylvia have spent several summers in Nauvoo, Illinois, as in-house historians. They are parents of eight children.

George developed an avid interest in LDS Church history upon learning of ancestors who joined the Church in upstate New York in 1830. His other published titles include *In Old Nauvoo, The Nauvoo Fact Book, Out of Palmyra,* and *The Hired Man's Christmas.*

George currently spends his time teaching Gospel Doctrine in the Lynchburg, Virginia First Ward and traveling around the country giving firesides on Church history.

9 26575 76518 5